Principles of Educational
&
Vocational Guidance

Published by :
Lotus Press Publishers & Distributors

Principles of Educational & Vocational Guidance

Dr. S. Rajjappa

Lotus Press
4735/22, Prakash Deep Building
Ansari Road, Darya Ganj,
New Delhi - 110002

Lotus Press : Publishers & Distributors
Unit No. 220, 2nd Floor, 4735/22, Prakash Deep Building,
Ansari Road, Darya Ganj, New Delhi- 110002
Ph.: 23280047, 98118-38000
• E-mail : lotuspress1984@gmail.com
www.lotuspress.co.in

Principles of Educational & Vocational Guidance

ISBN: 81-8382-148-0

Printed & Published by : **Lotus Press Publishers & Distributors,** New Delhi-02

PREFACE

Principles of Educational & Vocational Guidance is perhaps the newest addition to the professions where chief purpose is to help people with their problems. As a new discipline dedicated to the helping process it has much in common with the already professions, but it is also distinct from them, for it makes contributions to human welfare which are not forthcoming from other areas.

Vocational guidance at its present stage of development has various responsibilities which differ from each other, not only in objectives, but in the levels of skill necessary for specific functions and in the special knowledge required for particular areas.

The editor expresses his deep thanks to

- The Ministry of Human Resource Development, Government of India for its useful work in and
- The field of vocational guidance which has been of immense help in the preparation of this look.

Thanks are due to Shri A.J. Sehgal, Director of Lotus Press, in building out this new venture.

Author

CONTENTS

1

The Nature of Vocational Guidance

Vocational guidance is perhaps the newest addition to the professions whose chief purpose is to help people with their problems. As a new discipline dedicated to the helping process it has much in common with the already existing professions, but it is also distinct from them, for it makes contributions to human welfare which are not forthcoming from the other area. What vocational guidance is, depends to some extent on one's personal views. Some see it primarily as a service established to help people make a satisfactory economic adjustment. Others view it chiefly as a preventive or prophylactic aid for in-school youth. Still others tend to extend the scope of vocational guidance to include problems in social and personal adjustment. Several adequate definitions of vocational guidance for students in that field exist. The present work will neither adopt already existing definitions nor attempt a new formulation. I believe that any formal definition of vocational guidance, no matter how carefully expressed, cannot be equated with guidance itself. As Carl Rogers says aptly in discussing therapy, "If one wishes to give such a real meaning he should put his hand over his mouth and *point*." Although the present work is a far cry from this direct and emphatic way of handling the problem, an attempt nevertheless will be made to convey to the reader the concept of vocational guidance as a living experience. Vocational guidance cannot be learned solely through books, nor can its significance be grasped fully in the classroom. It is only through daily practice in helping people and through competent supervision that a counsellor can develop a real understanding of the interpersonal relationship and process that go into giving and taking help.

Vocational guidance at its present stage of development has various responsibilities which differ from each other, not only in objectives, but in the levels of skill necessary for specific functions and in the special knowledge required for particular areas.

Concretely, some vocational guidance workers may be primarily concerned with the interpretation of vocational guidance to the lay public. They may also engage in fund raising and fund administration whether in the school system or in relation to the Community Chest. Vocational guidance if it is to exist needs money for its maintenance as a service. The same workers who are interested in interpreting vocational guidance and in the ways and means of financing it may also want to achieve a closer coordination between vocational guidance and other helping services. This may mean a greater participation in the Council of Social Agencies and other similar, bodies concerned with the general communal welfare. These and related activities are known as "community organisation" in social-work parlance. Although apparently university curricula in vocational guidance offer no courses in community organisation as do schools of social work, there exists a need for trained workers who can assume the responsibility for interpreting, promoting, and coordinating the different facets of vocational guidance.

Another area in vocational guidance which demands specialised training and peculiar skills is "group work." This term, too, is borrowed from social work, although it possesses a different meaning in the vocational context. Group vocational guidance is concerned primarily with dissemination of occupational information, broadening the occupational horizons, and stimulation of interest in vocational self-help among the individual members of a particular group. The Vocational Service Bureau of B'nai B'rith, for example, has been engaged in such activity for almost two decades by conducting occupational studies, publishing vocational guidance material, and employing professional counsellors to address various fraternities and clubs on matters pertaining to career planning.

The last area of vocational guidance to be considered is individual vocational counselling. Here one finds professionally trained workers whose chief function is to assist the individual client with his educational or occupational problem. The larger part of the present text is devoted to this area.

In practice, partly because of the newness of the profession, the vocational counsellor may be called upon to participate in community organisation and group vocational guidance, as well as individual counselling. The fact that his personal background, interests, and talents may not lie in all these areas is not always taken into consideration. What is particularly important from the present viewpoint is not so much the differences among the vocational functions as their similarities. Irrespective of the broad area of specialisation, all vocational counsellors possess certain fundamental characteristics which enable them to call themselves vocational counsellors and which distinguish them from, let us say, teachers or electricians.

The medical profession has set up, quite wisely, areas of specialisation which differ not only in function but also in degree and type of preparation. Thus we have physicians, nurses, laboratory technologists, hospital attendants, pharmacists, etc. Each one has his definite function defined by extent and kind of training, as well as by law. A nurse, for example, is not a miniature physician, nor is a pharmacist almost a medical doctor. One either is a physician or is not. The issue is not whether one is apediatrician, an obstetrician, or a psychiatrist. The question is whether one has met the state requirements for an M.D. degree or not. No such legal distinction exists in respect to vocational guidance; hence one is free to speak of levels among vocational counsellors. This is unfortunate; the concept of vocational counselling should be defined in terms of training, function, and legal requirements. A uniform standard for vocational counsellors would also leave room for all those who practice some form of vocational guidance or assist the counsellor, and yet do not meet the minimal requirements. Adequate legislation could protect the broad public from the unscrupulous and the incompetent, who may be found in the midst of vocational counsellors of today.

Vocational guidance is a helping profession. An important distinction between a helping profession and a trade lies not only in the extent and levels of training but in the fact that becoming a professional demands an active involvement of the self. A man may take a course in television mechanics, learn the necessary facts, acquire the appropriate skills, and still remain essentially the same person he was prior to his becoming a television maintenance man. On the other hand, a person studying for a profession which purports to assist others not only acquires the factual knowledge necessary for its practice but also develops as a human being. Unlike the television mechanic, the counsellor, the caseworker, or the physician is no longer his former self. Something has happened to him as a result of his training. This something is professional growth. But growth does not occur spontaneously and automatically as a result of mere contact with a textbook or a classroom. Growth is an experience which becomes meaningful only when the learner can internalize that which is happening around him. A personal involvement is essential in the growing process. This is perhaps why standard classroom lectures and laboratory procedures do not contribute significantly to the intrinsic development of the student. He may learn facts, techniques, and principles, which constitute an essential part of his professional background—but formal instructions rarely involve the active use of self. As a matter of fact, a large lecture room with an impersonal professor at the head is conducive to minimal participation on the part of the student. The relative anonymity of the individual in a group situation will be very likely to result in his avoiding the responsibility for the growing process. Professional growth cannot be expressed in terms of graduate credits, the number of advanced degrees held, or certification. This is not to imply that academic training is unessential or of secondary importance. Quite the contrary, it is a "must," but a "must" which, although necessary, is not sufficient in itself. A comprehensive training programme for vocational counsellors not only should consist of classroom instructions, and field-work experience, but also must afford the kind of supervision which will compel the trainee to examine his feelings and attitudes toward himself, his supervisor, and those who come to him for professional help.

Vocational Guidance a Misnomer

The term vocational guidance is an unfortunate one. It is used in this book as an expedient. Common usage makes it inadvisable to devise a new term, for this would create the impression that one is dealing not with vocational guidance but with some newly conceived entity. Perhaps the most desirable feature of the term vocational guidance is the fact that the occupational focus is implied in the very expression. Although historically the emphasis may have shifted from apprenticeship programmes, to aptitude testing, and finally to the helping process itself, the salient fact remains that vocational guidance has always been concerned with the individual and his adjustment to the world of work. Thus vocational guidance emerges as a discipline distinct from social work, psychology, or generic counselling.

But vocational guidance is not concerned solely with vocations in the traditional sense of the word. Although the emphasis is on occupational adjustment, vocational guidance also embraces the educational aspects of growth and certainly the attitudes, feelings, and anxieties that revolve around the all-important problems of work, occupational status, job satisfaction, security, and many other facets of earning a livelihood on which our society places such a premium. An atomistic breakdown of personality into interests, aptitudes, intelligence, and similar components and an artificial matching of the measured attributes with the existing labour market and occupational trends are a poor substitute for a helping process. Vocational guidance, if it is to be effective, must take into consideration the individual's needs, his drives, his aspirations, and his opportunities. It must weigh carefully the client's acceptance of himself in his new role as a carpenter, entertainer, or apprentice. Of equal importance is the client's ability to live comfortably with the new trade and the new reality which may have been brought about as a result of his occupational plans. Although the *content* of vocational guidance is the manner in which one earns a livelihood, the *focus* is the helping process, which enables the person to effect appropriate changes within himself and the environment about him.

It is within the function of the vocational counsellor to help an adolescent with high professional ambitions to accept the fact that he is not college material. Similarly it is within the scope of the counsellor's activities to assist an elderly worker to recognise that he has outlived his industrial usefulness but still may enjoy years of fruitful living. The European refugee, who may have commanded respect as a successful businessman abroad, may have to be helped to accept himself for what he is and what he can do in a new land. One could continue listing other situations which demand vocational readjustment, not merely as a step from one job to another, but as a *process* which enables the client to make a major change and "live with it." This is not to suggest that most of the counsellor's activities deal with misfortunes in life. Vocational changes in the positive direction, too, may arouse anxieties and doubts that go with added responsibilities and higher occupational status. The handling of feelings that may accompany a plan or a change for the better is also part of vocational guidance. Thus we see that the adjective "vocational," in the present context, embraces many activities which, although vested in occupational planning and work satisfaction in general, transcend the conventional limits.

The term guidance is also not only poorly chosen but actually misleading. Literally it means to direct, to conduct, or to pilot. Implicitly it suggests that the counsellor knows the path of action which the client should follow and accordingly guides the latter along the true course. As a corollary, the client surrenders himself to the omniscience of the counsellor, with minimal participation of his own. Nothing could be further from the truth. As we shall see later, the client's activity, if it is to be truly his, must always be self-directed. The counsellor's role is not that of a guide or of a catalytic agent but of a professional worker who, by virtue of his qualifications and affiliation with the agency, assumes the responsibility for helping the client with his dilemma. As Pray expressed it, "It is the process of helping, not the ultimate outcome for which the worker carries the responsibility."

The client-counsellor dynamics are exceedingly complex—so complex in fact, that a large portion of this work is devoted to discussion of this very important point. For the present it will suffice to note that the term guidance not only does not express what actually takes place during the vocational process but virtually distorts its true meaning.

Because of the unfortunate connotations implicit in the term vocational guidance, use is made of such expressions as vocational assistance and occupational planning, for they seem to be free from some of the objections raised to the term vocational guidance and also tend to emphasise the helping and the planning aspects of the programme.

But even these expressions fail to convey the active role of the client and the significance of the interpersonal client-counsellor relationship. Rogers's "client-centred" counselling (or therapy) seems to fall short of the desired mark, just as does Taft's "relationship therapy." Counselling, if it is to deserve that name, is always client-centred in the sense that it is the client who wants help and is, therefore, the central figure during the interview. With respect to relationship therapy Allen cogently remarks, "All therapy involves a relationship between patient and therapist". Perhaps the English language lacks the words that would incisively express the actual meaning of vocational guidance with all its implications. Even if an appropriate formulation were found, it could never be completely equated with the substance itself. The chapters that follow will attempt to describe and to illustrate what vocational guidance may signify to some counsellors.

The Focus in Vocational Guidance

The entire existence of vocational guidance, its very *raison d'être,* is predicated upon the fact that it is a helping discipline. Vocational guidance has no other justification for existence than to assist people with their occupational adjustments in a manner that will be truly beneficial to those in need of help. To attain this objective, the vocational counsellor will utilise his interviewing skills, his body of knowledge regarding occupations, his intimate familiarity with psychological dynamics and psychometric data. In addition to his professional training, the counsellor will also convey to the client that he is genuinely interested in the latter's problems, that he tries to understand the client's needs, and that he respects the client's right to differ from him. The professionally disciplined counsellor has no other interest in the client than to help him with the problem under consideration. He will therefore refrain from doing anything that does not in some way facilitate the helping process. For example, the counsellor will not ask any questions, no matter how intriguing they may seem to him, unless the answers to these questions help the client resolve his dilemma. He certainly will not administer tests to the client unless he feels quite certain that the test results will reveal some significant aspects of the client's make-up relevant to the problem at hand. Scientific curiosity, laudable as it may be in research, has no place in a guidance process. Taft, in discussing the nonscientific role of social casework, states:

"That social case work cannot become a science, is taken for granted by virtue of its practical basis. To establish truth, or to engage in scientifically valid research can never be its aim, since, always, whatever it does is vitiated for science by its avowed purpose, which is to help. Where helping human beings comes first, interests in furthering scientific observation must be sacrificed, for the one destroys the other".

Vocational counselling, too, is concerned primarily with help. Its cardinal aim is to assist the client rather than to establish scientific principles. Help is the first general objective of vocational guidance. As we proceed, we shall see how vocational guidance differs from other helping professions.

Areas of Research in Guidance

Those counsellors trained in psychological research, the experimental method, and statistical investigation may find it difficult to accept such an orientation as that just described. To allay their anxieties, it may be stated emphatically that the field of vocational guidance not only welcomes scientific studies in that area but is actually handicapped by an insufficiency of scientific evidence. This statement is probably equally applicable to other helping professions.

Specialists trained in vocational guidance and research have indeed contributed a great deal to a better understanding of counselling dynamics, the relative effectiveness of the techniques employed, and the outcome of the vocational guidance process. Numerous studies that analyse minutely electrical recordings of counselling interviews are available to those interested in research. And yet, despite all the accumulated knowledge, much additional investigation is needed into the dynamics of counselling itself and into the criteria for counselability, readiness, and movement. Similarly, little is known about the effectiveness and value of vocational guidance after the cessation of contacts with the agency—in other words, there is a definite need for follow-up studies. These are of interest not only to professional workers but to those vested with the responsibility of administering funds for vocational guidance. The results of such investigations are closely related to the whole question of promotion and interpretation of vocational guidance to the entire community. Still other areas that demand scientific research are psychometric and vocational testing in terms of their usefulness and validity in vocational guidance. What is the actual relationship between a test score and one's performance on the job? Can individual prediction be made on the basis of test evidence? There is also a demand for studies in occupational trends, in the training and supervision of students and vocational workers, in the setting up of professional standards and certification procedures. No discussion dealing with research in vocational guidance can omit the need for study of the special groups, *i.e.*, the adolescent, the aged, and the physically and mentally handicapped. The list could undoubtedly be extended, demonstrating further the necessity for objective evidence in the relatively nascent field of vocational guidance. Research in guidance becomes particularly tempting if one considers the fact that almost every agency practicing in that area probably has at its disposal hundreds, or possibly thousands, of individual case histories and psychometric data. Only recently the Veterans Administration (VA) expressed willingness to lend some 300,000 completed test blanks and answer sheets to qualified individuals or institutions interested in research. Although such information may be of limited value in certain investigations, much of it probably could be put to excellent use.

However, no matter how pressing the necessity for research and investigation in guidance is, the scientific activity, as such, cannot go on during the helping process. It is impossible for the counsellor to assume the roles of the helper and the scientist simultaneously during the interview, for the two objectives are contradictory to each other.

Help Centred Vocational Guidance

Philosophically help-centred vocational guidance differs from other types of vocational guidance in that its primary, and only, function is to help the client attain an occupational adjustment that is satisfactory from his standpoint. It is a system of thought based upon the principle that the client is the one to decide on whether or not he wants help, on the kind of assistance he is ready to accept, and on the direction in which he prefers to move. It bears some resemblance to the "functional" approach in casework, but it is not "functional guidance."

Very briefly, the distinction between the "diagnostic" and the "functional" philosophy is as follows: In the former, "help is conceived as a planned, goal directed treatment... the treatment objectives and techniques are variable, selected to meet the requirements of the diagnosis". The functional position is that problems arise out of a "destructive use of relationships." The new experience between client and counsellor enables the former to make a new and constructive use of himself and the latter. The activity is not guided by the diagnostic findings, nor is it initiated by the counsellor. In the words of the committee established to study the differences in orientation, "the client gives direction to his own processes of change, with the worker taking responsibility for his own part in helping the client to realise these processes".

The help-centred approach, too, upholds the client's right to self-direction and places confidence in his ability to help himself. The term "help-centred guidance" rather than "functional guidance" was selected because of several considerations. The word "function" has a definite, almost a technical meaning in social casework. It denotes a philosophy and an approach which came into being as a result of inner forces within that area and which should operate there. By comparison with vocational guidance, casework is an old art, which in the course of its growth has developed viewpoints and skills particularly suited to its objectives. Through its schools of social work, professional journals, and conferences, social work has evolved a body of practice dedicated to assist mankind with certain ills. That in the course of time differences in theory should have developed is not only to be expected but perhaps to be desired. Complete accord on every issue is rarely conducive to progress. Today, there are several schools of thought in social work, each contributing its share to human welfare.

Vocational guidance, as contrasted with some other helping disciplines, is strictly a neophyte. At the present stage of its early development it cannot identify itself totally with an existing philosophy of an already well-established profession. It still remains to be demonstrated ,that principles applicable to social work possess the same validity and significance in vocational guidance. To appropriate a label uncritically would be a folly that might hinder, rather than promote, the growth of guidance.

The term help-centred guidance was chosen for other reasons as well. First, and possibly foremost, it draws a line of distinction between itself and the diagnostic approach, which places a premium on genesis. Help-centred thinking by contrast emphasises not the past history but the present reality as it is perceived by the client. It furthermore assumes that with professional assistance the client will be able to move in the areas in which he can take help and in the direction of his choice. At no time does the help-centred worker question the client's right to have conficts, to have problems, or to do, or not to do, anything about these. Unlike nondirective counselling, help-centred guidance is not based primarily on "permissiveness" but is predicated on a clearly structured client-counsellor relationship. Although it respects the client's right to accept or to reject any part of the service, help-centred guidance offers the client an opportunity to examine the nature of his vocational problem and to decide whether he wishes to continue with vocational counselling. In other words, the client is always given a choice of action. Far from being passive, the worker plays an important and active part in assisting the client to express his doubts and negative feelings and to arrive at a decision for which he can assume some responsibility. The client also learns to work with limits by discovering that he can weather the painful aspects of being helped. These and other questions of equal importance to fuller understanding of help-centred counselling will be discussed later in the text.

A philosophy vested in the belief that the client can help himself is particularly suited to the treatment of vocational difficulties. We shall see later that such self-help does not arise spontaneously but is brought about as a result of psychological (affective) interaction between client and counsellor. People frequently have to be helped to help themselves. A clear understanding of the focus of the problem and the function of the worker keeps the entire relationship on a reality level without allowing it to become an experience in total personality analysis. The fact that the client can discuss his occupational dilemma without fear of becoming lost in the primordial jungle of the unconscious may enable him to proceed with the problem at hand, the problem which caused him to seek assistance in the first place. Even psychoanalytically oriented workers feel that the psychology of Freud has made relatively little contribution to vocational guidance because it tends to explain phenomena in terms of instinctual drives. The choice of an occupation, they contend, must be "approached primarily as a problem of ego psychology."

A fuller utilisation of the "ego," or "self," is the theme of the present work. Rogers, on one occasion at least, voices the belief that the client-centred counselling approach is of particular value because it is "much safer". The present thesis places the client in a central position, not because of the safety factor, but because the client is the only one who can decide what type of service he wants and what occupational choice he wishes to make.

Vocational help is essentially a process intended to enable the client to mobilise his inner resources to an optimum level. The counsellor's contribution lies in helping the client to verbalise his feelings and attitudes and thus possibly arrive at some occupational plan which is his own. But an expression of feelings on the part of the client cannot be conducted as a monologue. Nor is it sufficient to paraphrase or "reflect" these feelings. In order to be genuinely helpful, the counsellor has to demonstrate his sincere desire to assist the client and his genuine faith in the latter's right to arrive at his own decisions. The counsellor is nondirective only in the sense that he does not thrust his own values, attitudes, and goals upon the client. He is directive in the sense that he becomes a meaningful figure in the client-counsellor relationship. He may identify himself with the client at one point. He may differentiate himself from the client with respect to some other issues. In his professional role he may set limits, which the client may "fight" at first, only to emerge a stronger person somewhat later. We shall have occasion to return repeatedly to the important question of the part the worker assumes in the vocational counselling relationship.

This position is in sharp contrast with the psychoanalytical philosophy which implicitly postulates that the therapist "knows best" what is good for the client. Diagnostically oriented guidance is predicated on a comprehensive study of the individual in terms of his present, *i.e.*, his abilities, interests, aptitudes, etc., as measured by various tests, and his past, as revealed by a case history, school records, statements found in referrals, etc. The counsellor then analyses and interprets the accumulated data and subtly, or otherwise, suggests the appropriate plan of action as well as the most feasible objective. When the client is resistant to the counsellor's directives, the latter may attempt to overcome this by employing suitable professional techniques, such as persuasive interpretation, calculated to enable the client to accept the counsellor's viewpoint. Allen notes correctly that the client who gives himself up to the will of the therapist is considered "cooperative" as judged by an authoritarian worker. Conversely, the client who insists on his right to decide for himself may be labelled "recalcitrant." Neither term has a place in a system of counselling which upholds the client's right of self-determination.

At this point the reader should be cautioned not to infer that help-centred guidance completely disregards the value of psychometric testing and the case history. Both have a definite place in a comprehensive vocational programme. The emphasis, however, is not so much on factual information as on the feelings the client may have about the tests, what taking tests signifies *to* him, and how he can use the objective findings. The merits of factual information have probably been vastly overrated and at times have actually been employed as a poor substitute for competent vocational planning. Facts in themselves, although of potentially tremendous significance, are of value in vocational guidance only to the extent that they can be used by the client.

Traditionally psychologists and vocational counsellors have devoted a considerable amount of effort to the measurement of general ability, special aptitudes, manual dexterity, and other attributes on the assumption that a fuller understanding of the client's potentialities will suggest a more appropriate occupational choice and will increase his chances of vocational success. This general hypothesis is held by some vocational counsellors despite the overwhelming amount of empirical evidence that tends to point to the opposite conclusion. Even a variable such as academic ability, which lends itself to relatively precise measurement, is rather unreliable as an index of academic achievement and is still less reliable as a criterion for vocational success in the broader sense of the word. Instruments designed to measure such intangible entities as spatial visualisation and musical aptitude are still less reliable as tools for predicting success in a specific occupational area. Every counsellor is familiar with brilliant students who fail in school and mediocre individuals who nevertheless do entirely satisfactory work. In industry, where one's vocational success is not gauged necessarily by one's grades on an examination, success on a job is frequently determined by numerous variables other than finger dexterity or mechanical aptitude as measured by a test.

The relatively low correlation between the amount or degree of any single aptitude evinced by the individual and the extent of vocational success as suggested by job satisfaction, on-the-job proficiency, or income should be a matter of concern to all vocational counsellors. As previously indicated, a great deal of vocational guidance is predicated on the assumption that, once the counsellor and client can establish reliably the latter's potentialities, the client can proceed to plan accordingly. The fact that in practice this is not always so has not seriously challenged the basic belief in the almost supernatural value of factual data and information. Important as objective evidence may be, there is more to vocational planning than matching aptitudes with occupations. The fact that some capable persons fail at one time in their lives, only to do well during other periods, cannot be explained in terms of aptitudes alone. Nor can one explain satisfactorily by means of vocational tests why a less gifted person will at times do better than an individual endowed with superior abilities. The counsellor when confronted with facts that appear to be paradoxical, on the surface at least, will probably give recognition to forces that do not lend themselves readily to quantification. The counsellor will speak of personality components, emotional blocking, drives, readiness, habits etc., as factors that determine the dynamic functioning of the individual.

No factorial analysis of personality from a vocational standpoint seems ever to have been made. In other words, it is a matter of conjecture whether it is the aptitudes or the rather intangible aspects of personality that play a more decisive role in determining vocational success. Daily observation would suggest that one's concern over a vocational dilemma, one's desire to do something about it, and finally one's ability to mobilise and integrate one's inherent strengths constitute the major forces that determine movement. In school as well as on the job, success appears to be conditioned not so much by what the client may *possess* in terms of general potentialities as by his being able to *use* to an optimum extent that which he has. In short, educational or vocational progress may be considered as a function of the degree to which the client can use himself in that particular area.

The concept of self-use in a particular endeavour has little in common with that of total emotional adjustment. A "classical psychoneurotic" may do well in school or on a job, sometimes precisely because of his neurotic needs. It has been said wisely that "it is a sick oyster that yields a pearl." Similarly, a person may be well adjusted in his work but a failure as a sex partner. The counsellor's function, as previously indicated, is not to attempt to bring about total adjustment but rather to help the client in a given vocational area. Vocational adjustment, as suggested by Super, is a subjectively perceived experience. It is really a form of movement toward self-acceptance in terms of abilities, background, opportunities, and similar realities on the one hand and vocational objectives and aspirations on the other. Shostrom and Brammer perceive one's adjustment as "a manner consistent with his self concept". Such self-consistency is the goal of psychological counselling, which attempts to stress the client's feelings rather than objective facts.

It is both interesting and significant that the concept of psychological counselling appears to be extending beyond the rather narrow circle of workers devoted to the helping aspects of counselling. Thus at a conference of the Institute for Human

Adjustment held at the University of Michigan in 1949 and 1950, the following important conclusion was reached: "Even educational and vocational choices, however, entail more than a consideration of abilities and interests in relation to educational and occupational opportunities. Status needs, parent attitudes, and various interpersonal and intra personal pressures complicate the process of making choices". Having generally indicated the scope of the problem, the institute proceeded to spell out the major aspects of psychological counselling, viz.: *(a)* increasing the accuracy of the individual's self-percept; *(b)* increasing the accuracy of the individual's environmental perceptions; *(c)* integrating the individual's self-percepts and his environmental perceptions; *(d)* presenting relevant information; *(e)* improving the individual's planning and execution. To this list one might also add helping the individual to develop his ego strength, assisting him to assume responsibility for his choices, and giving him the right to self-determination.

Most vocational failures are not necessarily persons with low IQ's, reading deficiencies, poor spatial visualisation, or inferior finger dexterity. Actually, they often are persons whose various abilities are distributed along the Gaussian curve like those of the rest of the population. Wechsler questions seriously the concept that human attributes distribute themselves along the normal probability curve. From the standpoint of the present discussion the actual equation for the distribution of human capacities is of secondary interest. What distinguishes these individuals vocationally from others is their inability to integrate and to organise themselves in a constructive manner.

If the present thesis is correct, *i.e.*, if a person's vocational or educational success is determined chiefly by his ability to utilise his strength and assets, it follows that the counsellor's primary function is to assist the client to make a fuller use of his potentialities. An acceptance of this hypothesis must shift the emphasis in vocational guidance from diagnostic activity to that of the helping process. The objectives of the help-centred philosophy place emphasis not so much on the exploration of the client's attributes as on service that will enable the client to utilise more fully his potentialities and drives in keeping with his set of values and reality.

The present brief discussion on the difference between help centred vocational guidance and other forms of vocational assistance does not exhaust the subject. Further references to the question will be made throughout the text as additional concepts are discussed.

❑❑❑

2

THE HELPING PROFESSIONS

The Relationship of Vocational Guidance to other Helping Professions

Vocational guidance as a profession has a great deal in common with other disciplines whose chief function is to assist human beings with their problems, resembling to some extent psychiatry, psychology, and social casework. In practice it is at times difficult to draw a sharp line between the different professions. That it should be so need not be too surprising if one considers the fact that human sorrow rarely comes wrapped up in individual, clearly labelled packages. As often as not, relationship difficulties appear alongside of vocational conflicts, only to be superseded by problems in personality disorder. To disentangle the complex skein of professional responsibilities requires more than skills. What is needed is a clear theoretical understanding of the function of the professional worker and the focus of the problem.

Ginzberg *et al.* note that, despite the great abundance of vocational literature, the field itself is "conceptually weak.". They view vocational guidance as "an offshoot of the psychology of individual differences," as something that tends to be "atomistic" and "static." With the possible exception of Rogers and his colleagues, vocational guidance is rarely, if ever, perceived as a helping process. Most workers in the field regard it essentially as a diagnostic, goal-directed activity. The distinction between vocational guidance and other helping professions is frequently made on the basis not of the *nature* of the problem but of its *intensity*.

Thus, the treatment of severe personality disorders is usually undertaken by psychiatrists; when the disorders are less dramatic and less severe, they may be handled by psychologists; emotional problems of still lesser intensity may be assigned to caseworkers. By the same token vocational counsellors deal with problems that have only a minimal affective value.

Actual experience with clients completely rejects this system of classification. The intensity of feeling experienced by a client has little relation to the nosological diagnosis. A client may feel extremely threatened and disturbed over the loss of a job and yet show little concern over his obsessive-compulsive tendencies. The criteria by which the different professions can be distinguished are not the severity of the problem with which they deal but rather the kind of problem which the particular profession is qualified to handle. The distinction between psychotherapy as conducted by the psychiatrist and counselling as furnished by the vocational worker certainly is not that the former deals in "deep" therapy as contrasted with the "superficial" nature of the counselling process. Both professions encounter problems that require the highest degree of competence and skills as well as difficulties that can be ameliorated quite readily. One of the fundamental differences between the work of the psychiatrist and other professionals engaged in the helping process lies in the distinction between the concepts of psychotherapy and counselling. Dynamic psychotherapy deals primarily with internalized problems of the *total* personality and total reality; vocational counselling, on the other hand, concerns itself chiefly with those aspects of personality as related to a specific occupational problem.

Those trained to think in terms of the whole personality may feel that every facet of human activity derives its meaning from the total psyche. This indeed is so, except that in a helping relationship it is possible to differentiate between treatment of the entire personality structure and help with a particular problem. Psychoanalysis or any other system of therapy that has as its objective a remolding of the total inner make-up of the individual must be assigned to the psychiatrist. The question is not whether the problem is one of mild anxiety, insomnia, or acute hallucination. The issue is not how severe the disturbance is but rather what it is that prompts the client to seek help. A client may be seriously upset over his inability to succeed in his occupational endeavour. He may be equally concerned about his feelings of tension and disquietude. The former complaint should be handled by the vocational counsellor; the latter, irrespective of its affective intensity, has to be treated by the psychiatrist. In short, the counsellor is more likely to deal with the problems of daily living as opposed to those which embrace the entire self.

Opponents of this view may hold that assisting the client with a specific complaint is merely treating a symptom. This may or may not be so. A specific difficulty, such as inability to get along in a job, may be a problem in vocational fitness or a sign of schizophrenia. If it is the latter, it will be associated with a number of additional pathological indications that constitute the schizophrenic syndrome. If it is the former and the person in question comes to the counsellor for vocational assistance, the worker can assume the responsibility for helping him. It is entirely possible that the difficulties at work may be due to over-qualification (or underqualification), a lack of interest in the field, or the fact that the particular job fails to satisfy some of the basic needs for recognition, prestige, etc. The counsellor need not fear that he is treating symptoms as long as he understands the nature of the complaint and his own professional function. It would be most unfortunate for the client who wants help with an occupational problem to find himself plunged into a psychoanalytic abyss. At the risk of oversimplification, it should be remembered that one need not take the entire automobile apart in order to change the spark plugs. Counselling experience demonstrates that it is possible to assist a client with his educational, vocational, or social problems without having to resort to a complete personality reorganisation.

In the preceding section it was mentioned that one important goal of vocational guidance is to help the client. It was furthermore pointed out that such help does not lie necessarily in providing the client with a concrete answer or tangible results. Vocational assistance as envisioned here is a growth process which involves the discovery, awareness, and affirmation of the client's own strength. Now we come to the *focus*, which deals with assistance in specific areas. This is not a question of content or in density alone. The vocational worker in order to be helpful, will often discover that he may have to handle feeling of depth and poignancy. He may be called upon to exercise all his sensitiveness to the nuances conveyed during the counselling session in order to enable the client to move in the direction of his choice. However, the skilled counsellor will not allow himself to be drawn into areas outside of his professional domain. At no time can he assume the responsibility for practicing psychiatry or social casework. As Aptekar puts it, "The psychotherapist's centre of interest . . . is the person, and not the service . . ." The vocational counsellor's chief focus is the service, not the whole person.

At this point it may be helpful to distinguish between *content* and *focus*, especially since the latter term is not too frequently encountered in vocational guidance circles. Let us take a simple hypothetical case of a proofreader who comes for vocational guidance because his eyes are failing. He is concerned lest he be compelled to give up his job and learn a new occupation. This may be a problem in ophthalmology or vocational guidance. It may also be a problem in medical casework if it involves fears of becoming totally blind or a matter for psychiatry if the failing vision is a hysterical or a psychosomatic phenomenon. Let us consider another case, of a chronic alcoholic who because of his inebriety cannot hold a job. As in the preceding illustration the problem itself may lie in several areas. The content in both instances may be of a vocational nature, depending on the focus, or the area in which the client wants help.

It is apparent that the vocational counsellor would not attempt to treat the proofreader's eye condition any more than he would handle the problem of alcoholism. Both the content and the focus would be almost automatically limited to the occupational nature of the problem. The situation, however, is not always so obvious. For example, a neurotic person may request help which is vocational in content and yet really seek assistance with his neurosis, which would be the psychiatrist's function. The distinction between content and focus lies not so much in the verbal presentation made by the client as in his actual motives for seeking help. Only recently such a case was described at a vocational guidance conference. A man who was fearful of women and who had given up his job at a plant where many women were employed came to a vocational counsellor for help. After listing to the general problem, the counsellor indicated to the client that the agency could help only with occupational difficulties and suggested an appropriate referral if he wanted help in the psychosexual area. The client accepted these limits but continued to revert to problems which seemed to cause him greater disturbance than the loss of a job. As the counsellor attempted to focus on the vocational aspects of the problem, the client would comply, only to return to the original and more burning issue. He used the vocational guidance content merely to retain his eligibility for service offered by the agency but was unable to accept the vocational focus.

For that matter, one would expect the client, rather than the counsellor, to select the focus, with the latter helping the client to clarify his request. The counsellor cannot tell the client in which area or for which problems he should seek help. An emotionally disturbed individual who shows a genuine concern over his occupational future may sometimes be helped in the vocational area despite his emotional disequilibrium. The counsellor should not assume that the client wants psychiatric treatment simply because it seems to be indicated. If the client is able to focus on the vocational aspects of the process, the worker may want to go along with him even if the client appears to be emotionally disturbed. On the other hand, vocational content alone, if unsupported by the client's desire to be helped in the occupational area, will not provide a basis for a vocational counselling relationship.

As the client and the counsellor work jointly on a specific problem, the former may show growth, not only in relation to the particular area under consideration, but with respect to his total ego strength. Counselling often proves to be a therapeutic experience which enables the client to make a fuller use of self, even in situations not directly related to the issue in question. We shall see later that coming for vocational assistance is frequently a difficult step to take. Entering into a helping relationship with a counsellor is almost invariably a psychological experience. What the outcome of the vocational contacts will be cannot be determined in advance, although it is probable that the client will emerge with a greater amount of self-reliance as a result of the counselling sessions. Needless to say much will depend on the client's readiness and capacity for movement. So in a sense the broader aspects of personality are involved after all.

The significant contribution of the focus-oriented type of counselling is that it helps the client to grow, not by grappling with the entire personality configuration (as he would in the psychiatric situation), but by working within a clearly defined area. This area, or focus, is determined by the nature of the problem and the counsellor's readiness to assume responsibility for helping the client with the particular difficulty. Clients will sometimes introduce into the vocational counselling experience problems which, although genuine, nevertheless lie outside the occupational focus. When such a situation arises, the counsellor cannot take it upon himself to assist the client in the new area as well. Recognition of the fact that several related problems may coexist should not tempt the counsellor to handle all of them. Quite the contrary, a fuller understanding of the counsellor's own function and that of other professions should be conducive to closer cooperation among the different helping professions. It is entirely possible that the difficulties revealed by one and the same client may require the joint participation of an entire "team."

The relationship between vocational guidance and other helping professions can be discussed on two levels: the theoretical, which points out the similarities and the differences between vocational guidance and another profession, and the practical, which helps one understand how vocational guidance and another profession can utilise each other's respective knowledge and skills.

Relationship between Vocational Guidance and Psychiatry

We have already touched on some fundamental differences between counselling and psychotherapy and by implication made the distinction between the counsellor and the psychiatrist. We have also noted that theoretically the role of the vocational counsellor is differentiated from that of the therapist in that the former is responsible for the administration of a concrete and tangible service whereas the latter concerns himself with the total personality structure. The psychiatrist rarely takes it upon himself to change the patient environment by, let us say, finding job for him. When he does so, be referring the patient to an employment agency, the job itself is not the ultimate objective, but merely an intermediate step toward a broader and total goal. The patient comes to the psychiatrist not with his placement problem but with his intrapsychic difficulties with which he wants help. Here once more we see the difference between content (placement) and focus (psychotherapy).

Other differences between the two areas exist that are too obvious to require discussion, such as the difference in training for physicians and for vocational counsellors. A significant aspect in the training for the two professions, however, is sometimes overlooked. Although a medical background supplemented by post-graduate study in psychiatry may qualify a physician to claim exclusive rights to the fields of psychopathology and psychosomatics, it does not in any way prepare him for practice in vocational guidance or related areas. Actually when psychiatrists have occasion to work together with vocational counsellors, this vital point is at times ignored.

The question of practical cooperation between vocational guidance and psychiatry is gaining some prominence in vocational circles. At the 1951 session of the National Conference of the Jewish Occupational Council, for example, an entire meeting was devoted to this issue. Some private vocational guidance agencies are seeking psychiatrists to work jointly as either consultants or members of the staff. The inclusion of psychiatrists in the vocational programme raises numerous practical questions which demand careful consideration.

Among the first questions one may want to consider is the readiness of the staff to make full use of the psychiatrist. Coleman notes that workers who are compelled to carry large case loads with infrequent contacts between worker and client are generally not prepared to utilise the contributions of the psychiatrist. Relatively untrained workers and those who feel professionally insecure are even less ready to benefit from the experience of having a psychiatrist work alongside them.

As a corollary, the psychiatrist who does not understand clearly his role in a vocational agency may also feel threatened by the nonmedically trained workers around him. Developing a good intrastaff relationship may be harder for the psychiatrist than for the counsellor; for whereas most counsellors are acquainted with the functions and responsibilities of psychiatry, few, if any, psychiatrists have had any orientation in vocational counselling. This is because academic curricula in guidance, psychology, or casework almost invariably include courses in abnormal psychology, pathology, or psychiatric casework but the protectoral training of the physician or his postdoctoral courses in psychiatry do not, at any point, deal with occupational counselling or related subjects.

Even prior to the psychiatrist's becoming a consultant or a full-fledged member of the staff, it is imperative to define the exact function of each member in his new partnership. To facilitate matters, it must be clearly understood that at no time is the psychiatrist to become a guidance counsellor, any more than the counsellor is to become a psychiatrist. There can be no hierarchy in a "team" relationship, for each professional contributes that which is unique to his own training and experience. It is only by fostering mutual esteem for the respective contribution of each discipline that one can expect truly integrated achievements to take place.

The concept of a "clinical team" has captured the imagination of many professional workers in the helping area. But by no means all advocates of the team approach recognise the functional implications of this idea. The strength of the team does not arise out of an algebraic summation of its components. It is rather a *Gestalt-quality* that emerges out of the *unity of differences* among its constituent members. In other words, the value of the team lies not in the additive combined efforts of several individuals performing approximately the same function but precisely in the differentiation of functions and the specific contribution each member of the team can make. In a team relationship it is imperative to define the responsibilities and functions of each participant in order to effect optimum helpfulness for the client. However, a hierarchical or paternalistic structure within the team itself is not likely to elicit his fullest contribution from each member. Rather, mutual respect for the knowledge and skills of the respective professions will probably reduce some of the tensions that can arise out of professional mistrust and personal insecurity.

At this point it may be in order to consider some of the specific contributions of a psychiatrist to a vocational service Unfortunately, vocational literature does not seem to deal with this question too comprehensively. When the role of the psychiatrist is mentioned, he is viewed primarily in his relation to the client. That is to say, the psychiatrist is seen as a diagnostician, as one "of great assistance in detecting cases of incipient dementia praecox", and as a therapist. The present question, however, is not what the function of a psychiatrist is in general but what his part is in a vocational guidance setting. Once again one is compelled to refer to casework for a possible answer to' this important problem.

Caseworkers, by virtue of their function, have for a long time come into active professional contact with psychiatrists. Specially trained "psychiatric" as well as "generic" social workers have, for years, worked alongside medically trained doctors on problems of emotional adjustment. In the course of time, they have developed a functional rationale based on a division of responsibilities toward the client. This is not to imply that a professional utopia has been attained. There still exist psychiatrists who see the caseworker chiefly as a subordinate whose primary job is to collect factual information, just as there are social workers who view the psychiatrist with a great deal of professional mistrust. Further interprofessional difficulties occasionally arise out of the attitude of some in the medical field that social work and social services are essentially for the economically underprivileged masses and that social work must therefore be an inferior discipline; hence the caseworker is assigned a lower professional status. The significant question, however, from the present standpoint is not the degree of harmony that may exist between psychiatry and casework but the fact that, as a result of continuous and close cooperation between the two professions, casework has developed both a theoretical and a practical *modus vivendi*. Vocational guidance, or for that matter clinical psychology, because of the newness of the situation which demands joint participation, has not had an opportunity to develop a philosophy of its own. With proper modifications, some of the principles developed through close cooperation between psychiatrists and caseworkers could be applied with almost equal validity to a vocational guidance agency: *(a)* The psychiatrist, by virtue of his medical training, may be used as a consultant in individual vocational counselling cases. Specifically, he may make a psychiatric (a total personality) diagnosis if one is deemed necessary. He may enter into a brief therapeutic relationship with a client, if the latter demonstrates his inability to use vocational assistance or if a referral for psychotherapy appears to be definitely indicated. By virtue of his training in psychopathology, the psychiatrist is in a better position than the counsellor to evaluate the probable adjustment of prepsychotic or "remission" clients. *(b)* He may act as a teacher in psychiatric theory as it is applicable to the counselling process. *(c)* He may assist in differential diagnosis in terms of counselability and suggest appropriate referrals when necessary. *(d)* Lastly, the psychiatrist can help on the administrative level in the evaluation and improvement of the collaborative efforts.

The introduction of a professional trained in a fundamentally different area is likely to engender considerable anxiety and tension in an otherwise smoothly functioning staff. Those familiar with the operation of a professional "team" will recognise the fact that, in practice, harmonious interacting relationships are the exception rather than the rule. Several reasons suggest themselves for this condition, among which one can point to the failure of each member of the group to perceive clearly his own function and that of his fellow worker. A more sharply defined operational focus would probably alleviate some of the tensions that arise when several professionals begin to "step on each other's toes." Much confusion could probably be eliminated through a better understanding of the role of the vocational guidance agency. As Taft cogently remarks as she discusses the function of casework help. In other words, is casework help in the counselling case merely a stop gap, an inferior kind of helping for those who know or can afford no better, or is it a legitimate social service for which a social agency through its workers can take full responsibility without disguise or apology, and without psychiatric supervision. Vocational counsellors too, once fully convinced of their function, could take their stand proudly among the most specialised helping professions.

Relationship between Vocation Guidance and Psychology

Historically vocational guidance is more closely related to psychology than to any other field dealing with human behaviour. It has incorporated into its system, with only minor modifications, the methodology and principles of psychological diagnosis, psychometric testing, psychological concepts, and even psychological terminology. That such an intimate kinship should exist is understandable if one examines the growth of the two professions. Until very recently, and in certain circles even today, vocational guidance has been considered chiefly an adjunct of applied psychology. Psychologists who specialise in certain areas frequently select vocational guidance as their field of specialisation, in the same sense as others choose clinical psychology, speech correction, or remedial reading. Many of the workers in guidance, whether at the practitioner or at the administrative level, hold graduate degrees in psychology. It is only natural that their own training and orientation should have an influence on the development of vocational guidance. The fact that the American Psychological Association maintains a Division of Counselling and Guidance further strengthens the prominence of psychological thinking in the occupational field. The universities, too, which offer degrees with a guidance major, usually in the schools of education, tend to take their cues from the departments of psychology in the graduate divisions. Thus, not only are students majoring in guidance expected to have a thorough grounding in general psychology and psychometric testing, but even the teaching methods and techniques in the two areas are alike. Role playing, construction of sociograms, test administration, and analysis of electrically recorded interviews are some of the media through which the student is expected to acquire competence as a counsellor or therapist.

The somewhat uncritical absorption of so many psychological principles into the field of vocational guidance leads to several serious complications. One of these lies in the fact that psychology, as a profession, has not as yet resolved many of its own fundamental problems. Although psychology is spoken of frequently as a science and a profession, its claims to professional status are of relatively recent origin and do not meet fully the criteria established for professions in general. The Ph.D. degree awarded in psychology is primarily not a professional but an academic degree which attests satisfactory fulfilment of educational requirements. We also tend to ignore the fact that there are no professional schools of psychology in the same sense as there are schools of dentistry, medicine, or social work. Some of the theoretical and practical difficulties that beset psychology have to do with the role of the trained worker, his relationship to other professional staff members the training and supervision of students and workers ethical standards and practices, and licensing of workers as members of a full-fledged and clearly recognised profession.

Because of the close proximity of the two professions the inner struggles within the field of psychology are bound to have their effects on the growth of vocational guidance. Perhaps an even more serious criticism of the professional "crossbreeding" between different disciplines stems from a fundamental difference in their objectives. Traditionally, psychology has concerned itself primarily with scientific research, with statistical measurements, and only to some extent with psychotherapy. Whenever treatment has become the focus of the psychologist, it has usually been conducted within a clinical setting in close cooperation with the psychiatrist or other member of the medical staff.

It may be of interest to note that in the term "clinical psychology," coined by Lightner Witmer in 1896, "clinical" takes its root from the Greek word *kline*, bed, and hence by extension is defined as "pertaining to the sickbed." Such an orientation is probably not accidental. The likelihood is that the term was chosen deliberately to distinguish it from the then prevalent "psychophysical psychology" of Wundt and the Leipzig school. Although such a move may have served to shift the emphasis from scientific experimentation to that of working with psychotics, it also surrounded the clinical psychologist with a distinct psychiatric aura. The professional jargon of the clinical psychologist is replete with psychiatric terminology. It is probably significant that he often speaks of the client as "patient," of the student in training as "intern," and of the field-work training as "practicum." In practice, both the psychiatrist and the clinical psychologist are frequently engaged in psychodiagnosis and psychotherapy.

Presumably the vocational counsellor has no medical aspirations. His responsibility to the client is limited to assistance with educational and vocational planning and ceases the moment the focus becomes help with the total personality. The vocational counsellor does not diagnose or treat in the psychiatric sense but makes appropriate referral whenever he encounters cases that require other than vocational help. Although psychology can contribute considerably to the understanding of fundamental dynamics as they are experienced in vocational guidance, there is a sufficient difference between the two fields to warrant complete professional autonomy.

At present there is considerable evidence to suggest that vocational guidance is beginning to emerge as an independent profession, that is, not merely as an adjunct to the high school system but as a body with its own function, technical knowledge, skills, and rationale. The most significant aspect of its growth is the emergence of well-trained cadres of vocational counsellors to whom guidance is not an incidental avocation but a realisation of their own personal occupational goals.

Occasionally one meets vocational guidance workers who tend to set up a functional hierarchy among counsellors, implying that some occupational problems can be handled at a level requiring little or no professional skill, others by "advisory" counsellors, and still more complex problems by "clinical counsellors." Such a stratification is undesirable even if one considers the dearth of well-trained workers. It is reminiscent of the days of Paracelsus, when the duties of a medical doctor were distributed among barbers, surgeons, and physicians. The barber cured the "simplest" illnesses, the surgeon operated (a task held in low esteem), and the physician lectured and administered treatment with secret medicines. In defence of the sixteenth century, it should be said that its learned physician, even though wearing the traditional ermine hat, did not differ *so* much from the barber as does a counsellor qualified to practice his profession from one untrained. When ignorance is universal, the degree of inexpertness is secondary. The implication in professional stratification among vocational counsellors is that, the closer the training of the worker approaches the training required of a clinical psychologist, the more qualified he becomes as a vocational counsellor. Such an approach is unfortunate if one views vocational guidance and psychology as distinct fields. When a counsellor is entrusted with the responsibility of assisting a client, the question is not how difficult the case is or to what extent the counsellor's training resembles that of a clinical psychologist but, rather, how qualified the vocational counsellor is to practice his profession. Individual competence plays such an important role in counselling that, in the opinion of some workers, the methodology may actually be relegated to a secondary position. One may wonder whether workers with only minimal training should practice counselling at any level unless supervised by a more experienced counsellor. No practitioner can take it upon himself to decide on the seriousness of a conflict; only the client can say whether a particular fact is important to him. To assign a "simple" case to an untrained counsellor is to assume a major responsibility. Only when close supervision of the trainee is available can a case be assigned to a beginner.

At the practical level the presence of clinical psychologists on the vocational guidance staff may create problems in intraprofessional relationships. As in the case of the psychiatrist, the functions and responsibilities of the psychologist must be clearly defined before he is asked to join the staff. Since different vocational agencies may utilise the psychologist's contributions in different ways, his role must be spelled out in relation to the needs of the particular agency that is going to employ him. Most vocational agencies retain psychologists in a diagnostic capacity. The psychologist is frequently in charge of the testing programme and is responsible, as a supervisor, for the administration and interpretation of tests if they are given by nonpsychologists. In some agencies all testing done directly by the psychologist and his assistant. Almost invariably the individual general-ability tests as well as the projective devices are administered and interpreted directly by the psychologist. Some vocational agencies turn to the psychologist with problems in speech pathology, relationship difficulties, and personality disorders. Whether such problems fall within the functional scope of a vocational agency and whether they should be handled by a psychologist operating within a vocational setup is questionable. Lastly, the psychologist may contribute to the guidance staff by helping it familiarise itself more thoroughly with the psychological dynamics, statistical concepts, and psychometric measurement in general.

Clinical psychologists, however, are not the only ones who are active in vocational guidance circles. "Counselling psychologists," although at present theirs is still a new occupational classification, may be expected to become progressively more prominent in vocational and educational planning. According to the APA Division of Counselling and Guidance "the professional goal of the counselling psychologist is to foster the psychological development of the individual". Essentially he deals with the normal individual, stressing the positive and preventive aspects of adjustment. He may be expected to take an active role within the public school system, although he can also make significant contributions as a worker in industry, youth organisations, social agencies, etc. Professionally he is equipped with a doctoral degree which in addition to testing and counselling enables him to "carry administrative, supervisory, training, research, and public relations responsibilities".

At present it is still too early to evaluate the possible relationship between the counselling psychologist and the vocational counsellor. It is conceivable that in the course of time the clinical psychologist will gravitate toward the psychiatric field and the counselling psychologist will ascend in the vocational guidance area. Today, however, the counselling psychologist is still to a large extent a hypothetical entity, with clinically trained psychologists playing a major role in vocational counselling.

The foregoing discussion is in no way an attempt to delimit the functions of the clinical psychologist. Whether he sees himself chiefly as a therapist, a diagnostician, or a research worker has no bearing on the present topic. However, when—in whatever role—he becomes part of vocational guidance, the vocational counsellor must examine the contribution he is likely to make to the occupational helping process. The present discussion is concerned not with psychology in general but specifically with its relationship to vocational guidance.

In discussing the relationship between vocational guidance and other kindred fields, it becomes increasingly apparent that as a young profession vocational guidance cannot depend for nourishment solely on its own rather inadequate and limited experience. It has to borrow, and borrow heavily, from those disciplines which have contributed to the understanding of human dynamics and the helping process in particular.

Relationship between Vocational Guidance and Casework

Before discussing the relationship between vocational guidance and social casework, a few words about the growth of psychology and casework as professions are in order. By outlining the significant characteristics of the two systems, the reader may be helped to see why the vocational counsellor, in his new role as a borrower, is likely to gain more by establishing closer ties with one profession than with the other.

The development of psychology as an experimental science needs no recapitulation. Most vocational counsellors who have taken courses in psychology are probably familiar with it. What is important about its growth, from the present standpoint, is the persistent emphasis on observation, experimentation, formulation of hypotheses, and verification. Wundt, Pavlov, Cattell, and scores of other, investigators who laid the foundations for psychology took great pains to adhere as closely as possible to the laboratory conditions of a physical science and to the spirit of scientific methodology in general. In a sense, the history of psychology is a history of experimentation and measurement. Its roots lie in the early studies of the Leipzig school and extend through decades of attempted quantification of practically every psychological trait or attribute. In his development as a scientific investigator, the psychologist has always maintained an aloof and impartial attitude lest his subjective judgement or even his presence effect the outcome of the experiment or influence the data under study.

This impersonal approach did not confine itself to the laboratory but became the guiding principle in test situations and actually exerted its influence on counselling sessions. This is not to deny that, in dealing with people, psychologists quickly became aware of the need for a "rapport." But a rapport is an artifact when compared with a genuine interpersonal relationship. It is something that the psychologist deliberately "establishes" as a prerequisite to what is to follow. For example, it is well known that people who are frightened, tense, or uncomfortable are not likely to do as well on psychometric tests as those who are at ease. The psychologist attempts to establish a rapport in order to secure the subject's maximum cooperation and intellectual productivity. A rapport then becomes a device intended to bring about relaxation, as might amytal in the preoperative stage. From the present standpoint, the establishment of a rapport, in this sense of the word, is undesirable, for it tends to place the main burden of the relationship on the counsellor and appears to relieve the client of the responsibility of making the interview a valuable experience.

It is only recently that psychologists have become interested in psychotherapy; it is even more recently that they have begun to differentiate between medical psychotherapy and counselling. Today, by virtue of his academic training and a long history of scientific tradition, the psychologist has attained considerable maturity in research and test construction, but he is still relatively a novice in dealing with problems that arise out of daily realities. Luchins, noting that the majority of clinical training programmes are "tool-centred" and that not enough educational activity is devoted to clinical practice, remarks, "However, from what is known of the psychology of learning and transfer of training, it cannot be assumed that principles and cautions reiterated in the classroom, or even in the clinic, need carry over to the actual clinical practice". The psychologist as a professional still has not defined too clearly his function and place among the helping services, nor has he developed a training and supervisory programme that enables him to assure comfortably the role of a helper.

Social casework, in contrast to psychology, has no scientific ancestry to fall back on. It cannot claim its descent from Plato or Aristotle. It has a strictly "plebeian" origin in the slums arid tenements of the modern city. However, its most significant feature, from the present standpoint, is the fact that social work came into being as a direct answer to some of the people's needs. Furthermore, from its very outset, it assumed the responsibilities of a service intended to ameliorate these needs, a service so structured as to help people with certain immediate problems.

During its earlier stages social work was almost exclusively concerned with the financial aspects of life. The "lady bountiful" often connected with a philanthropically minded woman's club or a religious group would judiciously dispense food and used clothes to the "needy and deserving." The administration of such financial assistance was usually spiced liberally with virtuous advice and sanctimonious admonition. In the course of their daily contact with the impoverished sections of the population, the workers in the field were constantly faced with problems of family relationships, broken homes, alcoholism, juvenile delinquency, prostitution, and hosts of other evils that were an integral part of the lives of the poor. It was only after years of struggle with these everyday situations and occurrences that social work began to evolve techniques skills, and a philosophy of its own. It took years of helping experience to transform "eleemosynary work" into modern casework practice.

It would be a gross oversimplification to say that casework today has all the answers. As a theory and as a practice, casework, too, is grappling with a host of problems in the training of students, supervision of workers, and interpretation of its role to the boards and the community, to mention only a few. But it is precisely because of these years of constant struggle at the administrative, supervisory, and practitioner levels that casework managed to develop as a helping profession uniquely suited to deal with certain kinds of life situations.

Apparently there exists its no unified casework theory any more than a unified theory of personality. In its theoretical orientation much of casework, like psychology and psychiatry, is greatly influenced by the teachings of Fraud and his followers. Individual social-work agencies as well as individual caseworkers may modify their philosophy in accordance with the teachings of Adler, lung, Rank, Homey, Fromm, Sullivan, and others. Some case-workers profess eclecticism and synthesise several doctrines to their own satisfaction. As one compares the literature in psychology and social work, one cannot help being impressed by the difference in the quantity of space devoted to theoretical considerations. Whereas psychology still seems to be profoundly interested in the study of personality and human behaviour per se, casework appears to be chiefly concerned with the practical aspects of living and adjusting. Many caseworkers are totally oblivious to the major contributions in the realm of personality theory made by psychologists but seem to be able to assist their clients with their daily relationship problems. Conversely, some psychologists, although probably thoroughly familiar with the works of Thorndike, G. Allport, or Lewin, may encounter considerable difficulty in applying their theoretical knowledge to a practical situation.'"

Research, or as it is usually called in social-work circles, "social research," is also relatively new. Although, as a profession, social work has recognised its value and importance for some time, tradition and lack of funds still hamper its fuller development. A notable exception are the studies conducted by the Institute of Welfare Research, Community Service Society of New York, under the direction of J. McY. Hunt, a psychologist.

Some Similarities between Casework and Vocational Guidance

To return to the question of the relationship between vocational guidance and social casework. The preceding discussion, sketchy and incomplete as it may have been, has attempted to point up one fundamental distinction between psychology and casework, viz.: the philosophy of psychology is that of a science; the philosophy of casework is that of a helping profession. Fortunately both psychology and casework can contribute a great deal to the theory and practice of vocational guidance. Which of the two disciplines bears a closer kinship to vocational guidance deserves further consideration.

An examination of both vocational guidance and casework reveals several important similarities:

1. Both vocational guidance and social casework are services. This means that their chief objective is to help people in the community with their specific needs, questions, and problems.

2. Both vocational guidance and social casework encounter not only situations that demand a tangible and concrete service but problems that cannot be satisfactorily resolved by environmental manipulation. In the latter instance psychological counselling is frequently employed in order to help the client arrive at certain conclusions and decisions. By psychological counselling is meant a professional relationship which takes into account the client's feelings, his attitudes toward himself, the counsellor, and the vocational goals, as well as his interests, levels of aspiration, and characteristic adjustment patterns. It is predicated not on the intellectual knowledge of relevant facts but on their emotional acceptance. Psychological counselling as practiced by both professions establishes a further likeness between them.

3. Vocational guidance and casework are nonmedically oriented helping professions which nevertheless utilise medical and psychological findings in assisting the individual to move toward a particular objective.

4. Vocational guidance and casework alike are concerned chiefly with those aspects of total adjustment with which the client wants help and which the agency is qualified to handle. When the whole personality becomes the focus of the problem, both professions may be expected to make an appropriate psychiatric referral.

5. The fact that some vocational agents and social-work agencies may derive their funds from the Community Chest, belong to the Council of Social Agencies, and participate in joint communal planning further strengthens the bond between the two professions.

It is not the intention to suggest that vocational guidance imitate slavishly the field of social casework. Social casework itself, as previously mentioned, is confronted with some serious problems in both the theoretical and practical phases of its development. Among its theoretical difficulties one might mention the fact that, although social work has made significant contributions to the practice of assisting people with their variegated problems, it has not established a correspondingly clearly articulated rationale. Social work is founded on pragmatism, but a pragmatism that is frequently unsubstantiated by scientific research and investigation.

From the practical standpoint social work is severely handicapped by the profound differences that exist between its professional levels of aspiration, as revealed by a keen understanding of the psychological dynamics of the helping process on the one hand and a very limited ability to apply these principles to everyday situations on the other. This unfortunate condition stems from the extreme heterogeneity in training and background that is to be found among social workers. If one is to assume that the professional caliber of an occupational field is dependent upon the competence of the individual members of that field, it becomes apparent that a great variation in composition will produce a correspondingly wide divergence in the quality of performance.

In an extremely comprehensive and lucid treatment of social-work education Hollis and Taylor caution the reader on the use of statistics on this field by saying, "It is an understatement to say the statistics on social work and social workers are incomplete, unreliable, and generally chaotic." Bearing that admonition in mind, they proceed to analyze the data, with the most appalling results. For example, one discovers that "Between three fifths and three fourths of the public assistance and related social workers of the nation have not had any professional education: moreover, with the general education of nearly half of this group being less than college graduation, a substantial proportion is not eligible to undertake graduate professional studies." The situation is only slightly better in private agencies, which frequently pride themselves on their high standards. In the same study Hollis and Taylor continue, "One third of the 1,100 persons classed as professional social workers by the public welfare agencies of Boston had no formal education beyond high school graduation. Three fifths of the private agency group workers had no professional education in group work or in any other field of social work, and among case workers—usually considered the best developed field of social work education—17 percent had no professional case work training."

This raises the important question whether or not social work is a profession. Still more important from the standpoint of the present discussion is the professional stature of vocational guidance. Does vocational guidance meet the criteria generally established for a profession? Will a closer identification with social work help vocational guidance attain a higher degree of professionalisation?

Anderson suggests that "In a profession, the control of the training or education of the professional practitioner and the determination of the standards for his practice rest with the members of the profession itself." He furthermore holds that "the professions establish and enforce a code of ethical behaviour for its members" and that "the practice of a profession . . . transcends the performance of skills and use of techniques." Hollis and Taylor submit a number of criteria which appear to be quite inclusive:

1. Does the profession have a well-defined function, the nature and scope of which can be identified?

2. Does the profession have a philosophy, code of ethics, and other means of self-regulation which assure that its practice transcends the bounds of political, sectarian, and economic self-interest?

3. Does the profession have a unified pattern of organisations that can speak for it with one voice?

4. Does the compensation received by the professional practitioner indicate that the public is willing to pay him as a skilled and responsible professional worker?

5. Is the practice of the profession limited, or tending to be limited, to persons with approved general and professional preparation?

6. Is there, in fact, a recognised systematic body of knowledge, skills, and attitudes which can be identified and transmitted as a regimen of professional preparation?

7. Is the regimen of professional education recognised as of a quality appropriate for inclusion in the graduate and professional offerings of a university?

It should be noted that the application of the above criteria to social work and to vocational guidance tends to bring out the fact that the two professions share in their strengths and weaknesses. Although neither casework nor vocational guidance can reply in an unequivocally affirmative manner to any of the points raised, an element of confirmation is present in all criteria. Casework is perhaps somewhat ahead of vocational guidance professionally in some respects. The significant features, however, are that both occupations seek a fuller professionalisation as their goal. Both occupations are moving in that direction. Thus a further bond between social work and vocational guidance may be established in that both disciplines struggle with similar problems and work toward similar objectives.

Some Differences between Casework and Vocational Guidance

The chief differences between vocational guidance and casework lie in the specific content that each profession is competent to handle and in the student training programme. Out of these two distinctions flow a multitude of other attributes which, in practice, certainly make the two professions quite distinct in relation to each other.

With regard to content, by virtue of his training the caseworker is qualified to handle problems that arise out of interpersonal relationship in general; these include difficulties that stem from parent-child inter-relationships, marital incompatibility, budgeting, and the like. The functions of caseworkers are usually defined in broad terms to meet the particular needs of the community. Whereas one frequently speaks of family caseworkers, child-welfare worker, medical social worker, and psychiatric social worker, the specific duties and responsibilities of the individual staff member may be determined by particular agency. Some caseworker, for example, engage in psychotherapy under the supervision of a psychiatrist. Others may be primarily service-oriented, whereas still others may see counselling as their chief function. Agency policy and agency philosophy will often define and delineate the activities of the members of the staff. As a profession, social work is governed by general code of ethics and personnel standards and practice. The list of services mentioned here by no means exhausts' the gamut of functions usually assigned to the caseworker. It is intended merely for illustrative purposes.

The vocational counsellor, too, because of his specialised background, is in a position to make contributions that differentiate him from other professionals. His special knowledge of occupational trends, vocational opportunities, college entrance requirements and curricula and the labour market is but one item in his professional armamentarium. The vocational counsellor's knowledge of psychological measurements and their application to comprehensive occupational planning further adds to his professional identity. Lastly, through the use of his counselling skills, the vocational counsellor is in a position to help the client to integrate the objective situation with his personal needs, interests, and abilities into a vocationally sound plan. Through psychological counselling the counsellor helps the client to make a vocational choice, to put his special aptitudes to an optimum use, and to progress toward his objective.

An elaboration on the use of tests in vocational guidance may be in place since, in the minds of many, testing constitutes the crux of occupational planning. A fuller discussion of the subject will be found in the section devoted to the role of psychological testing. At present it may suffice to indicate that the application of quantitative data to educational and occupational planning and evaluation of vocational fitness in general is the specific function of the vocational counsellor. Although psychological tests are used widely by psychiatrists, clinical psychologists, and educators, the kind of tests employed and the purpose for which they are administered differ in many respects from the manner in which the vocational counsellor utilises test evidence. The distinguishing characteristic of the vocational counsellor lies in his dynamic use of measuring devices in relation to occupational adjustment. Perhaps the word "dynamic" should be stressed for it intended to convey not merely a static quantitative appraisal of the clients vocational potentialities but testing which is integrated with the total vocational counselling process.

With respect to the training programme, most schools of social work offer a two-year course accredited by the American Association of the Schools of Social Work. Vocational guidance as a profession has no such uniform standards. There are no comparable schools of vocational guidance, nor is there a recognised accrediting apparatus. The methods of training differ significantly, too. Schools of social work tend to emphasise supervised field-work experience, as opposed to the more academic classroom instruction methods of the schools of education, which are usually vested with the responsibility of training vocational counsellors.

The similarities and the differences between the two areas are equally important for the growth of vocational guidance. An understanding of the differences will not only eliminate the duplication and confusion in the functional roles but can actually strengthen the new field of vocational guidance by pointing up and delimiting its contributions to human welfare. Simultaneously, the similarities between the two fields can assist vocational guidance immeasurably if it should allow itself to profit from the years of accumulated experience in generic social work.

Some Practical Considerations

Vocational guidance can adopt, with appropriate modifications, some of the student training and supervisory activities of social work. Social work, perhaps more than most other professions, has devoted much thought and energy to the question of student education within its various schools. Integration of academic training with field-work practice has been given careful consideration in order to produce a programme that will provide the student with theoretical information as well as opportunities to apply such knowledge to actual casework situations. Student supervision has also been incorporated into the curriculum of most case-workers. By contrast, vocational guidance has not developed similar educational facilities, nor has it shown as much concern for the training of graduate students, uniformity of professional standards, supervised field work, or ethical practices. Some significant steps have, indeed, been made toward professionalisation of vocational guidance and vocational counselling in particular. But by comparison with social casework the advances made are sporadic and not characteristic of the field as a whole.

Vocational guidance can also take a cue from the professional periodicals and professional organisations in the field of social work in order to develop more fully its own equivalent adjuncts. In the present instance, once again, vocational guidance lags sadly behind its cousin professions, psychology and social work.

Whereas both psychology and casework can pride themselves on an array of periodicals in their respective fields, vocational guidance has actually only one professional organ of nationwide distribution. The periodical in question is the *Personnel and Guidance Journal,* the successor to *Occupations. Occupations* was published only during the school year and was oriented primarily to the needs and problems of the school counsellor. The content and treatment were in the majority of instances on an elementary level, intended apparently to be read by schoolteachers not trained particularly in the vocational area.

The *Personnel and Guidance Journal,* thus far, has not departed significantly from its predecessor in its format, editorial policy or professional caliber. This is understandable if one considers the fact that most vocational counsellors are teachers who deal with problems as they may arise within the school system. The general level of the periodicals may also be justified on the grounds that a large proportion of its readers have not had the benefits of graduate training in vocational guidance and consequently would not find some of the more advanced articles particularly stimulating or meaningful. This may be so, but inherent in such thinking is the danger that the counsellor is being "sold short." Surely one or two incisive and searching discussions included in every issue are not likely to prove editorially detrimental to the magazine. Then it may be well to consider the numerous counsellors who do hold graduate degrees in vocational guidance and probably would welcome a thought-provoking discussion at a higher professional level. A "call for papers" on the part of the *Personnel and Guidance Journal* might result in a sizable output of original and worthwhile ideas. My own association with workers in the field suggests that there is no dearth of intelligent thinking among the rank and file.

What is possibly lacking is an encouraging and welcoming attitude toward mature theoretical contributions.

At this point one should also mention the *Vocational Guidance Quarterly* published by the National Vocational Guidance Association to meet the more specialised interests of those working within the vocational guidance field. There can be little question that, because of the diversity of interests in the vocational field as a whole, vocational counsellors do need a professional periodical devoted to their specific problems and needs. A quarterly that is freed from the responsibility of meeting the demands of the various subgroups within generic guidance could devote itself wholeheartedly to the issues that are of primary concern to the occupational counsellor. Such a periodical could treat in considerable detail such theoretical questions as counselling dynamics, the role of the counsellor, supervision of field-work students, the role of the family in vocational guidance, and the like. It could also deal with the more practical matters of professional and ethical standards, certification of guidance workers, intake policies, and promotion and interpretation of vocational guidance to other professions and to the community at large. Finally, numerous pages could be devoted to actual case recordings, follow-up studies, counselling with special groups (*e.g.*, the handicapped, the aged), and research in guidance. Book reviews, placement notices and "gossip" columns would probably prove to be of interest to many subscribers. Some of the latter items might cement the professional bonds among the readers. One would like to envision the *Quarterly* as a many-paged publication perhaps similar in format to *Mental Hygiene* or the *American Journal of Orthopsychiatry*, replete with significant material, a real inspiration to the vocational counsellor. Unfortunately the *Vocational Guidance Quarterly* as it appears today does not in any sense approach such a standard. It seems to fall short both quantitatively and qualitatively as a professional periodical.

Articles dealing with vocational tests, counselling, and work with special groups, such as the handicapped, may be found in other periodicals which are not published primarily as organs of the vocational guidance field. Among the latter one may mention

Journal of Applied Psychology American Vocational Journal, Educational and Psychological Measurements, Journal of Consulting Psychology, Journal of Educational Research, and *Personnel Journal.* There are also several periodicals that deal with the problems of the blind, tubercular, the hard of hearing, etc. The Federal government issues monthly publications that dear with labour trends, personnel, industrial production, employment data, and the like. Occasionally articles related to vocational counselling may be found in *Social Casework, Jewish Social Service Quarterly, Mental Hygiene,* and *American Journal of Orthopsychiatry.*

One could continue listing other aspects of casework which could readily apply to the field of vocational guidance. For example, vocational guidance as a profession has not devoted sufficient time and energy to interpreting its functions and the contributions it can make to other agencies and the community at large. A great deal of ignorance exists in the minds of many as to what vocational guidance is, what it has to offer, and how it can be integrated with other social services. Through misinterpretation vocational guidance is at times confused with aptitude testing, with the result that its most significant and vital aspect—the vocational guidance process—is at times completely overlooked. And yet vocational guidance has much to contribute to the occupational adjustment of in-school youth, young people who leave school and enter industries, college students, veterans, employed and unemployed adults, the mentally retarded, the physically handicapped, and the aged. Although the potential needs may exist, the public at large or, for that matter, the various social agencies have not as yet recognised the contributions the trained vocational counsellor can make toward helping the individual client attain a more satisfactory occupational status. Communitywide interpretation is imperative if vocational guidance is to make its services available to the public. Here too, vocational guidance might benefit if it were to study more carefully the methods and techniques employed by the already existing social agencies.

The concept of community interpretation, or "promotion," is not new to vocational guidance agencies. Many vocational services issue periodically circulars dealing with their work, cause newspapers to describe their activities, or participate on radio and television programmes. As long as promononal work is conduced through the medium of words, no serious difficulty need be encountered. But some vocational agencies wish to convey their message through cartoons, drawings, and photographs. Since it is impossible to express pictorially the vocational process as a whole, the temptation is to rely on an item that is photogenic, *i.e.*, the performance tests used in vocational guidance. Hence one encounters in the Sunday rotogravure sections scenes depicting the psychologist with a pad and stop watch (facing the camera) and the "client" busily placing disks in holes or assembling puzzles. Such a scene, although possibly dear to the heart of the newspaper photographer, is ethically questionable and probably harmful to the field of vocational guidance. The harm comes from an overemphasis on testing, which in turn contributes further to the misconceptions about guidance in the minds of the lay public.

The idea that vocational guidance and casework have a great deal in common is not new. Almost two decades ago Washington suggested that vocational guidance can gain a great deal by identifying itself more closely with social work than with education. Grumer, too, feels that the objectives and skills of both professions are sufficiently similar to permit vocational guidance to absorb some of the casework principles. At this point it is imperative to realize that the incorporation of some of the ideas prevalent in casework in no way implies that a caseworker is competent to practice vocational guidance. The situation is analogous to the relationship between guidance and psychology, already discussed. The naive counsellor may reason as follows: Knowledge of psychological dynamics and their application is essential to vocational guidance; psychologists are the ones who possess the most advanced training in psychology; *ergo*, psychologists should make the best vocational guidance counsellors. Similarly, caseworkers have accumulated a great many skills in human relationship; these skills are indispensable to professional counselling; therefore, caseworkers are the vocational counsellors par excellence. There are, indeed, psychologists and caseworkers who believe this to be so.

In practice, it is important to keep separate the functions of the psychologist, caseworker, and vocational counsellor. Each profession has still a great deal to learn about its own field without taking cities offering specialised services, there seems to be no valid (reason why one profession should take over the responsibilities of another field). Agencies that attempt to handle each and every problem which clients may bring them, at times when they may not even have the staff qualified to handle the particular problems, create unnecessary confusion within the community.

The Generic Counsellor

It is held by some that a clear-cut definition of function in the field of counselling is not only unnecessary but actually harmful to the profession. A counsellor, according to some workers, is a trained in helping people with their personal, emotional, and social problems. It matters little, it is asserted, whether the client is worried about his occupational future or about his relations with his wife, or is troubled by excessive masturbation. Since the basic dynamics, skills, and techniques are practically identical, irrespective of the content, the competent counsellor should be able to help the client with whatever problem the latter presents. The proponents of this viewpoint appear to confuse the genesis of counselling with the end product itself. Or, more precisely, they fail to distinguish between generic counselling and the generic counsellor. Whereas generic counselling is a broad body of professional knowledge, skills, and techniques centred around the help-giving and help-taking process, the generic counsellor is a human being who attempts to apply his own rather limited skills to helping his fellow man. All helping disciplines have much in common, but the similarity, among them should not blind one to the differences that distinguish one field from another. Those acquainted with vertebrate embryology are probably impressed by the profound morphological likeness that exists, especially during the early developmental stages, between, let us say, the fish, the reptile, and the mammal. And yet no one could seriously question the differences between a salmon, an alligator, and a pig. Coming for assistance to an agency with one's personal problems whether they have to do with total personality adjustment, relationship difficulties, or occupational conflicts, sets into motion feelings, fears, and doubts irrespective of the actual focus. The general manner in which the client is received by the worker, as well as the over-all professional atmosphere that characterises the contacts is again typical of all helping situations. An unwritten code of professional ethics and broad interviewing procedures have been established for all helping disciplines. This situation is akin to the morphological similarity mentioned previously. As the worker (therapist, counsellor) enters into a meaningful relationship with the person in need of assistance, the generic aspects of counselling begin to assume a secondary role. The specific problem with which the client wants help (focus) and the specific service the worker is prepared to offer (function) become the dominant forces in the relationship. In practice, especially in localities that lack many essential community resources, a counsellor may be called upon to assist a client in areas in which the former has no particular training or qualifications. Such situations are analogous to the emergencies which demand that nonmedically trained persons deliver babies or perform surgery. The latter cases, however, are extremely rare and do not constitute a part of the daily experience of most people.

As an educational or professional objective, it certainly will not do to train counsellors to handle any and all problems that a client may present. The promulgation of a generic counselling programme is tantamount to a rejection of the specific contributions and services that each helping profession can make. Aside from the chaos and duplication of functions that would result from such an undifferentiated attitude, the client would actually suffer in the end, for he would be denied the benefits of the specialist with his years of training and experience in a particular field.

As the total amount of knowledge in anyone field increases, it becomes progressively more difficult for the professional to keep abreast of all the developments and to claim equal competence in all subdivisions in his field. Whereas at one time the term chemist designated a specific occupation, today it may be delimited by modifiers to organic chemist, or organic chemist in plastics, or even organic chemist in vinyl plastics. Vocational guidance, too, as we have seen, has broad as well as specific areas of interest. These are sufficiently exacting to tax the proficiency of most individuals; to add to this large field other responsibilities, such as personality adjustment or familial relationship difficulties, is bound to produce.

This is not to deny the fact that many counsellors do take it upon themselves to practice professions for which they have but the minimal (if any) professional qualifications. Vocational counsellors do counsel in "personal" matters and offer assistance in marital counselling and related problems. In one instance at least, it would seem that a counsellor entered into a "dynamic psychoanalysis" with a schizophrenic patient.

A study of the 1951 National Vocational Guidance Association Directory reveals the wide array of activities in which vocational guidance counsellors appear to be engaged. A breakdown of services which the listed agencies and private individuals offer follows:

Couselling: vocational, educational, evaluation of vocational future, occupational planning, etc.	162
Testing: diagnostic, aptitude, psychological, etc.	162
Industrial: appraisal of workers, job analysis, etc.	44
Group discussions, lectures, speakers	36
Personal counselling	33
Personality adjustment, psychotherapy, mental hygiene	24
Placement	19
Marital adjustment	15
Clinical psychology	14
Remedial reading, speech correction	12
Childhood behaviour difficulties, play therapy, adoption evaluation	8
Scholarships	8
Family relations	5

It will be noted that some terms are rather ambiguous. A clearer professional nomenclature would do away with much of the misunderstanding that arises from confused terminology. The Ethical Practice Committee of the NVGA might prepare a glossary of vocational terms to define clearly the sundry functions of vocational counsellors and request that these definitions and terms be employed by agencies when they apply for the next listing.

Vocational counsellors, however are not the only who tend to extend their services in areas in which they do not have the necessary background and training. Some psychiatrists, psychologists, caseworkers and school counsellor although frequently jealous of what they consider to be their own domain, seem to have little respect for the uniqueness of other professions. It has never been quite established what courses in the medical curriculum entitle a physician to counsel in vocational or casework matters; nor has it ever been demonstrated that a "manual training" teacher possesses, *ipso facto,* the necessary professional background to enable him to assist a student with his occupational choice.

A survey of psychological services conducted by Trow reveals several significant facts about psychology as a profession. Among these one notes great variability in the size of staffs, case-load range, techniques employed, and training. "In training, the staff members range from one to two people with ambition and very little else to groups of experts with post-doctoral training and years of clinical experience". The types of problems accepted for diagnosis and treatment included mental retardation, mental acceleration, school adjustment (scholastic), school adjustment (personality), sensory (speech), educational guidance, vocational guidance, marital adjustment, conduct (delinquency), alcoholism, personal problems (emotional), psychoneuroses, psychoses, and "other."

The fact that considerable confusion appears to exist among the various practitioners certainly does not strengthen the cause of those who advocate generic counselling. The generic counsellor, because of his lack of specialisation, as implied in the term itself, is likely to create additional interprofessional problems and may duplicate some of the work which could be done more expertly by trained workers in the respective areas.

The proponents of generic counselling, furthermore, do not seem to take into account the fact that the worker's role as a professional counsellor stems not only from his training and experience but also from his being employed by an organisation or agency dedicated to render a specific service to the community. A private practitioner is free to define his own functions and to set his own limits. Under the present laws, unfortunately, he can do pretty much as he pleases, as long as he does not offend the ethics of the American Medical Association (AMA). Thus, along with vocational guidance, marital counselling, and psychometric testing, he may read tea leaves and construct horoscopes. However, as long as he is employed by an agency that has a specific function in the community, his own role is immediately defined in terms of the service the agency is set up to offer.

Familiarity with other helping professions is indeed desirable and should constitute a part of the training programme of every counsellor. Such understanding and general knowledge, however, must not entice the counsellor to take over the responsibilities of workers in other fields; quite the contrary, an appreciation of what other professions have to contribute to the helping process should help the vocational counsellor to delimit and to define his own functions.

Practitioners in vocational counselling sometimes raise the question of the advisability of subdividing vocational counsellors into two categories, those especially proficient in vocational diagnostic testing, and those particularly qualified to sustain a counselling relationship. It has even been suggested that academic curricula be designed to prepare the student for either diagnostic or counselling activities. Such overspecialisation does not appear to be either necessary or desirable. Extensive psychometric or vocational testing if indicated can be left to the agency's psychologist. The clinical psychologist's training in the area of measurements is usually sufficiently wide and flexible to enable him to do a thoroughly comprehensive job in vocational guidance as well.

Perhaps a more serious objection to such a functional division is its artificial dichotomisation of the vocational process. If one perceives the vocational process as a helping relationship, vocational testing also becomes a part of that experience. Tests or test findings have no meaning in themselves: they derive the meaning from the totality of the counselling situation. Gurvitz notes that "diagnosis and personality evaluation is made not by a test or by a battery of tests but by a psychologist who interprets in the light of his clinical experience." The vocational counsellor must extend this concept even further, for as a helper he is concerned not only with his own clinical experience but also with what testing may signify to the client. Vocational testing, although perceived by many counsellors as an auxiliary or supportive activity, is viewed by some clients as the most significant feature of the vocational guidance programme. Other clients may see it as a threat or as an anxiety-arousing situation. The vocational counsellor who is trained in both counselling and testing is in a better position to handle the anxieties and misconceptions which the client may have about taking tests.

Occasionally a situation arises which calls for the administration of a test which the counsellor does not feel qualified to give. In such instances the client may be referred to the psychologist. When such a referral is made, the counsellor should attempt to place the test in question in its true perspective in the total vocational planning situation and to assuage the anxieties such a procedure may arouse. This is quite different from what can happen if two vocational counsellors, one trained in testing and the other in counselling, work with the client simultaneously. Testing, instead of remaining a fact-contributing activity, may then very well move into the central position of the entire programme. The client-counsellor relationship, which is one of the most important features of the vocational process, may become attenuated to the point where it becomes a relationship among three individuals. It is in the light of such considerations that it seems advisable to preserve the present status of vocational counsellors without creating new hybrids between vocational counsellors and clinical psychologists and caseworkers.

From the above discussion it can be seen that vocational counsellors can define their role as broadly or as narrowly as they wish. On the one hand, vocational counselling can be conceived in such general terms as to make it virtually indistinguishable from psychiatry, psychology, or social casework. At the other extreme, vocational, counsellors can be restricted to areas that deal exclusively with vocational face-to-face relationships or solely with vocational guidance testing. The help-centred approach would probably choose an in-between position which would describe the activities of the vocational counsellor in terms of the professional responsibilities he and his agency are prepared to assume, the services he is qualified to offer, and the focus of the problem around which the client wants help. Such a professional service would integrate vis-a-vis vocational counselling with aptitude testing into a meaningful vocational process. The vocational counsellor in turn would be expected to be equally competent in counselling and vocational measurements. The role which tests play in the vocational guidance process is discussed more fully under Test Evidence.

❑❑❑

3

THE PRO-COUNSELLING PHASE

General Consideration

From the vocational agency's standpoint appointment making is daily occurrence. It is frequently handled routinely by a member of the clerical staff. At the end of the month, the number appointments kept is counted and entered into a ledger as part of the agency's statistics. From the client's standpoint making an appointment may signify a major event. It may represent the culmination of months of doubts and anxieties about some painful issue—or it may be just a response to some mild stimulus.

Making an appointment with a vocational guidance counsellor means different things to different people. Although each individual brings his unique self into the new situation, it is assumed that certain universal characteristics are present in varying degrees in all clients. For example, it is held that those coming to an agency for vocational assistance have an occupational problem with which they want help. There is probably some doubt or possibly anxiety about a particular course of action or vocational plan. Some individuals seek an objective verification of their potentialities; others may be in quest of occupational information. Still others need help with a choice of a career, self-acceptance on a job, or adjustment to a difficult dilemma that may have arisen in connection with their schoolwork. Awareness of a problem, be it intense or superficial, is one characteristic shared by all adult applicants who come for vocational guidance.

When the client keeps the first appointment he brings with him more than the question that prompted his coming for vocational guidance. He also brings with him his attitudes and feelings toward himself, toward the counsellor, and toward the very idea of asking for vocational help. The likelihood is that, the more meaningful the problem is to him, the more strongly he will feel about his entire predicament. How he is going to react to the first interview is an individual matter.

The counsellor can never expect to know the client fully; nor will he ever know the total significance that the appointment may have for the client. What the counsellor is confronted with are the feelings of the client in his first tenuous and exploratory contact with the vocational service. The client may appear to be bitter or optimistic, demanding or timid, belligerent or dependent. He may attempt to control the worker, may remain outwardly indifferent to what is going on about him, or may actively reject any attempt to be helped. Combs holds that these attitudes and feelings are "more critical in the motivation of behaviour than intelligence, aptitude, physical, strength, or dexterity."

The reasons for coming for vocational guidance are many and complex. I say reasons, realising very well that the forces that bring the client to any agency never operate singly; nor do they necessarily work in harmony with each other. A conflict among wishes, attitudes, and emotions is the rule rather than an exception.

Ambivalence

As we examine our feelings about any action we are about to take, we discover that we rarely think of it as being all positive or all negative. A woman may be tempted to take a candy, only to remind herself of her diet. A man wishing to buy a new car will also consider the expenses that go with the purchase and upkeep. He wants the car, and yet he may not want to part with his money or go into debt. The greater the investment, or the more there is at stake, the more thought is likely to be given to the problem and the sharper will be the ambivalent feelings.

What happens before the client makes his first appointment? Generally and empirically, the counsellor knows that most people experience difficulty in accepting help. On the one hand, there is the problem, which disturbs and upsets the person's equilibrium. He wants to do something to diminish or actually remove the forces responsible for his disquietude. On the other hand, he is afraid to change, is fearful of the unknown, and is reluctant to bring himself into conflict. Although circumstances may compel him to seek assistance from the outside, he resists any change and clings tenaciously to that which has become a part of himself. Unacceptable as his present reality may seem, he has developed some modicum of adjustment to it. It is difficult for him to give up that which is known in exchange for something new and threatening. This is particularly so since he has little control over the new experience.

To some people taking help means other things as well. There are those who see in the helping relationship an admission of inadequacy or failure. Still others will take the attitude that they either need no assistance or cannot be helped, for whatever reason. It is perhaps because of a fear of personal involvement that so many vocational guidance clients insist that psychometric tests be administered to them. They secretly hope that the answer to their difficulties may come through an objective and impersonal medium and leave them essentially untouched. They want their vocational problems solved without having to *do* anything about them.

Considering the ambivalence that one is likely experience, coming for help must represent a culmination point in the struggle between wanting to come and the negative forces that prevent one from making use of the agency. It may be that a client has lost his job, or has failed in college, or is confronted with a vocational dilemma which he cannot resolve. Asking for help represents an attempt to get out of the predicament. It is an expression of positive action, which necessitates taking on some responsibility for one's plans.

Freud recognized this psychological ambivalence as basic to all feelings and actions. Rank termed it the counterwill *i.e.*, the negative component to every positive endeavour. It is in view of this polarity that accompanies human action that it is so difficult to "give reasons" why people make a vocational guidance appointment. Listing reasons is an artifact, more precisely, a methodological expedient, provided one bears in mind the highly complex and fluid nature of individual behaviour.

Reasons for Making an Appointment

An examination of the forces that prompt an individual to make an appointment for vocational guidance reveals that, in life, causes rarely operate singly; nor are there clearly defined "chain reactions." From the biological standpoint the organism always reacts as a whole and in the direction that tends to reduce tension or to effect a temporary equilibrium. Psychologists and psychiatrists alike have frequently adopted this viewpoint in explaining psychic phenomena, Strecker *et al.*, for example, quote from Goldstein: ". . . it is the real goal of alleviate and to discharge the tension, and to bring the organism into a state of non-tension, *i.e.*, it is the goal of the drive to release itself." This principle has influenced the thinking of many vocational counsellors, despite the fact that it seems to have overlooked, somewhat, the dynamic nature of purposeful behaviour. Although an amoeba if placed in an unfavourable environment may react in a manner that will reduce tension, by either withdrawing or rolling up in a ball, a human being may take a course of action that appears to be contrary to his present needs. Thus, a worthwhile vocational plan, even if perceived as a remote objective, may outweigh the unpleasant features of the immediate counselling situation. The client may want to "go through with it," painful as such experience may appear at the moment.

Three commonly occurring factors that bring the client to the agency will be discussed presently. It is well to bear in mind that, as often as not, the reasons given by the client are not identical with the forces that impelled him to make and to keep an appointment, Frequently the client himself is not too sharply aware of what actually brought him to seek help; at times he is not ready to face it or to share his doubts with the counsellor.

Although, in a general sense, making the first appointment may signify that the positive forces have transcended the mere wishful stage and have become integrated into concrete action, with that integration new negative forces come into being. Of these the most conspicuous is fear—fear of the unknown and of what is going to happen to the client once he becomes involved in the vocational process. However, not all people feel equally strongly about anything. The extent of trepidation and ambivalence that a client will experience prior to his coming to the counsellor will depend largely on the degree to which the vocational problem has become endowed significance. In one instance at least, an examination of scores of registration blanks with the intention of classifying the causes that precipitated the client's coming for vocational assistance failed to reveal any clearly defined categories. Quite often the reasons given in writing did not indicate the problems with which the client wanted help. It was only by working with the client vis-a-vis, sometimes for two or three hours, that the true nature of the problems would come into focus.

In a very general sense, some of the reasons that bring the client to a vocational agency are the need for occupational information, verification of abilities, etc.; by someone; and anxiety. It was mentioned previously that more than one reason usually operate at a time. Consequently, the rather arbitrary classification is based not so much on overt verbalisation as on the dominant feeling tone.

1. *The need for occupational information, verification of abilities, etc.* A large number of adults who come for vocational services tend to intellectualise their problems. They usually seek concrete "advice," or wish to verify (with the aid of tests) their "aptitudes," or desire specific information regarding training and job opportunities in a particular occupation. Some applicants have independently worked out their vocational plans and really need little else than concrete information. They make a limited but evertheless a legitimate use of the agency. Such clients, however, are in the minority. The fact that at first a client verbally presents his problem in an intellectualised manner—by a request for a specific service, such as testing—does not mean that this is the only thing he wants or can use. It is the responsibility of the counsellor to let the client know that sometimes vocational problems involve more than getting information about a given field.

Working with the client around his specific request helps him clarify his own needs. He may decide that factual information is the only thing he can use at the moment, or he may wish to explore with the counsellor other opportunities open to him. It frequently happens that the client is pleasantly surprised to learn that there is more to vocational guidance than testing. He may have asked for a test thinking that this was the only service available to him. Other clients ask that tests be administered to them because they are not ready to share in the fuller process. The request for any particular form of vocational assistance is never as important as what it may signify to the client.

It is of interest to note how failure to respond to the actual need of the client may bring about an avalanche of criticism. In a study of negative reactions to counselling, Sheer presents a table of causes for dis-satisfaction expressed anonymously by college students:

Interview unplanned	23
Recommendations vague	20
Counsellor talked too much	19
Did not consider student.	16
No purpose or goal	12
Preestablish pattern	7

Although one cannot be certain how much of the criticism was entirely justified, a good deal of the dissatisfaction may have sprung from the fact that the counsellor possibly did not respond to the nuances of feelings expressed by the client. Had the student been given an opportunity to work through his problem as he himself saw it, it is likely that he would not have wanted the counsellor to give concrete advice or make definite recommendations.

The counsellor conveys to the client that he may, if he so desires, make a fuller use of the agency by sharing with the counsellor some of his thoughts and feelings regarding his vocational plans. As the counsellor clarifies for the client how the vocational agency may or may not be able to meet his needs, he also acquaints the client with certain restricting factors inherent in the vocational situation. For example, the client is helped to accept the fact that the counsellor can offer aid only in the occupational area and cannot assume the responsibility for assisting him with problems of a nonvocational nature. Similarly, the client is helped to recognize the relatively brief nature of the vocational contact. Time is introduced as a dynamic which may aid the client in mustering his resources more effectively. These restricting forces are sometimes referred to as "limits." As the counsellor identifies himself with the client in recognizing what the problem seems to be and its inner significance to the latter, he also sets up limits as to the kind and extend of assistance the agency can offer.

The client thus experiences the situation of coming face to face with a person who is understanding of his feelings and needs and yet who is not permissive to the point of allowing him complete freedom. Both the client and the counsellor become part of a structure that enables the former to evaluate his own desires and their relationship to his total situation.

When a client comes with a specific request for information or placement, the counsellor makes no attempt to create a problem where there does not appear to be one. At the same time he does not act as a mere information clerk. The distinction between a professional service as rendered by the counsellor and the activities of a nonprofessional worker is that the former assumes the responsibility for the *helping process,* whereas the latter is responsible for providing that which the client requests, without any other consideration.

The case cited below illustrates the distinction between a professional service created to assist the individual and one which interprets its function literally, with little regard for the client's welfare:

A mother of two small children, whose husband was chronically ill, asked our agency to help her find work. She was upset and frightened by that might happen to her and her family if she did not obtain employment immediately. In her hurry to find some work she had made practically no provision for her children or her bedridden husband. Taking a full-time job not only might fail to solve her problems but might actually make the situation worse. Instead of offering her employment she was helped to see why it would not be to her advantage to go to work at this moment. It was indicated that other community resources were open to her if she wanted to make a worthwhile plan. The client then asked that she be referred to a casework agency.

A non-professionally oriented agency might have referred the above client for employment with no regard for what such a step might mean to the entire family. The fact that a client asks for a job and nothing else does not absolve the worker from the responsibility of suggesting the advantages of a more comprehensive service. The very fact that the counsellor understands the client's plight and is there to help him distinguishes the counsellor from a professionally untrained worker.

If the woman in the above illustration had insisted on immediate employment and had rejected the opportunity to plan with a caseworker a concrete course of action, the counsellor could have done nothing about it. He certainly could not have forced her to accept his judgement, but he probably would not have capitulated to her demands either. Although the counsellor respects the right of a client to make his own decisions, he also has a responsibility to his agency, which is set up to *assist* people, not merely to grant their wishes. After attempting to help the client see the nature of his problem and what the agency has to offer toward its resolution, the counsellor can present the client with the choice of accepting the service *in toto,* making a limited use of it or rejecting it completely. This is by no means an ultimatum. The client often needs help, not only with the specific problem, but also with the process of being helped. The decision to accept or reject assistance, however, must lie with the client.

A responsible vocational service will not administer tests, provide specific occupational information, or find employment for people unless such activity is part of a helping process. It was emphasised that a vocational agency is concerned almost exclusively with *helping* the client attain his occupational or educational objectives. Although the agency cannot take on the responsibility for the outcome of the guidance process, it certainly should meet its obligations as a professional vocational service by offering the kind of assistance it is set up to render. New concepts in guidance are constantly being developed. It is encouraging indeed to witness a shift in emphasis from psychometric diagnosis to that of a helping process and a corresponding reformulation of some of the fundamental concepts.

Only recently, a man requested over the telephone that he be given an appointment in order to take a Binet and a Kuder Preference Record. It was indicated to him that the chief role of the agency was to assist people with their vocational planning and that, if that was what he wanted, an appointment would be made with him. It was not the function of the agency to administer tests in vacuum.

At this point one may wonder what the basic distinction is between the present case and that of the woman cited previously. An outline of the factors in operation may be helpful.

WOMAN	MAN
The woman was distressed by her economic plight (the problem).	The man gave no indication as to the nature of his problem, if one existed at all.
She came to the agency to be helped with the problem.	He was unable or unwilling to come to the agency for help despite the fact that an appointment was offered to him.
She asked for a job as a possible solution to her problem.	He asked over the telephone for two specific tests as a possible answer to his problem.
She was helped to realise that getting any kind of job was not likely to help her situation but would create additional problems.	He denid himself the opportunity to discuss his vocational problems with the counsellor.
An opportunity was offered to her to work out her problem through other means than immediate employment.	
She chose a course of action which seemed to be most acceptable to her and asked for an appropriate referral.	
A referral was made to a social agency.	

A formal statement of why the client came to the agency frequently tells the counsellor very little about the real nature of the situation. By asking the client to elaborate on some aspects of the problem the counsellor affords the applicant an opportunity to examine his original request. Simultaneously he helps the client to crystallise and to organise his own thoughts and feelings around the issues that seem to concern him. Frequently, at this stage of discussion, a great deal of hitherto latent anxiety comes to the problem is more serious or more compelling than he imagined at first. Often he will verbalize it candidly by saying in effect, I guess tests alone won't help" or "I see this is quite a mess I am in." It is not uncommon to witness the latent anxiety break out to the surface accompanied by a great deal of emotion or even tears. Thus, the client has moved from an almost impersonal request for an "aptitude test" to a point where he is able to share with the counsellor some of the aspects of his dilemma that are both meaningful and painful. Sometimes, however, the client, after having examined his original request, still feels that factual information, or whatever it was that he came for, is all he can use. If the particular request falls within the scope of services offered by the agency, there is no reason why the counsellor should deny the client the right to avail himself of it.

The case of Miss A illustrates the use of the vocational guidance office in a limited but nevertheless clearly focused and professional manner:

> Miss A is a retired schoolteacher. She is living on her pension and has an additional small *income*. Although financially independent, she would like to augment her means by tutoring deaf-mute children. Miss A has had extensive experience as a teacher for the deaf-mute. Since Miss A is a newcomer to the community, she would like the agency to help her establish contact with prospective employers or organisations that may want to use her skills.
>
> The counsellor discussed with Miss A the local employment opportunities in her field and mentioned the several names of individuals and agencies that might either employ Miss A directly or refer her to someone who could give her work.

Several features stand out about this brief contact. Miss A appears to be qualified to do the work she is looking for. This is borne out by state certification and many years of practical experience. As far as the counsellor was able to surmise during the brief contact, Miss A seems to be free from any disabling characteristics that might interfere with her employability or require a retraining programme. At present, Miss A is not interested in vocational guidance as such. She wants to utilise her special knowledge and skills as a teacher but, being a newcomer in the community, is not familiar with the different organisations that could use her services.

This is cited as an example of how a vocational guidance service can render concrete and tangible assistance without the employment of psychometric testing or extensive counselling. Both the client and the counsellor worked jointly toward a common objective at a level entirely acceptable to the client and within the functional framework of the agency. The significant aspects of the case are *(a)* Miss A had an occupational problem; *(b)* she attempted to resolve it by coming to a vocational agency for assistance; *(c)* one counselling session was sufficient to demonstrate to her and to the counsellor that she was able to use constructively her own assets and the information supplied by the agency.

Sometimes clients, especially adolescents, visit the agency out of sheer curiosity and perhaps a vague feeling that the vocational guidance process "can't hurt." Young people are often exposed to group guidance experience—a lecture, a discussion, or a film that stresses the need for occupational exploration. Their curiosity aroused, they accordingly make appointments to "take an aptitude test." Here again, there is no evidance of a vocational referrals from teachers, physicians, school counsellors, and parents. Each referral is unique in its feeling tone, structure, and objective. Social agencies, schools, and other public institutions frequently view the vocational guidance service as a diagnostic laboratory. The letter of referral usually contains a statement about the client's family and his employment history and a general request for psychological testing, When the client arrives, he is often test-oriented. Rarely has he been told that vocational guidance is a process that extends beyond numerical manipulation.

Generally, referral making, too, stems from a relationship between the person who makes it and the person who is referred.

Referrals may be made by friends or relatives or by a professional. The latter case deserves particular consideration because such referrals are a part of the process in which both the client and the worker are participating. Making a referral invariably entails responsibility. In order that the referral be effective, it is essential' that the client share in that responsibility. Being referred to the counsellor (or by the counsellor) often becomes a meaningful experience to the client. Although the worker cannot quite realise its full implications for the client, he can help him accept such a referral as a part of the counselling process.

This is not to imply that the person making the referral is expected to "do the intake" for the worker to whom the referral is made. For example, if it is the caseworker who is making a referral to the vocational guidance counsellor, we cannot expect the former to help the client overcome all the anxieties and negative feelings he may have about such a referral. It is of course a help if the caseworker in question understands the role of the vocational counsellor and can convey to the client something of what vocational guidance is. However, it is not the responsibility of the caseworker to interpret the vocational guidance process to the client or to begin vocational counselling with him. At times, workers in the various areas themselves have but a vague notion of the actual function of a vocational counsellor. They may perceive vocational guidance as a process of tests and sound advice giving, in which case they are likely to transmit their own misconceptions to the client. Such a misunderstanding is not too helpful, but it need not be fatal to the vocational process. The fact that the client is not entirely clear as to how the vocational counsellor can help him or is actually labouring under a misapprehension as to what vocational guidance is may be quite understandable. The counsellor always begins with the reality as it appears to the client. Intellectual misconceptions can usually be handled provided the client really wants assistance with his occupational problems.

How the *referral* was *structured* is another point to consider. Was the client told that he was coming to take tests, was he given the impression that the counsellor would solve the problem for him, or was it perhaps implied that the counsellor's decision would actually affect the rest of his life?

The structuring of the referral, although not necessarily crucial to the outcome of the counselling process, may help or hinder its initial development. It may come as a shock to the client who comes solely "to take an aptitude test" to discover that he will be asked to assume the responsibilities for making a difficult vocational decision. Similarly, the advice-oriented individual who comes to the counsellor as an expert may not be ready to take his real place in the counselling relationship. Sometimes an exasperated principal or a teacher may send a student to the counsellor as a last resort. Such a student views the counsellor with suspicion and hostility. He considers him as an adjunct to the school system—a symbol of authority—not as a professionally trained person who is ready to assist him with his educational difficulties.

The last important point to be considered in connection with referrals is how *the client perceives the referral and what use he makes* of it. Perception of an event is almost invariably coloured by the immediate and the fundamental psychological needs of the perceiver. The person referred for vocational guidance by a professional worker is going to perceive the referral in a manner characteristic of his total make-up and in harmony with his drives and wishes as they appear at the moment.

The situation is not unlike that encountered with the Rorschach ink blots or the Thematic Apperception Test (TAT), where an essentially ambiguous but potentially meaningful stimulus is interpreted subjectively by the teste in a manner peculiar to his entire personality. For example, a well-adjusted individual with a positive outlook on life may see in the Rorsohach blots dancing people, gaiety, and flowering meadows. The same ink blots may be perceived by an anxious and hostile patient as people fighting, destruction, and dripping blood. The manner in which an individual interprets a projective test is rarely, if ever, accidental. The interpretation is usually characteristic of the individual's fundamental personality make-up. How the client sees the referral, the counsellor, and the test data is also going to be determined largely by his basic personality structure and his most pressing needs.

This raises the important question of apperception, which Bellak defines as "an organism's (dynamically) meaningful interpretation of a perception." Elsewhere he speaks of apperception as "all sorts of perception that in one manner or another are influenced by selective, personal drives and thus suffer some distortion from the hypothetically purely cognitive percept." It is well to remember that these distortions are likely to be of a wishful nature or to have some need-satisfaction value. Far from being of solely theoretical interest the concept of apperception has definite practical implications. What the counsellor says to the client, what the tests may reveal, what occupational plans appear to be indicated will be influenced (or even distorted) by the client's subjective perception of events about him. It is postulated that the more immature the client is, the greater will be the extent of apperceptive distortion. It is further-more held that directive counselling which utilises advice giving and literal test interpretation and which emphasises factual data in general is subject to greater mis-interpretation (*i.e.,* distortion) by the client than counselling that is based on the latter's self-directiveness.

Though accepting a referral for vocational guidance, the client is likely to abstract from the total situation only those elements with which he can cope at the moment. Thus he may focus on the psychometric aspects of the programme and relegate to the back ground the more painful process of counselling; or he may insist on projecting an authoritative role on the counsellor and place himself in a strictly receptive position. These personal interpretations of the service are particularly common with self-referred individuals and those referred without the benefit of a pre-counselling experience prior to coming to the agency. Self-referred persons frequently learn of the vocational service through newspapers, through mailed interpretative material, or by word at mouth from someone familiar with the agency. In addition to a desire to be helped, they have only a vague notion as to what a vocational guidance service can offer. Furthermore, they perceive the service almost entirely in terms that are acceptable and palatable to them.

Referrals made by professional workers in another field are often coloured by the client's subjective interpretation as well. Even a carefully structured referral is likely to be perceived by the client in his own personal manner. Here again, the vocational counsellor may have to work with the forces responsible for the particular way in which vocational assistance is perceived by the client. If the client, for example, tends to place the entire onus for the vocational decision on the counsellor, the latter may have to try to help the client to see that such an attitude is but an evasion of his own responsibility in the plan. Similarly, an undue emphasis tests may signify unreadiness for taking hold of the problem. In both instances, the client lets the external forces (*i.e.*, the counsellor or the tests) do the deciding for him. How the client has perceived the referral, and what use he can make of it, becomes important as a starting point around which the counselling relationship may develop.

The preceding discussion centred itself primarily around the situation wherein the client was referred by someone, *i.e.*, teacher, caseworker, psychiatrist, to the vocational agency. A few words about the converse condition may be in order. The vocational counsellor, too, is frequently called upon to make referrals to appropriate services when the client wants help with a nonvocational problem. Many of the dynamics discussed thus far apply with equal force to a situation wherein the *vocational counsellor* is the one who makes the referral. That is, the worker is likely to encounter resistance to such action. There may be ambivalence on the part of the client about accepting such a referral and considerable anxiety about the new situation. The vocational counsellor may have to handle these feelings to enable the client to move to a point at which he can take it upon himself to make the decision.

In connection with referrals made by the vocational counsellor, Arbuckle raises a rather interesting point when he poses the question as to what is to be done when "there is simply no one to whom the client can be referred. . . if the counsellor represents the client's last hope in the way of professional assistance." Actually, two separate ideas are implied in this statement: *(a)* that there exist no community resources whatsoever that are set up to handle nonvocational problems and *(b)* that the counsel or may have to assume the responsibility of offering assistance in an area outside his professional competence.

With respect to the first, it is extremely unlikely that a community sufficiently advanced to offer vocational services will not have at its disposal some psychiatric or casework facilities as well. If anything, the reverse is much more common. Generally, outpatient psychiatric departments of hospitals, mental hygiene clinics, and social agencies antedate vocational guidance services. Even medium-sized communities are likely to have child care agencies and child guidance clinics. Communities that are too small to have in their midst some psychiatric or casework resources certainly are not likely to have much of a vocational guidance programme either. Perhaps the "impossibility" of the vocational counsellor making an appropriate referral comes not so much from a complete absence of suitable resources as from the vocational counsellor's unfamiliarity with such services.

The second point, the possibility that the vocational counsellor may have to offer help in an area for which he has no particular competence or qualification, has been touched upon previously. So unsafe a practice can be justified only under the most unusual conditions. As already implied in the preceding paragraph, wherever there are vocational counsellors, there are also likely to be psychiatrists, psychologists, and caseworkers. Before undertaking a task which lies outside his professional field, the vocational worker should familiarize himself thoroughly with the resources in his community. In practice, however, situations do arise which make it extremely difficult to obtain psychiatric assistance even when such facilities do exist in the community. The outpatient psychiatric departments and mental hygiene clinics frequently have waiting lists that are so long as to make their services, from the practical standpoint, almost inaccessible to most people.

Only recently a young chemist came to see us about his vocational plans because he was dissatisfied selling sewing machines from door to door. During the first interview it was established with a fair degree of certainty that his vocational maladjustment stemmed from a more general personality imbalance. The client in question verbalized quite readily his feelings about having failed not only in occupational areas but in his relationship with people and in life in general. Although he came to be assisted vocationally, he was also deeply concerned with his total malfunctioning and toward the closing of the first session wondered whether he needed psychiatric help. Quite understandably the client had considerable fears about a psychiatric referral and wanted to know whether it was really imperative that he avail himself of psychotherapy or whether he was likely to resolve his conflicts unassisted. Because of that consideration and in order to ascertain the extent of his vocational "counselability," it was mutually decided that a total personality test might prove to be helpful. The Rorschach was administered, and it was learned that the client suffered from a pronounced anxiety neurosis accompanied by marked depressive tendencies. It was therefore felt that at the moment the client was not likely to benefit from vocational guidance but could be helped through psychotherapy. During the third and last session, in which the question of a psychiatric referral was taken up once more, the client expressed a definite desire to begin psychiatric treatment at once. Since he had no money, attempt was made to have him accepted by the existing but patient clinics. A telephone call to a hospital revealed that a waiting list made it impossible for him to be seen for next two months. A call to a mental hygiene clinic brought similar results. A telephone conversation with a psychological training centre finally elicited some assurance that the client could be seen by the intake worker in about a week. This looked promising. The client hurried away saying that he would make an appointment immediately.

About two weeks latter we received a telephone call from a family social-work agency. The caseworker there indicated that our client had been referred to that agency by there psychological centre to which our original referral had been made. Although she did not claim to be a psychiatrist, she thought that she might help." Such an uncritical understanding of the nature of the problem and the function of the worker, as a specialist, is regrettable indeed. It still has to be demonstrated that casework treatment can serve as a valid substitute for psychotherapy.

Lastly, one may wish to pose the question of whose responsibility it is to expand or to modify the existing psychiatric services in a manner which allows for an accommodation of a greater number of applicants. Is this a problem for the already existing psychiatric profession, which currently is concerned with the prevention and treatment of emotional disorders, or is it an issue which is to be decided by general counsellors and caseworkers? In other words, are counsellors and caseworkers justified in attempting psychotherapy (even if it be designated by some other term) simply because psychiatry has failed to develop a type of service that meets the needs of the community? Clearly the initiative for the establishment of adequate psychiatric facilities is the responsibility of the medical profession. It is not the function of nonmedically trained workers to attempt to fill the existing gaps.

3. *Anxiety.* Anxiety is another important factor that impels people to seek vocational assistance. From the vocational counsellor's standpoint, anxiety may be viewed as a condition that is brought about when two or several antagonistic forces come into open conflict with each other. Barring the situations where anxiety is so acute as to incapacitate the individual, it may be considered a desirable adjuvant in the counselling process. When examined carefully, it represents the conflict between opposing drives, needs, and desires in the educational or vocational area that motivates the client to ask for professional assistance. Unless the client feels anxious, unsure of his plans, or ambivalent about some occupational choice, he does not need the help of the vocational counsellor. The very essence of counselling lies in helping the client to recognise the conflicting feelings inherent in every occupational problem and to accept them as a part of his real self. There can be no genuine vocational counselling without the client's experiencing some anxiety in that area.

It was stated earlier that causes prompting one to seek vocational assistance rarely operate as single entities. Almost invariably several drives, toward and away from the helping process, take place simultaneously. Completely integrated into the maze of contradictory forces are the anxiety components, which further, contribute to the discomfort and doubts of the individual. When the client comes for help, he brings with him his conflicting feelings, attitudes, and wishes. It would be most unusual, indeed, if the client openly announced, "I am afflicted with anxiety; help me!" He is more likely to couch his fears in terms of vocational indecision, fear of failure, lack of specific occupational training or information, doubts about the soundness of a plan, etc. As he expresses his difficulties, he may reveal considerable defensiveness about asking for vocational assistance. He may try to minimise the seriousness of the situation or actually flinch when the word "problem" is used. Many persons like to think of vocational guidance as an impersonal, possibly test-centred process that places only superficial demands on their participation. Characteristically, they ask for assistance but simultaneously resist becoming involved in a helping relationship!

Among the anxious adults who come with their vocational problems are those who are afflicted with an all-embracing anxiety that appears to permeate most of their activities. There are also those who, although essentially stable, show concern or even anxiety over a particular vocational development. The former group need interest us only to the extent that it can be helped vocationally. The treatment of anxiety, per se, is obviously not the counsellor's job. The capacity for planning, the ability to make use, of self, as well as the desire to progress vocationally, however, are very much the concern of the vocational counsellor. For that matter, clinical diagnosis, whether made by the counsellor or by a psychiatrist who may have had previous contact with the client, is not a part of the helping process. The counsellor becomes a diagnotician only after the client has demonstrated his inability to take hold of the vocational programme and has shown an incapacity for growth or movement. Only then is it in order to ask why the client has failed to benefit from the vocational experience, what factors prevented him from using himself, and what is to be done next.

The term "diagnosis" as employed in the preceding paragraph has deliberately been given a rather static connotation in order to emphasise the ineffectiveness of pigeonholing as part of a helping procedure. "Dynamic diagnosis," that is, diagnosis that evaluates the individual in terms of integrated functions, has much more to contribute, not only to understanding the client, but to the process of assisting him with his problem.

But dynamic diagnosis, even at this stage, becomes much more effective when it is the client who wants to know why he has not been helped. The counsellor should not administer a Rorschach in order to vindicate himself or to satisfy his intellectual curiosity. If personality tests are to be administered, this should be done because the client himself is concerned over his inability to progress vocationally and is possibly attributing his failure to move to his total emotional difficulties. Such testing may lead ultimately to a psychiatric referral.

The fact that a veteran may have been classified as a case of anxiety neurosis does not mean that he cannot have genuine vocational or educational problems. It is true that the particular problem with which he wants help may be merely an outgrowth of a deeper, total disturbance. Nevertheless, the occupational dilemma may be real. The counsellor cannot very well assume that, when the major disturbance is alleviated, the vocational difficulties will disappear of themselves; nor can he decide a priori that free-floating anxiety must always be so severe as completely to paralyse the client's capacity to be helped vocationally. In such a case the counsellor has only one recourse, and that is to attempt to enter with the client into a professional helping relationship. Should the client demonstrate that, because of his anxiety or any other disabling psychological condition, he cannot make a constructive use of the vocational programme, the counsellor may then assume the responsibility for suggesting an appropriate referral or for terminating the service.

Anxiety may at times reveal itself in the client's persistent attempts to find relief for his emotional distress without being able to come to actual grips with the disturbing situation. In the occupational area such anxiety may be recognised through frequent changes in employment, vocational dissatisfaction, and sporadic attempts to procure professional assistance.

Among those seeking vocational help as an answer to their multiple problems are people who seem to be merely "shopping around." Shopping around is a descriptive rather than a nosological term. It is intended to embrace a large category of persons who are frequently encountered in vocational guidance work and who seem to have one feature in common: they are aware of something being wrong, but they are incapable of going through the helping process. They seem to have just enough energy to bring themselves to see the counsellor, only to reject the entire experience. Many have genuine problems in the vocational realm, although the focus is usually not the vocational difficulty, but the total personality. The vocational problems are merely derivative, inasmuch as they stem from basic total maladjustments.

Such persons have usually applied to several agencies. In all probability they want help without realizing their inability to mobilise their resources or to make use of the existing facilities. Consequently, in their view it is usually the agency or the worker who is at fault. They want help, but only on their own terms. The whole helping process is a challenge to them—a battle of wits in which they are victorious beforehand. They are masters in dueling, but, should the counsellor refuse to be used as an antagonist, they lower their visors and withdraw.

It is questionable whether or not such persons are counselable or can really profit from occupational planning. Although they appear to ask for help, they do all they can to resist making a change or becoming emotionally involved. In effect they say to the counsellor, "Wash me, but don't get me wet." Another reason for their limited counselability is the fact that they themselves are not too concerned with the vocational focus. To them vocational guidance is but a safe avenue toward psychotherapy. They themselves realise the derivative nature of their vocational guidance problem and are actually more concerned with problems of the whole personality. As the various community resources fail them, they ultimately come to the vocational guidance agency holy to discover that it, too, does not meet their particular needs.

Still other manifestations of generalised anxiety are at times encountered in a vocational guidance agency. Overt forms of anxiety, although of interest to the clinical psychologist and the psychiatrist, need not preoccupy the vocational counsellor too much. The counsellor's chief responsibility is not to diagnose a particular neurosis or to treat it but to help the client with his vocational plans. It is safe to assume that virtually every counsellor who has been in the field for any length of time has encountered almost the complete gamut of psychological disturbance.

Without too much effort I can recall meeting professionally both mild and severe psychoneurotic, admitted homosexuals, drug addicts, alcoholics, and unmistakably delusional, paranoiac, hallucinatory, and schizophrenic clients. Some were under psychiatric treatment; others were on the way to, or on convalescent care from, a state hospital. The worker's role, no matter how mild or severe the client's disturbance may be, is always that of a vocational counsellor; at no time should he undertake the role of the psychotherapist or attempt to treat the disturbance itself.

The second group of applicants to be considered are those individuals who, although essentially psychologically sound, develop an anxiety in response to an environmental difficulty such as loss of a job, failure in school, or inability to make a choice between alternate occupational or educational plans. It is presumed that the anxiety engendered by the particular predicament will be ameliorated when the client mobilizes his own resources and comes to a definite vocational decision. The ambivalent forces that are at the root of anxiety may impel the client to seek vocational assistance and simultaneously may enable him to participate in a psychologically meaningful manner in the counselling process. Quite obviously, a person so motivated is not free from the negative and oppositional feelings that are bound to be encountered in every helping situation. The client is in conflict, not only about his occupational dilemma, but also about his wanting and not wanting help.

As the client grapples with the original problem with which he came to the agency and the new problem of entering into a helping relationship, he is likely to demand, at first, an unusual amount of support. This need for support is likely to express itself as a desire for reassurance and confirmation. The amount of support required by the client will vary with the individual and the specific predicament that prompted him to apply for vocational assistance. This need may manifest itself in general dependence, seeming helplessness, fearfulness, or professed ignorance of the occupational world. In essence what the client is attempting to do is to place himself in a subordinate position and cause the vocational counsellor to do the planning for him. The significance of these dynamics as they apply to adult and to adolescents will be discussed at a later point.

□□□

4

THE FIRST INTERVIEW

The Client Make an Appointment

Generally speaking, the vocational counselling process may be considered to consist of three parts: the request for vocational assistance, the handling of the problem, and the termination of the relationship with the counsellor and the institution which he represents. In the light of the preceding discussion, it may be difficult to draw a sharp line between the beginning and the rest of the process. For example, one might ask, Did the process set itself into motion with the first thought or realisation of the client that he wants help? Or was it initiated with the actual making of the first appointment? In other words, do the predisposing factors that prompt one to make an appointment, *i.e.*, the need for specific information, the doubts and anxieties, become a part of the couselling process?

It has already been suggested that the dynamics of helpfulness are pivoted around the interpersonal relationship between the counsellor and the client. Since no such relationship can be established prior to the client's keeping his initial appointment, the struggles that precede the first interview cannot be considered as part of the process. The process then must begin with the first actual contact between the client and the counsellor. However, between the desire for help and actual help lies the narrow area in which the client makes the appointment. This may be replete with psychological significance, for it represents, from the client's point of view, the first step toward movement.

Sylvester holds that the helping process "begins with a person's coming to an agency because he feels a need for something beyond what he thinks he can obtain solely through his own efforts". She furthermore feels that the relationship established between the worker and the client is not only a part of the process itself but "the medium for movement in that process."

Tenuousness of the First Contact

It has been stated previously that many vocational agencies usually schedule the first appointment over the telephone. The incoming call may be handled by a clerical worker unless the applicant has questions, in which case the call may be switched over to a member of the professional staff. How the request for vocational assistance is structured, what the problem appears to be, and how the future client perceives the helping process and his place in it may be revealed in the brief telephone conversation. Ideally one would expect that all telephone appointments be handled by the vocational counsellor rather than his secretary. In practice this is not always feasible, for the counsellor cannot be interrupted when he is interviewing or in conference. Since it is not always possible to return the call, it may be necessary to let the clerical worker handle "routine" appointments. Understaffed or one-man vocational agencies may be compelled to rely on this expedient. An intelligent and sensitive clerk can be trusted to distinguish between a client who asks for an appointment in a straightforward, businesslike manner and one who apparently has many reservations about becoming "involved" with the agency. Such procedure represents a compromise between the more desirable situation in which a counsellor is always available and that in which the worker is either too busy or out of the office much of the time.

The significance of what transpires over the telephone is not so much any diagnostic value, but lies in the client's tentative acceptance of the service. It is the client's privilege to enter this new relationship with some questioning or even with marked trepidation. It is perfectly understandable that he should leave some doors open behind him in the event that the new experience proves to be more, than he ran handle. It is well for the counsellor to be attuned to the nuances of feelings that may be expressed over the telephone. Although this aspect of getting vocational help has been generally overlooked, it nevertheless deserves consideration. Over the telephone, as during the interview proper, clients allow themselves all the shades of feeling with which they approach the counselling situation. Here again one may see complete rejection, passive tolerance, or a genuine interest in planning.

Does the Client make the Appointment Himself?

Ordinarily one might expect an adult to make the appointment himself. This, however, is not always the case. Wives, mothers, caseworkers, and physicians frequently make the original telephone contact. This expedient is usually indicative of the feelings the potential client may have about receiving vocational help. It may be reasoned that circumstances sometimes make it easier for someone else to telephone. This is rarely so. A person actively motivated by the prospects of vocational help will want to become engaged in every aspect of it as soon as possible. Considering all the misunderstandings and delays that may arise when someone else makes the appointment, the client, if actually ready for the experience, will not permit anyone else to usurp his part in this important venture.

It follows, therefore, that, when the client relegates appointment making to someone else, he has for whatever reason rejected becoming involved in the vocational guidance programme. The more feeling he has about not wanting help or the more anxious he is about the process itself, the more likely he is to let someone else make the appointment for him. This is his way of saying, "*I* want no part of it." It may also mean, "I want it, but I am afraid of it." Whether the initial telephone call is made by the would-be client himself or by proxy is an indicator of the extent to which he is willing or able to identify himself with the vocational programme.

How does the Client Formulate the Request?

The fact that the client calls up himself and makes the appointment is no proof of his accepting wholeheartedly what is to follow, although it may represent a step forward as compared with someone else taking the initiative for him. How he verbalizes his request for assistance is all-important. For example, he may say, "Miss X said I should call you." Here he is obviously trying to convey the idea that the request does not originate with him and that therefore he is not responsible for what will happen. He is keeping himself entirely out of the picture. He is merely a messenger delivering someone else's request. Or he may say, "I want to make an appointment for an aptitude test." In this instance the "I" is more prominent. He no longer places the entire responsibility on Miss X. However, he is still feeling his way along cautiously. He is not quite ready to become a part of the process. Significantly, he is not asking for assistance with his problems, only for aptitude tests. Essentially his attitude is noncommittal, though also exploratory. Next on the hypothetical scale is the prospective client who in effect says, "I want to talk to you about my vocational plans." Verbally, at least, he not only assumes full participation but also reveals an understanding of why he is asking for an interview.

One would be rash indeed to categorise a person by the way he words his request for an appointment. An individual who on the telephone appears to be capable of accepting his role in the vocational process may still not be able to go through with it in an actual face-to-face situation. However, to employ appointment making as one single criterion of the client's readiness to share in the counselling process, one cannot help feeling that, psychologically, it makes a difference whether the client has someone else make the call for him, whether he places the entire onus on another person, or whether he can take it upon himself to ask for vocational assistance.

If it is the counsellor who speaks to the client in making the telephone appointment, he has the definite responsibility of attempting to help the latter decide whether he actually want to avail himself of the service the agency is prepared to offer. The counsellor may also have to handle some of the anxieties that accompany the taking of vocational help. The case of Mr. L, a young attorney, illustrates some of the difficulties one may experience in making an appointment. The telephone conversation is reproduced practically verbatim:

L_1. I understand you give aptitude tests to help people with their vocational problems. Is that right?

C_1. Well, we try to assist people with their vocational and educational problems, and we do give tests when that seems to be necessary.

L_2. How do I go about taking those tests?

C_2. You can make an appointment right now, and I shall be glad to talk to you about your vocational problem.

L_3. It is not really a problem; it is just that I want to be sure that I am doing the right thing.

C_3. You would want us to verify your plans.

L_4. That's right. I thought that by talking to someone I could make up my mind regarding certain plans.

C_4. I shall be glad to talk to you about these plans, and possibly we might be able to help you decide for yourself what you want to do.

L_5. *(After a few seconds' pause)* Excuse me, are there any fees for the service? I am not working now, but I can pay some money.

C_5. There are no fees whatsoever. We are a Red Feather Agency, supported by the Community Chest.

L_6. I am very glad to know that such services are available to the people of Buffalo. One more question, however—when I come up, do I ask for you or someone else?

C_6. That will depend on when you can come in. Either I or another vocational counsellor will see you.

L_7. Are the other counsellors qualified to handle my case?

C_7. You seem to be concerned that you will be mis-understood. Although I am not certain who your counsellor will be, I feel that our counsellors are quite competent.

L_8. All this is confidential, I presume.

C_8. Definitely.

L_9. What about your stenographic help? Do they ever discuss the cases they type?

C_9. I can appreciate how you feel about coming to us for vocational help. You want to be certain that we can help you, and naturally you don't want anyone else to know that you are coming to see us.

L_{10}. That's correct. You know how people talk.

C_{10}. Yes, I do. As I said before, whatever takes place in the office is in strict confidence.

L_{11}. Do I know any of the counsellors?

C_{11}. I don't know. There is Mr. A, Mr. B, and myself.

L_{12}. *(Pause)* No, I don't know them.

C_{12}. Shall I give you an appointment?

L_{13}. Oh, yes. How about this coming Wednesday morning?

It is unsound to speak of "typical" cases in vocational guidance, and yet conversations such as the one just cited are common indeed. It is interesting to note how cautiously the client approaches the counsellor. He wants to be quite certain that *tests* are administered by the agency. In his second remark he is still careful to indicate that it is testing that he is interested in. In his third comment he apparently resents the word "problem." Evidently he prefers to think of his vocational dilemma in rather vague terms. Significantly, in his fourth comment he abandons testing in favour of "talking to someone. His fifth remark suggests that he is still uncertain about coming in and is searching for a valid reason that may keep him away. Simultaneously he does not want to reject the service (ambivalence). Mr. L says he can "pay some money." The sixth remark depersonalises the experience, for he is now talking about the "people of Buffalo" as if head nothing to do with the situation. (It would be a great deal more difficult to say, "I am glad that such services are available to *me.*") Anxiety is revealed again when Mr. L asks whom to ask for. It becomes more pronounced when he questions the qualifications of the other counsellors. He is now asking for re-assurance and a guarantee (L_7). The eighth question is still replete with anxiety and ambivalence. Mr. L is now concerned with the confidentiality of the records although he probably knows perfectly well that all information is confidential. He is given reassurance, but he pursues the same point in question L_9. In the tenth remark he is still testing the situation and asking for additional support. The pause after the twelfth comment is significant. Mr. L has no more questions to ask. The time has come to decide whether he will or will not make an appointment. The feeling tone in L_{13} comes almost as a relief. He has decided what to do and is eager to start.

The counsellor's part during the telephone conversation has been to convey his recognition of the difficulties one .may have about taking help and to give reassurance. Very briefly the counsellor has suggested the nature of the service (C_1, C_2, C_4), recognised some of the feelings the client has about vocational assistance (C_7, C_8), and offered some reassurance regarding specific questions (C_5, C_7, C_8, C_{10}). Such reassurance, although probably unhelpful in an actual counselling situation, has aided the client in his immediate anxiety, enabling him to continue with the telephone conversation. A less supportive attitude at this extremely tenuous stage of relationship may very easily miscarry. Since one cannot do actual intake over the telephone, the counsellor must assist the client to overcome his initial fears in order that he may bring himself to the first face-to-face session.

The First Session

Much of what takes place during the first interview has been anticipated in the preceding pages, in order to convey some of the feelings that may be at work within the client even prior to his first contact with the agency. It is also hoped that the foregoing remarks pertaining to the first counselling session will in a sense set the stage for what is to follow.

A brief recapitulation may be in order. It has been assumed that an adult client comes for vocational assistance because he is concerned over some aspect of his occupational status. The problem may be pressing and immediate, or it may deal with more general plans projected into the future. Whatever the case may be, in working with adults a vocational (or educational) problem is the *sine qua non* in vocational guidance.

It has been pointed out that every meaningful psychological act is accompanied by conflicting feelings. Applying for vocational assistance is no exception. The ambivalence that accompanies the client's first impulse to come to the agency for vocational assistance stems from his basic fear of a change versus a desire to effect a change. This resistance to change usually remains, in varying degrees, throughout the counselling process.

What happens during the first face-to-face contact? By necessity one has to be very general, for no two individual will react in an identical manner to the first interview. Either the counsellor or the client may open the discussion. There need not be any rigid rules about this. As the client begins to talk, he usually states why! he came and what he expects from the service. How he perceives himself in the vocational process, how he thinks he can be helped, and what he hopes the counsellor can accomplish are important. It is possible that he conceives of vocational guidance as a strictly diagnostic procedure, or he may impute to it activities that ordinarily would belong to family casework or psychiatry.

The counsellor, recognizing the difficulties that a client may experience in bringing his problems to the agency, helps the latter mobilize his inner strength by identifying himself with the client's feelings. But such an identification is by no means total. As previously mentioned, the counsellor does not strive to create a completely permissive atmosphere. Although he tries to understand the feelings and undertones expressed by the client, he also *sets up differences.* That is, he reserves the right to differ from the client, to disagree with him, or not to grant certain wishes.

The distinction between what the client may want and what the counsellor can grant need not be a mere theoretical abstraction. The issue in which such a conflict centres may be very meaningful to the client. He may insist that the counsellor go along with his request and become hostile or actually abusive if the counsellor refuses to submit to his demands. The fact that the client may raise his voice or pound on the table is no reflection on the professional tone of the interview. It simply indicates that the client is really struggling with his own conflicts and the limitations imposed by the counsellor on a subjectively meaningful issue. The client may be testing himself and the counsellor to determine how much he can "get away with." Or he may be angry because he has discovered that, although the counsellor is sympathetic and understanding, he refuses to be used as a crutch. The client may also be projecting his negative feelings on the counsellor by making him the arch villain in the present situation.

Recently a client became quite voluable because the counsellor would not call up the client employer and ask him for a raise. The counsellor was understanding and sympathetic with the client's desire for an increase in salary, but he refused to negotiate for the client, feeling that he was too fearful and dependent in his relationship with people. It would have been much easier for the counsellor to talk to the employer, but such a course of action would deprive the client of the valuable experience of using himself constructively. The client revealed considerable strength in opposing the counsellor—perhaps he could mobilize part of that strength in trying to have his salary raised.

A complete acceptance of the client for what he is almost fatalistic in its philosophy, for implicit in such acceptance is a denial of his will to change. When the counsellor assumes the responsibility for assisting the client with his vocational problems, he takes for granted that the client wants to do something about his occupational predicament, although he may need help to bring about certain changes. The counsellor's role then becomes not only that of a sympathetic listener but one in which the counsellor participates dynamically in effecting a transformation. Sometimes a fuller employment of self can be elicited from the client through identification with his needs; sometimes differentiation from the client is more effective in stimulating his latent potentialities for growth. The case of Miss illustrates this point:

Miss J is a laboratory technician who through circumstances found herself stranded in the City. The family agency agreed to help her financially until she found employment. Although in the course of a month the employment counsellor referred her to several places where vacancies existed, Miss J was not hired. As the counsellor worked with her around her inability to find work, he learned that Miss J was evidently a fearful and dependent individual, incapable of utilising her training. If someone had approached her and offered her a job, she would have accepted it. But following leads and then being refused was more than the client could cope with. It soon became evident that Miss J was totally dependent on the counsellor, not only for employment, but also for emotional support. At that time Miss J was described as a "weak, clinging person."

In order to help Miss J to muster her strength, the tactics had to be changed. A time limit was set during which she was to find employment or lose her eligibility for financial assitance. Miss J fought this move. As the time of separation grew nearer, she became progressively more hostile toward the agency. She used insulting language and chart the counsellor with every conceivable sin. The counsellor nevertheless held firm. He tried to help Miss J realise that she could not expect to be supported indefinitely and that the decision made by the agency was not punitive but merely a part of reality which made further financial help impossible. "The weak and clinging person" became transformed into an aggressive and articulate individual. She loudly denounced the agency, saying that she would never return for any kind of assistance.

Miss J did not keep her last appointment. The following day we received a call from a hospital. The pathologist in charge of the laboratory was about to hire Miss J. She had applied unassisted for a job and apparently had made a good impression. Miss J had given the counsellor's name as a reference.

There can be little question that it was not easy for Miss J to use herself constructively. On the other hand, continued passive acceptance would probably merely have fostered further dependence and would not have helped Miss J make a fuller use of her potential strength. The counsellor utilised time as a dynamic in bringing out Miss J's true abilities, which she could not organise in a less definitive situation. Although Miss J severed her relationship with the agency in anger, she has also learned to get along without the agency's support. The counsellor has helped Miss J to become independent, although such independence was won at a considerable cost.

Parenthetically it may be remarked that a vocational guidance agency cannot rely on testimonials from satisfied "customers." Taking help is usually a difficult and emotionally painful experience. Not all clients leave the agency with a feeling of glowing satisfaction, ready to recommend the service to their friends. They may have been helped with their vocational difficulties, but, because of the frequently painful nature of the helping process, they may have terminated their contacts somewhat prematurely. Having to decide for themselves, having to face reality, unpleasant as it may be, and finally having to choose a course of action contrary to one's actual desires is not a pleasant experience. This is not to imply that the counsellor forces the client into anything against his own wishes. The client himself always decides what he is going to do, but his decision is not always to his liking. Frequently he has to compromise or abandon some of his cherished ambitions because reality dictates otherwise. Even after the counselling experience the client may still feel fearful of making a change, afraid of the future, and ambivalent about his plans.

Ambivalence, however, is not the sole force that hampers the capacity of the client to benefit from the vocational guidance process; inability to assume responsibility for his action and plans, lack of self-confidence coupled with a need for continued reassurance, and failure to accept the vocational focus as against total personality treatment are some of the other components that militate against his profiting from the counselling experience. The foregoing discussion has also attempted to convey some of the subtler nuances of feeling that go with efforts to secure vocational help. We have seen how the client vacillates, how he tends to narrow the service to its mere psychometric aspects or to expand it to embrace the total personality, and how he tries to externalise the whole problem by holding someone else responsible for whatever he does about getting help. It is against this background of conflicting feelings that the client finally comes to the vocational agency.

The most significant aspect of the first interview is the fact that represents a meeting between two human beings. This point cannot be overemphasised, for whatever follows in the course of the counselling process will be contingent on the kind of relationship that emerges between the counsellor and the client.

The first interview, of necessity, must begin with a face-to-face encounter. Whatever the client says or does during this session is always in relation to the counsellor, who for that hour becomes the pivot around which the feelings, complaints, and hopes of the client turn. The client never behaves in a vacuum, as if the counsellor were not in the room. If he did so behave, he would not utter a word unless he were in the habit of talking to himself. It is precisely because the counsellor is very much a part of the process that the client reacts to him as to a human being and as professional.

How the client uses the initial contact is an individual matter. He may perceive in the counsellor an antagonist and start out with an attack. He is just as likely to see the counsellor as a judge, a father-confessor, or a witch doctor or to impute to him any role that fulfils his needs at the moment. How the counsellor reacts to the client's behaviour and feelings willing turn set off the emotional interplay which is the core of the professional relationship. I say professional relationship because the counsellor's role in this intercourse is not indiscriminate and random, as it might be when two people meet on a train. The counsellor, by virtue of being on the staff of an agency, has definite responsibilities toward the client. He has also specific functions which he may exercise and which are determined by the over-all structure of the agency and his place in it. Because of his training he is in possession of certain skills, knowledge, and ethical principles which distinguish him from a well-meaning amateur. In the course of the interview the counsellor will allow his professional self to react to the feelings expressed by the client in a way which will promote a freer flow of expression and a better understanding between the two. This, however, is not a "technique" or a professional trick calculated to promote spontaneity in the client. The positive relationship that ensues stems from the fact that the counsellor is genuinely interested in helping the client to make the most of his visit. A counsellor who, because of his personal needs, is judgemental or hostile toward the client or blocks the latter's right to feel about things as he does is not fulfilling his professional obligations.

The rationale of this book is predicated on the uniqueness of the dynamic relationship that is established between the client and, the counsellor. Perhaps for the first time in his life the client meets a person, who although want and sympathetic, does not attempt to take the problem away by trying to solve it for him. A new climate is created wherein the client can develop his ego strength by grappling with his problems as they arise. The counsellor, during this struggle, is very much a part of the newly created reality. The client can use the counsellor to test out his own strengths as well as his weaknesses. Because limits are set up as to what he can expect from the agency, the client learns to make use of what is, instead of losing himself in the search for what he would like. The new relationship is indeed very painful at times. The client must often give up much of what he had cherished in himself in order to attain his new goals. The counsellor's understanding of some of the struggles that go into the process accompanying a change helps the client to move and to grow.

The counsellor, as envisioned here, is a far cry from the all-permissive, Buddha-like worker; nor is he a warm, all-embracing "alter ego" who tries desperately to become a mirror image of the client. Quite the contrary, he embodies an active force which assists the client to express some of his feelings, sharpens his awareness of his problem, and facilitates movement.

The client-counsellor relationship that is usually established during the initial interview is not the only important aspect of the first contact. The initial, or intake, interview enables both the client and the counsellor to examine the nature of the problem with which the client wants assistance and to ascertain whether the vocational service is set up to handle such a problem. Fees, if any, duration and frequency of interviews, kinds of psychometric tests to be administered, and other limits may be discussed. The definite client thus gets a distinct feeling that he is functioning within a definite structure and that it is up to, him to make whatever use he can of it. The concepts of *function,* or the kind of service the agency is prepared to render, *focus,* or the specific problem with which the client wants help, *structure,* or the framework within which the helping process takes place, and finally *limits,* or the reality factors which circumscribe the entire experience, are the bases on which the present work is predicated. The intake interview is the medium through which these dynamics are set into motion. Needless to say, they are not brought up mechanically or artificially—quite the contrary, they arise spotaneously and indigenously as the very essence of the first client-counsellor relationship.

Limits

In the preceding chapters reference has been made to limits, as an important aspect of the counselling process. Those acquainted with the vicissitudes of vocational guidance are probably aware of the constantly shifting focus in this field. Thus in earlier days the emphasis appeared to be on the specific attributes of the individual as related to his occupational choice, suitability for particular training, or qualifications for a definite job. Psychometric evidence, spatial visualisation, finger dexterity, and hand-eye coordination were the criteria by which the individual's fitness for a certain plan or undertaking were estimated. In the course of time interest inventories and adjustment questionnaires were added to the "vocational battery." Ultimately vocational counsellors began to realise that the vocational process extends considerably beyond the informational or diagnostic range. Today an ever-increasing emphasis is placed on the total individual and on the helping aspects of the guidance process. Comprehensive guidance no longer consists in an analysis of aptitudes and their application to a particular endeavour; helping the client achieve his objectives has become the paramount concern of the vocational guidance worker.

It happens frequently that, when a new profession embraces a new creed, it tends to become completely preoccupied with it, so much so that, in its eagerness to apply the new principles, it may discard some of the older but nevertheless worthwhile concepts. The emergence of a person in need of help from behind the screen of psychographs and quantitative data has been somewhat of a revelation to many counsellors. Quite understandably, in their new role as professional helpers they at times transgressed the conventional bounds of vocational guidance and became case-workers and psychotherapists. One often hears remarks such as "We deal with the whole individual" or "We are concerned with the total personality." This reaction against faculty psychology and static compartmentalisation of the individual may be a step forward when viewed scientifically. It may also have its undesirable features when viewed professionally.

The significance of *function* as an aspect of a professional service has already been discussed. In our enthusiasm as helpers we at times overlook the necessity for a clearly structured and sharply focused relationship. Although the total personality is represented in every facet of human behaviour, as vocational counsellors we are concerned only with those areas which pertain to educational and occupational adjustment in the broader sense of the word.

This sense of responsibility for our contributions as professional workers leads us not only to a better understanding of our role but also to a more definitive application of our skills. For example in situations where psychometric evidence is of value, the non-diagnostically oriented worker is likely to employ testing with considerable discretion. To use Goldman's terms, he is more likely to resort to "precision testing," than to "saturation testing." The nondiagnostic counsellor is also likely to adhere to the focus of vocational guidance and not allow himself to be used as an expert in another field.

What constitutes the area of vocational guidance has to be defined rather arbitrarily. As I read the mail that comes to my office, I am at tunes astounded by the vanity and, breadth of subject matter that seems to fall under the heading of "guidance material" and is supposed to be handled professionally by school counsellors. For example, Science Research Associates issues booklets, guides, and posters addressed to high school youth and school counsellors that deal with such topics as Understanding Sex, How to Live with Parents, Looking Ahead to Marriage, You and Your Health, Where Are Your Manners?, Facts about Alcohol, and Facts about Narcotics. This by no means exhausts the list of interesting titles published by that organisation. Such a wide range of supplementary reading material may be justified if one regards the school counsellor as a polymorphous expert prepared to assist the student in almost any area. The vocational counsellor who is attuned to his own function and the occupational focus might find such an array of topics somewhat distracting. Thus once more it becomes imperative for the counsellor to understand and to spell out what his precise role and responsibilities are in a particular setting.

Lastly, he is going to use time as an important element in the relationship process. Therapeutically it is desirable for the client to learn the meaning of time. Vocational appointments not only are set at a definite hour but have a fixed duration as well. The counselling hour (or whatever unit of time is employed) belongs to the client. He is free to make whatever use he wants of it. He may waste it in discussing trivia, or he may use it constructively. He may come late for the appointment, in which case only the remaining time belongs to him. It is well to determine the number of counselling sessions in advance, for this too endows the whole experience with a new definitiveness. Time thus becomes an active aspect of the guidance process and reality. It is also a limiting factor which is set jointly and at times at the beginning of the first interview by the client and the counsellor and which cannot be disregarded or manipulated to meet the counsellor's or the client's momentary needs; to treat it so would, in the words of Aptekar, "make the helping situation a make-believe world.

The concept of limits is not new. We live in a regulated society which permits us to do some things and forbids us to do others. But the control is not always total; thus we may drive a car at 40 miles an hour but not at 70. Under certain conditions the speed must be reduced to 20. A child may enter the first grade at the age of six but not of four. As we pause to think, we realise that we are surrounded by various restrictions, or limits.

The vocational counselling situation, if it is to have any meaning, must also be regulated by certain limits. The agency will usually set limits as to the type of assistance it is qualified to render (function), the kind of people eligible for assistance (intake policy), and in some cases the number of interviews and their duration. When the client meets the counsellor during the intake interview, he is likely to derive a great deal of satisfaction from the fact that he is encountering, perhaps for the first time in his life, a clearly structured reality. The atmosphere is friendly and positive and yet not so completely permissive as to become bewildering. This may give the client considerable security, for he soon learns what he can expect from the counsellor, as well as what are his own contributions and share in the relationship.

But limits are not always easy to accept. Although they may contribute to the positive experience, they may also be perceived as a challenge. At times the client as a means of asserting himself will attempt to reject the limits set by the counsellor. He may also use the limits in a symbolically destructive way, by coming late for the appointment, by not appearing at all, or by actively fighting the existing structure. In the latter instance he may be testing his own strength against that of the counsellor. Irrespective of how the client uses that limits, they provide him with something tangible that offers opportunities for identification and differentiation. Fees, time, and other aspects of the agency's structure can be used therapeutically in helping the client accept the restrictions of reality and discover that he can still survive. Some case-workers feel that "clients thus derive the greatest help in the casework situation from becoming aware that there are limits to the service being offered."

The Short-Term Contact

What is a short-term contact? This term has been used in social work to designate a brief and usually specific service. Wilson views it primarily as a concrete form of assistance on some particular issue that enables the worker and the client to establish contact. Such assistance usually does not concern itself with problems that have no direct bearing on the immediate situation. In a research study conducted by the Family Service Association of America the short-term contact was defined in terms of the number of visits rather than type of service. It mattered little whether the client was "participation-slanted" or "service-slanded." In each instance the worker began at the point at which the client was, even if the initial request for help was not entirely "appropriate."

The short-term contact is a relatively recent feature of the helping process. In medical Psychotherapy and social casework it is not un-common to carry a case for two or three years, with the client making one or more visits a week. In the past several years, however, it has become apparent that prolonged treatment is not always necessary and at times actually retards the client's progress. It was perhaps under the pressure of necessity that psychiatrists and caseworkers began to cast about for a less time-consuming and expensive procedure. By reducing the amount of time allotted for each client, more people can avail themselves of the therapeutic services and at a smaller per capita cost.

Expedience alone, although important, is by no means the sole justification for the short-term contact. The basis for the shorter programme is the fact that not all patients (or clients) need prolonged treatment or can benefit from it. Some individuals possess sufficient ego strength to make use of a large number of therapeutic sessions. Others, although theoretically in need of numerous helping contacts, are not ready or cannot for whatever reason allow themselves, to become involved in a prolonged relationship. At the outset they may want help with a specific problem and not with the total personality.

Experience demonstrates that a client will move only in the areas in which he himself desires help, and not necessarily in those designated by the counsellor. Thus far nothing has been said about the intensity, or depth, of treatment. The reason for this is that there does not exist a one-to-one relationship between the frequency of contacts and the intensity of the process. Short-term treatment, although brief in terms of total time, may be both meaningful and "deep." Frequent visits, on the other hand, especially if under some form of duress, may be therapeutically un-productive and superficial. It therefore follows that it is neither the frequency of interviews nor the duration of the entire process that determines its therapeutic or helping value. The short-term contact is not a poor man's substitute for a lengthy and exhaustive programme. It possesses unique merit of its own and may be applicable to situations wherein more inclusive and prolonged treatment may fail.

Short-term contacts lend themselves particularly well to problems that can be assisted through occupational and educational information, referrals, psychometric diagnosis, and brief counselling. For that matter the largest portion of vocational guidance is carried on through the medium of the short-term contact, even if vocational workers themselves have not as yet incorporated that term in their thinking.

The vocational guidance process, unlike psychotherapy or case-work treatment, is by necessity almost always limited to a few sessions, The number of contacts is frequently determined by the institution that is conducting the programme. Thus in the school system the student may be seen only once, whereas the VA Advisement Office or private agencies may offer four or five sessions divided between counselling and testing. It is not un-common for the vocational agency to allocate its contacts in the following manner: the initial interview, two or three visits devoted to sundry testing, and the final (counselling) interview It is un-usual, indeed, in a vocational agency for the client to return more than five times. In support of this the frequencies of the number of visits made by vocational guidance clients in one agency have been tabulated. A random sampling of 100 adults (twenty years and over) revealed the following distribution, which is presented for illustrative purposes:

Number of Visits	Number of Clients
1	16
2	14
3	42
4	20
5	8
	100

The average number of visits per adult client was 2.90, which would still keep the number well within the commonly accepted bounds of "short-term contact." Although he made no attempt to analyse the reasons why the contacts were terminated at a particular point, Thomas lists six causes that play a part in the termination of a social service: *(a)* client unwilling to continue; *(b)* client did not follow through despite plan to do so; *(c)* modification unlikely; *(d)* service not available in community; *(e)* referred elsewhere; *(f)* service completed. These reasons are equally applicable to vocational guidance. Additional factors in voluntary dis-continuance of counselling contacts are discussed by Kirk and Headley.

Whereas other helping disciplines may be confronted with making a choice between prolonged and brief treatment, such a choice does not usually present itself to the field of guidance. The vocational counsellor is operating within the framework of the short-term contact, and it is up to him to make that experience both meaningful and lasting to the client.

Occasionally exceptions arise when the adult client may require more than the average amount of counselling to help him resolve his occupational conflicts. Such situations may be encountered when the client's tentative plans and aspirations are greatly at variance with his potentialities or the existing opportunities for carrying out his ideas or are out of keeping with reality in general. Prolonged counselling may also occur in working with the physically handicapped, especially when the client finds it almost impossible to accept his limitations. Most adults, however, do not seem to feel the necessity for prolonging their vocational guidance contacts for excessively long periods of time. Three or four sessions generally suffice to help them focus on the specific vocational problem, to integrate the objective findings about themselves with the acquired information, and finally to arrive at some tentative solution of the problem under consideration.

Vocational counselling programmes that do not specify the number of contacts in advance seem to bear out the contention that adult clients, even if offered an opportunity to return for further counselling and testing as many times as they wish, do not as a rule persist in their visits indefinitely. The dynamics underlying this phenomenon are not perfectly clear. It is possible that some clients after three or four counselling sessions become discouraged because there does not appear to be a ready solution to their occupational problem. It is equally probable that the short-term contact provides many clients with sufficient information about themselves and the vocational plan in question to enable them to proceed unassisted. There have been instances where a client has been seen by the vocational guidance counsellor fifteen to twenty times during the year, but significantly, in all cases without exception, the focus lay outside the occupational area. These clients were using vocational guidance merely as a pretext for personal counselling, because they were unable to bring themselves to visit a psychiatrist.

As already indicated, much ambiguity may exist in the mind of the client as to the actual nature of vocational guidance. Some seek it because they see in it an attenuated psychiatric programme;

others stay away from it for the very same reason. The vocational counsellor can dispel a great deal of unfounded anxiety or misconception by helping the client focus on the occupational aspects of his problem. Thus the client need not fear that he will be expected to talk about areas in which he is not ready to be helped, nor will he expect to get the kind of assistance the agency is not set up to offer.

The concept of the occupational focus lends itself particularly well to a clearly structured, brief helping process. Setting up time limits at the outset is another way of making a fuller use of the short-term contact. Knowing in advance how many meetings will take place helps the client to make the most use of the time allocated to him. Time limits established in advance have a therapeutic value in that they promote a more active participation on the part of the client. He can no longer sit back passively, saying to himself, "If I don't get there today, I'll get there tomorrow." It is true that time limits set in advance may engender some anxiety, but such anxiety can be used constructively by the competent counsellor.

The short-term contact may also help the counsellor decide how much time should be devoted to psychometric testing, to the giving of occupational information, etc. Different individuals require different programmes that emphasise their particular needs. Some may require much counselling and no testing; others may benefit most from a series of sessions devoted to both counselling and testing; still others may want nothing more than occupational information. The counsellor is often called upon to decide which aspect of guidance should be stressed. He does this, not arbitrarily, by fiat, but by working with the client's feelings and by helping the latter accept the real problem as his own. It is not uncommon for a client to request that he be given tests, only to have him say at the closing of the first session that really he never had too much confidence in the tests anyway.

In some ways the short-term contact may be more trying for both the counsellor and the client than the kind that can go on for an indefinite period of time. The relationship, if it is to be meaningful, must be intense, and yet there are only a few sessions during which it can be cultivated. By restricting the matter under consideration to vocational planning, much anxiety that might otherwise be aroused is fenced off. This enables the client to move more rapidly in the direction of his own choosing. The brief time limit set becomes integrated into the process itself. One of the values of short-term counselling is the fact that it is brief.

❑❑❑

5

Some Specific Dynamics in Vocational Counselling

Vocational Guidance in an Authoritative Situation

In discussing referrals it was emphasised how important it is for the client to perceive the referral not as a rejection, not as a punitive measure, but as something constructive and helpful. It was stressed furthermore that it is extremely desirable for the client himself to express the wish to do something about his problems and to consider the referral as a step in that direction.

In practice, however, not all professional workers who make referrals understand completely the functions of a vocational guidance service, nor do all clients, thus referred, really want to take advantage of the opportunity. Some clients, when they do arrive, maintain a cautious and exploratory attitude. Others are more outspoken in placing the responsibility for coming on the person who made the referral. Still others are openly hostile to the entire venture. These attitudinal gradations can be found among all clients and need not always be indicative of the skills of the worker who made the referral.

Situations arise, however, in which the client is compelled to "receive" vocational guidance irrespective of his personal wishes. Under certain circumstances vocational guidance is a prerequisite to another objective. For example, VA requires that disabled veterans go through testing and "advisement" before their plans can be officially approved Some prison classification boards require the psychologist's statement of his findings before the inmate can be assigned to a job Some private social agencies that offer financial assistance ask for a vocational counsellor's evaluation of the soundness of a person's plan prior to granting that person's request for aid. Can one, `under these circumstances, speak of the will to make a change, of movement, or of a positive client-counsellor relationship?

These questions cannot be answered categorically with a simple yes or no. A philosophy of guidance predicated on the concept of self-help in a vital occupational problem appears to be challenged seriously in situations in which the client rejects help and wants to have the experience done and over with as quickly as possible.

Experience in psychotherapy indicates, nevertheless, that people can be helped even if they themselves have but asked for help in the first place. This phenomenon becomes understandable if one considers that neither the acceptance nor the rejection of the therapeutic experience is ever, total. We have already dwelt at some length on the factors that hinder the client from taking help even if he actually wants it. Now it may be in order to examine some of the forces that prompt him to accept help even if the request for assistance did not originate with him.

Let us consider two hypothetical situations: *(a)* that in which the client comes to the agency with the idea that all he wants is to take some vocational tests; *(b)* that in which the client comes for vocational assistance in order to establish his eligibility for a business loan, which is administered by a social agency.

In the first instance the client may have a fairly definite idea that taking a few "aptitude" tests will help him to decide whether or not he should follow a particular plan or what he, is "best suited for." He has not as yet, by himself, examined the implications of his plan, the conflicting feelings he may have about his choice, or his own strength and ability to carry on. Furthermore, he may regard the counsellor merely as a vocational expert, qualified to advise on the steps to be taken.

It may require several interviews to help the client come to the realisation that occupational planning consists in more than testing. It may take even more time for the client to assume responsibility for his actions and to stop regarding the counsellor as an advice giver. But as a result of a successful experience in counselling, although the client came with a specific request for testing or advice, he leaves the agency with a better understanding of his problem and, it is to be hoped, with a greater ability to handle it. This is not analogous to the sales technique whereby a customer intent on buying a pair of socks leaves the store laden with a suit, hat, overcoat, and shoes. What actually has happened is that the counsellor has helped the client see the nature of his vocational problem and has placed the agency's resources before him. It is evident that vocational assistance does not stop with vocational diagnosis. The second hypothetical case is based on the assumption that the client wants no help but comes to the vocational agency in order to meet certain requirements imposed upon him. The two cases are similar in that neither client has conceived of vocational guidance as a helping process. The first individual has focused exclusively on testing; the second person has rejected even that limited aspect of the programme.

The skilled counsellor may be able to help the second client realise that the other agency's request that he consult with a vocational counsel or is not unreasonable. In so doing the counsellor may have to identify himself with the negative feelings the client may harbour toward the agency that made the referral. Even in an authoritarian setting the client has frequently the choice between doing something about his occupational predicament or withdrawing from the vocational counselling situation. The counsellor may have to be particularly careful to identify himself with the way the client feels about the referral rather than with the agency which made it. It is possible that the client has worked out some business plan which he thinks is sound. He may actually feel that all he needs is the money to finance it. He believes he can take care of the rest. This is analogous to the first situation, in which the client thinks that all he wants is a test or two. It is entirely possible that the first client needs nothing but psychometric verification; it is equally probable that the second client requires nothing but the cash. But neither the client nor the counsellor can know in advance the value of any plan. The client has to be given an opportunity to reexamine his request in order to make a definite decision.

The foregoing discussion suggests that vocational planning is possible in an authoritative relationship and need not be contradictory to a philosophy of self-help. There are, of course, individuals who regard the counsellor and the agency with so much preconceived hostility that it is practically impossible to establish any kind of positive relationship. Many such persons, although possibly in need of vocational help, are too disturbed to plan for secretively or to take advantage of professional assistance even if it is offered to them. Such individuals may also evince many other pressing problems outside the vocational realm where, too, their tensions seem to have an inhibitory effect on their desire to bring about a change. When circumstances demand it, they may go through the motions of being helped by complying with the formal requirements imposed on them by the authoritarian situation but still remain psychologically untouched. Fortunately, relatively few people are quite so complete in their rejection of helping services. In these rare cases, one is probably justified in suspecting rather serious personality disturbance.

Re-assurance

Reassurance as a means of assuaging anxiety plays a definite part in the counselling interview, provided its role is clearly understood. There exist numerous situations where anxiety stems from the client's lack of information or misconception about some important matter. A simple statement of fact may be both helpful and reassuring.

For example, an ambitious young businessman spends an uncomfortable week wondering whether a business loan for which he has applied has been granted; a college man becomes anxious pending the outcome of his examinations; an applicant for a job is in a state of nervous agitation awaiting the employer's confirmation that he has been hired. Sometimes the counsellor is in a position to impart the much-wanted information to the client and thus relieve him of many doubts. Such reassurance or confirmation is not only in place but actually desirable.

However, the need for reassurance does not always arise out of relatively simple situations that can he handled by imparting the required information or by providing the client with some specific set of factual data. Quite the contrary, the support and reassurance sought are usually an expression of an emotional conflict of considerable duration and intensity. Like the other phases of the helping situation, the need for reassurance will probably be structured in an intellectualised manner, with the emphasis on a narrow and rather inconsequential detail. The client is usually too fearful to express openly the deep inner significance of his problem, the full implications of which might be quite unacceptable to him. He would much rather have the "expert" tell him what is the matter with him or what specific action he is to take. A person in distress at times welcomes being told that things are not as bad as they appear or that there is a happy ending to every story.

But like every other psychological phenomenon, reassurance does not possess a uniform meaning to all people. A need to be reassured usually stems from an inner anxiety which has not been dealt with by the worker. It occurs frequently toward the ending phase of the relationship, when the client experiences new fears because of the approaching termination of the helping contacts. Although some progress may have been made, the client has by no means relinquished all his fears and doubts. He may have merely held them in abeyance pending the outcome of the interviews or the psychometric programme.

As the date for termination draws closer, the client may be afraid at the prospect of carrying on alone. At this point he may ask for reassurance once more by trying to place all the responsibility for his occupational choice on the counsellor. In his attempt to prolong the counselling relationship, he may say, "You really didn't tell me anything I did not already know" or "So you think I ought to quit my present job." In a sense he is momentarily regressing to the level where he was at the beginning of the first interview. Without quite realising it, he hopes that, by minimising the value of the guidance process, he will not only induce the counsellor to continue to offer help but actually compel him to make definitive statements of a diagnostic, advisory, or reassuring nature. It may require considerable self-discipline on the part of the counsellor to bring the ending phase of the counselling sessions to an end in a manner acceptable to the client. We have seen that during the early stages of the counselling process it is imperative that the client take the initiative for seeking help despite the resistant and negative feelings that usually accompany help taking. During the ending phase the client, once more, has to take an active part in the counselling process, only now he should direct his efforts toward ending the relationship. Considerable ambivalence may be aroused, for ending a meaningful contact may be as difficult as initiating it. It should be recalled that it was the client who originally consulted the counsellor because he felt he needed assistance in the vocational area. Now it is again the client who wishes to terminate the contact because he believes he can continue to function unassisted. In either instance it is the counsellor's responsibility to help the client to become engaged in the relationship process and to become disengaged from it.

Movement in counselling does not proceed in a straight line. Much more often it can be an uneven, sporadic development characterised by sudden insight and as sudden regression. To use the well-known phrase, the client sometimes has to get worse in order to get better. An attitude which implicitly calls for reassurance can therefore be considered as part of the struggle the client is experiencing with himself and the counsellor. No amount of reassurance on the part of the counsellor will be effective; if anything a forcibly expressed reassurance may have a blocking effect on the client and actually hamper his expression of feelings.

What is the client actually saying when he asks, "Is my boy normal?" "Am I college material?" "What would you suggest I do now?" Does he really believe for a moment that a reply to his question will free him miraculously of his cares, or is it rather his way of grappling with a problem which is beyond his present strength? It is essential that the counsellor recognise the feeling tone of the question rather than its literal meaning, It requires considerable self-discipline on the part of the counsellor not to be swayed by the impulse to help the client by taking his problem away from him. By telling the client not to worry, the counsellor in so many words suggests that the problem is not worth worrying about or is not there, thus completely disregarding its meaning to the client. It is at this point that it would be extremely helpful if the counsellor realised that the question raised by the client, although direct and specific in nature, is but an intellectualised abstraction of the real problem that disturbs him. A verbally expressed question cannot be equated with the anxiety it represents. This is one of the reasons why handling emotional problems in actually is so ineffective. Demonstrating logically the irrationality of a phobia or a compulsion is of no therapeutic value; by the same token, reassuring the client that his problem is not real denies him the right to seek assistance with it.

Winning Confidence

In the literature on vocational guidance one often encounters the admonition that before attempting to counsel it is necessary to win the confidence of the client. Presumably, once confidence is won, the client will express himself more freely, state the nature of his conflict with less hesitation, and become more amenable to the counsellor's suggestions. This theory is methodologically related to the question of support and reassurance, for winning confidence is essentially a device intended to allay anxiety within the client. Like reassurance it is likely to fail in its objective and may actually block, rather than promote, expression.

I do not mean to convey the impression that report or confidence in the counsellor is unnecessary or harmful in a working relationship. Quite the contrary, a warm understanding and trust in the counsellor's genuine desire to help are the cornerstones for a personal and yet professional relationship. However, establishing a rapport and winning confidence become stumbling blocks when they are treated as an end in themselves. A counsellor who is free from preconceived ideas about the client or what is good for him need not feel guilty about his own attitudes. Similarly, a counsellor who sincerely believes in the client's capacity for self-help and respects the latter's right to have negative feelings about the vocational process does not have to resort to artificial devices calculated to lull the client into a state of false security.

Distrust, like any other feeling or attitude expressed by the client, has to be met and handled as a part of the reality of the counselling situation. The counsellor cannot very well say to the client in so many words, "I want you to trust me" or "Don't be afraid to tell me; what we say here is strictly confidential." The counsellor must recognise that the client may be unwilling or unable to share with him certain facts about himself or his past. If this be so, the counsellor should indicate to the client that it is his right to confide in him or to withhold as much as he desires. Such an attitude is likely to reduce the guilt the client may experience from holding back information he is not ready, to give Instead of urging the client, "Tell me all about it," the counsellor may say to the client in effect, "You may tell me whatever you wish about yourself. You need not tell me things you are not ready to disclose."

Such an attitude is in sharp contrast with that by which the counsellor makes a studied effort to create a psychological setting which will impel the client to say more than he is ready to. The inexperienced counsellor may subtly cajole, threaten, or bribe the client into sharing with him matters he would rather not discuss. The interview then becomes counsellor-directed, with the client taking little responsibility for what is taking place. As a matter of fact, once the client begins to feel that he is being manipulated into divulging facts he does not wish to disclose, he may react to the counsellor by withdrawal.

Lack of trust in the vocational worker, the agency, or the vocational process itself must be viewed as a part of the working reality. Such a lack of faith cannot be disregarded by the counsellor. Quite the contrary, it must be met and handled like any other attitude or feeling expressed by the client.

Taking help is difficult. It may be particularly unpleasant for a fundamentally insecure and anxious individual. We have already spoken of the conflicting forces that prompt a person to seek assistance and to reject it at the same time. During the first interview the client may prove to be demanding and aggressive, or he may be completely submissive, maintaining the "you know best" attitude. It may be easy to "establish a rapport" with an articulate dynamic individual. It may be equally easy to "win the confidence" of a dependent, trusting client whose very passivity stems from his fear of becoming personally involved in the counselling relationship.

Verbal fluency and poise on the part of the client, although suggestive of a "good rapport," may be devoid of feelings or inner meaning. They may be but a protective device against the potentially threatening counselling process. The moment the suave or purely intellectual attitude is pierced, the client may become defensive and hostile. The good rapport may be gone, but the client may be beginning to take hold of the real situation.

It may be a great deal more pleasant for both the counsellor and the client to conduct the interview on a "gentlemanly" level, where the problems are discussed in an impersonal and almost scholarly manner. But such counselling is also singularly ineffective. The rapport may be excellent, the confidence may be completely won, and yet the client is merely participating in an interesting and warm chat. It is almost axiomatic that whenever the interview becomes too congenial, the counsellor is not "hitting the mark." Real helpfulness cannot be achieved without some discomfort, resistance, or even pain. The more meaningful the vocational process, the less pleasant it is likely to be.

In a counselling situation, the worker does not attempt to "put over" anything on the client. If the client is fearful, the counsellor recognises the dynamics underlying such fears; if the client resists change, the counsellor express his understanding that leaving the old for the new is often difficult and painful. In short, he does not minimise the validity of the client's feelings but tries to work with them. The counsellor deals with what is, be it lack of trust, unacceptance of self, unrealistic occupational aspirations, or profound feelings of inadequacy. This is the reality for both the client and the counsellor that has to be faced and dealt with. Winning confidence as a technique has no place in a genuinely straightforward relationship, in which both worker and client try to work on a disturbing problem. The client will indeed develop confidence in himself and the counsellor once he becomes a part of the helping process. Lack of trust or confidence in others often stems from inability to trust oneself. This condition cannot be overcome by denying its existence. It has to be faced and worked with as an integral part of the total problem.

Advice

Perhaps no concept is as firmly rooted in vocational guidance as that of advice. Advice is the pivot which a great deal of occupational planning appears to turn. This is not to say that its weakness as an empirical method has not been recognised by numerous workers in the field. Williamson speaks of its ineffectiveness time and again, and Jones whimsically remarks, "It is never safe to give advice except when you know that the other fellow will not follow it."

There are several reasons why direct advice seems to lend itself particularly to the kind of vocational guidance that is not: too concerned with the question of the dynamics of the helping process. Because it is frequently specific, it may produce the illusion that practical help is being offered. Perhaps even more important is the fact that it is easy for the counsellor to give advice. Advice giving may not only satisfy some of the counsellor's authoritarian needs but also relieve him of having to struggle with the client's doubts and indecisiveness. Giving advice is the layman's way of handling the problem. The less professionally trained the counsellor is, the more likely he is to resort to advice as a direct expedient. Rogers notes correctly that such expressions as If I were you. . . ," "I would suggest. . ." are essentially forms of advice and psychologically equivalent to the more direct forms.

Advice giving as a part of the vocational guidance process is predicated on several implicit assumptions, some of which are: *(a)* The counsellor knows what is "good" for the client or what general plan of action he should follow. *(b)* The counsellor is ready to assume the responsibility for both success and failure stemming from his advice. *(c)* The client is ready and able to make use of the advice. These points deserve further consideration.

We have already dealt with some of the dynamics that accompany vocational assistance. It has been indicated that adults usually find it difficult to ask for help. The counsellor, no matter how sensitive or skilled, cannot be familiar with all the factors that brought anyone particular individual into his office. One session or, for that matter, several sessions with the client still leave a tremendous amount of psychic material unexplored. The administration of a few psychometric tests or a highly comprehensive battery will shed but a few feeble rays of light in Stygian darkness. Myers admonishes the counsellor, "Before interviewing a man, you should learn all about him that you can." This is neither possible nor desirable. In working with a client the counsellor has to accept the fact that he is working with a small portion of the total individual—the portion the client cares to reveal. That the consullar has a professional obligation to attempt to uncover those aspects of the client's life which he is not ready to discuss is questionable. At no time is the objective evidence sufficiently complete, or for that matter valid, to enable the counsellor to state with any degree of certainty that the client will succeed in a particular endeavour. The counsellor can improve on his vocational prognostications when his findings are stated negatively; *i.e.*, he can be reasonably confident that a person with an IQ of 60 is not likely to graduate from college, that a man scoring in the first percentile on a finger-dexterity test will not succeed as a watch repairman, or that a one-legged person will probably fail as a tightrope walker.

Possibly more important than a comprehensive diagnosis of the client's vocational potentialities is an appraisal of his perception of himself, *i.e.*, the extent to which he is able to utilise that which he knows he possesses. Does he see himself as bold or timid, as intelligent or mediocre, as a tradesman or professional? What are his vocational goals in relation to self-acceptance? In short, what is his reality, and how does he fit into it? There is a distinction between an objective diagnosis and a subjective perception of self; whereas the psychologist may be concerned with the former, the counsellor is more interested in the latter. This is understandable in terms of respective functions, and the fact that the helping process must always begin with the client's point of view, rather than with scientific facts as seen by the psychologist.

This does not mean that the counsellor by virtue of his knowledge of the different occupational fields and his awareness of the strengths and weaknesses of the client cannot form an opinion as to the client's probable success in carrying out a particular plan. But there is a basic difference between the counsellor's belief about the feasibility of an undertaking and the client's acceptance of this view. It has been stated time and again, in vocational guidance literature, that an intellectual explanation or interpretation of objectively established acts does not necessarily enable the client to change his attitude or course of action. One of the counsellor's major contributions lies not in his diagnostic skills, not in his knowledge of the world of work, but in the extent to which he is able to help the client effect a change.

Thus far we have stressed the fact that the counsellor can never be in full possession of all the relevant facts. What would the situation be if through some magic the counsellor knew all there is to know about the client? Would this justify advice- oriented counselling? Even if, the counsellor could realistically appraise the vocational picture, such an evaluation would not be of much value to the client. Advice, in the psychological sense, represents the imposition of one person's set of ideas upon another person. It disregards the client's right to hold on to his own plans. The fact that the client frequently may ask for advice and assure the counsellor that this is really all, he needs, especially since he, has no concrete plans of his own, still does not prove that advice will be effective. Such an attitude may be suggestive of the client's inability to face his problems, rather than of his and readiness to follow explicit instructions. No matter how cogent and realistic the suggestions may be, the client will almost invariably follow his own plan. Or if he goes through the motions of carrying out the counsellor's decisions, psychologically it will always be someone else's choice and hence unsatisfactory to him.

Less experienced counsellors may at times be tempted to suggest concrete action for the client to follow. The adult client may then counter by saying, "I tried it already, but it does not help," thus projecting his failure on the counsellor from the start. Even when the client assumes a completely receptive and dependent attitude, professing that he has no motion whatsoever regarding his vocational preferences, he is likely to oppose specific suggestions the counsellor may make. The reasons why an adult client cannot formulate a concrete vocational plan are not, as a rule, his ignorance of occupational facts or inability to appraise his intellectual potentialities. The true causes for his vocational indecision must be sought in the inner conflicts between his aspirations and reality, in his inability to mobilise his strengths or to utilise his assets, in the anxiety-engendering forces that block him in virtually every undertaking. A counsellor who can recognise the psychological dynamics underlying a vocational problem should be able to see readily enough why, even from a theoretical standpoint, advice giving is bound to be ineffective as a counselling technique. Most adult clients do not come to a vocational agency because they lack wisdom in solving their occupational problems; they come because they are unable to apply satisfactorily their store of knowledge and experience. Consequently, providing them with, specific information is not likely to help them significantly, for it is not information per se that they lack, but rather the ability to use that which they already possess.

The next point to be considered is the responsibility the counsellor assumes when he gives advice. In advising, the counsellor implicitly takes over the client's problems and arrives at a relatively independent solution. He thus denies the client an opportunity to grapple with his dilemma—an experience which often proves to be of therapeutic value. Instead of helping the client grow as a result of his contact with the agency, the advice-giving counsellor tends to discourage the client from active participation. "The client's own impulses and feelings tend to become blocked; he figuratively steps aside and lets the counsellor do the planning for him. Once the client withdraws from the counselling situation, the entire experience is doomed to failure; for there can be neither process, nor movement, nor relationship without the client's active participation.

Some counsellors may feel that they, as vocational experts, know what is good for the client. They may hold further that it is not necessary for the client to go through the painful experience of being helped in order to attain certain occupational objectives. These counsellors may take the position that, once the client has applied to them for vocational assistance, it is their responsibility as counsellors to give sound advice based on their professional training and knowledge. Counsellors who reason thus take a grave responsibility upon themselves. Perhaps even more important from the client's standpoint is the fact that an advice-guided counsellor will, at best, assist the former with a specific and probably relatively insignificant issue. The client as a result of his counselling experience will not have learned to utilise his own strengths and resources. As soon as new issues or questions arise, he will be tempted to return to the counsellor for further advice and guidance simply because he has never learned to use himself in a new situation.

Vocational advice, aside from being incompatible with the; philosophy of self-help, poses certain practical considerations. As a private individual, the counsellor may in a nonprofessional capacity give advice. As a professional counsellor, in the employ of an accredited agency, however, he bears a responsibility to the client, the institution that employs him, and the community, He should not be placed in a position where his advice might prove to be detrimental to the welfare of the client. This is not to suggest that non-advice-oriented service is in a position to "guarantee" a successful vocational outcome. As previously indicated; the counsellor and the agency can assume the responsibility for offering vocational assistance, but not for the consequences. A vocational service that helps the client to arrive at his own plans is less likely to lay itself open to criticism than the agency that provides the client with a specific blueprint.

The last point to be examined in connection with advice-oriented counselling is the question of its effectiveness as a psychological dynamic. As already implied, advice-centred guidance is predicated on the assumption that once the client becomes aware of his own assets and limitations, as well as of the occupational opportunities in a particular field, he is ready to go ahead with his plans.

The theoretical fallacy of the above hypothesis is discussed by when he distinguishes between truth and reality Rank holds that "truth is what I believe or affirm, doubt is or rejection. But the reality which penetrates consciousness through our sense organs can influence us only by way of the emotional life and becomes either truth or falsehood accordingly. . . . Even the purely sensory consciousness is not merely receptive, but is guided and restricted by will. I see or hear what I want to, not what is."

Daily experience with clients is replete with instances that tend to support Rank's statement. One has only to recall the attitudes some clients take away with them. This is particularly revealing in the case of adolescents who share their impressions with their parents or other members of the family. One frequently hears such remarks as "You told my son not to go in for medicine, but advised him to take up engineering." This despite the fact that the counsellor may have spent a whole hour explaining patiently he does not "give advice" and that it is up to the client to decide what occupation to choose. Similarly, a careful explanation of an interest pattern such as is revealed by the Kuder Preference Record may be distorted by the client in order to suit his needs. Although the counsellor may have stressed the fact that the test indicates patterns of interests rather than of abilities, the client may blissfully conclude, "I guess I am good in sciences." Psychometric data and other objective evidence may be disregarded by the client as so much rubbish if they happen to be at variance with his total goals and needs. A young man intent on studying dentistry, for example, is not going to be deterred from his course of action by a set of tests that suggest that he is not likely to meet even the minimal college entrance standards. Only recently we came across a dull young man whose goal in life was to become a machinist. The fact that, according to the tests, he lacked each and every attribute characteristic of a successful mechanic meant very little to him. Some people seem to be able to reject facts as completely as if they had never existed.

The counsellor may occasionally encounter situations where bright, capable, and energetic young people do come for a verification of their abilities. They are interested in the service as an intellectual experience. The tests are a stimulating challenge. Some of these clients happen to be in a financially fortunate position, with an abundance of good contacts in different business and professional areas. Whatever their plans may be, they have little concern about their futures. The counselling interview offers them an opportunity to demonstrate to themselves and the counsellor their poise, good judgement, and superior acumen. They are so confident in themselves that they actually welcome suggestions "from above." They feel sufficiently secure not to be disturbed by the counsellor's directiveness as long as he informs them of what they already know and what they want to hear. Such cases are, however, in a distinct minority.

The majority of applicants are not certain of their occupational plans, they are disturbed by the ambivalence inherent in every situation, and they may not have the strength to face the vocational realities about them. It is indeed difficult for a young adult to accept the fact that the two years of struggle in an engineering school must come to an unsuccessful end because he never had the abilities to carry him through a four-year programme. Nor is it easy for parents with high professional aspirations for their son to accept the fact that he is not even college material. No amount of intellectualising will help the client accept himself for what he is. Attitudes, deep-seated wishes, and psychological defence mechanisms cannot be handled on the strength of logic alone. No amount of objective psychometric evidence will convince a client that a certain plan is doomed to failure if his heart is set on such a plan. Even years of empirical evidence are sometimes insufficient to convince a person that he is striving against his best interests.

The fact that advice is deemed an ineffectual helping technique need not cast any reflection on the value of objective data in the counselling situation. Factual information may be seriously misused if directed against the client's emotional set. It may be employed constructively if the counsellor is working with the client, rather than against him. Reality is always a phenomenological experience. Objective data *and* the vocational counsellor are a part of that experience. Even adverse test evidence can be used positively if the client is helped to perceive the entire vocational situation, not as a challenge and a battle, but as a self-initiated helping process. It is because of these invariably present negative attitudes that it is usually so difficult to sustain a helping relationship. The counsellor who is not completely attuned to the attitudes and feelings which the client may be expressing during the interview is likely to strengthen the latter's rejection of the factual information and his tendency to negate the potentially helpful aspects of the programme. Advice, especially if couched in directive terms, may serve as a nucleus around which the client can mobilise his negative feelings; when pitted against an emotionally charged idea, advice is of no value what soever.

❑❑❑

6

The Role of Diagnosis

The Diagnosis Approach

In the preceding chapter references have been made to helps centred counselling as a form of vocational assistance which focuses primarily On the *helping* aspects of the process rather than on diagnosis. Although nondiagnostic counselling does not deny the value of objective evidence as secured through tests and other means, it subordinates such information to the client's ability to own it (*i.e.*, accept it on an emotional level) and use it in formulating his vocational plan. It was furthermore stressed that it is not necessary to know everything about the client or his past to be vocationally helpful. Conversely, an impressive accumulation of information about the client need not be of decisive value in helping him make an occupational decision. A comprehensive and precise diagnosis in no way implies that the treatment that follows will be of commensurate caliber. As Rogers correctly points out, therapy is not "diagnosis in reverse."

On the other hand, it would be theoretically impossible and, from the practical standpoint, undesirable to rule out all vestiges of diagnosis in vocational guidance. The question is not whether to diagnose or not but rather what the function of diagnosis in the helping process is. Gomberg notes that "it is unfortunate when approaches to treatment are distinguished from each other on the basis of acceptance or rejection of diagnosis." Diagnosis plays a definite role in vocational guidance, but its role has been vastly overrated. A fuller consideration of the place of diagnosis in guidance follows.

Diagnosis as a feature of the healing art has been revered since the days of Hippocrates and Galen. It was held in unquestionable esteem during the Middle Ages, and even today it is considered an essential aspect of the therapeutic process. In the olden days the magus would visit the patient, squint at his urine, and then solemnly announce the name of the malady first in Latin, then in the vernacular. The purpose of the present discussion is not to ascertain the value of diagnosis in medicine but rather to trace the effect of medical thinking on the nonmedical helping professions and on vocational guidance in particular. It has already been pointed out how vocational guidance, by virtue of its being one of the latest additions to the helping disciplines, found itself in a position wherein it had to learn a great deal from psychiatry, psychology, and social casework. As it absorbed the philosophies, skills, and techniques from the other areas, it incorporated into its own structure both desirable and unsuitable features of each field. Vocational counsellors did not always pause to examine the applicability of every characteristic as it was taken over. It was rather naively assumed that a technique appropriate to, let us say, medicine was equally applicable to vocational guidance.

Alexander and French formulate clearly the objectives of psychodiagnosis by stating, "In diagnosis, we wish to obtain a psychodynamic explanation of the client's difficulty—how and why it arose, what present and previous factors contributed to it, and what, if any, possibilities for solution are now available." Implied in this statement is the idea that knowing a great deal about the etiology of the problem will enable the therapist to help bring about a desirable change. There can be little question that therapists so oriented have helped their patients with the different problems that demanded attention. It remains to be demonstrated, however, that a full understanding of the vocational dynamics by the counsellor contributes to a better occupational adjustment of the client. Even if it were possible for the therapist to grasp fully "the way in which the ego attempts to balance the conflicting forces of superego, id, and external reality" there is no assurance that such a conceptualisation on the part of the therapist will in itself help the patient.

As a corollary the counsellor, relatively thorough understanding of the client's interests, aptitudes, and aspirations and even some aspects of his emotional make-up need not in any sense safeguard or facilitate the helping phase of the situation. Practitioners in guidance are only too familiar with the ever-present phenomenon of clients persistently seeking to attain occupational or educational objectives which are far beyond their reach. Some clients will go from one vocational agency to another and request aptitude testing, with the vain hope that the new tests may contradict or disprove the older findings. Other clients, when confronted with a psychometrically established unfavourable prognosis, may disregard it completely and proceed with their unrealistic original plans. Vocational counsellors at times fail to see the dynamics underlying such a request for further testing and continue with additional diagnostician as if an accurate appraisal could ever take the place of help.

The current consensus among counsellors is that the significant features of the helping process lie not in the application of a particular doctrine but rather in the manner in which the client and the worker employ themselves in relationship to each other. Adherence to anyone school does not in itself determine the outcome. There are competent counsellors in every ideological camp, just as there exist professional nonentities and ignoramuses. The present work does not attempt to point out the road of exclusive salvation. Instead it endeavours to submit a rationale in which the helping aspects of the service will supplant in emphasis the diagnostic and evaluative characteristics of vocational guidance which appear to be to the fore today.

Why diagnosis should play such an important role in the minds of many counsellors becomes quite understandable if one considers the fact that as a new profession vocational guidance has not had an opportunity to develop a philosophy and a methodology of its own. In medicine, for example, emphasis is placed on genesis, the physical examination of the patient, and laboratory findings. The physician asks questions pertaining to the present and past well-being of the patient, looking for signs that may serve as clues to the present condition. He examines the patient, still on the lookout for symptoms that will help him establish a diagnosis. The physical examination may further be supplemented by laboratory tests which can shed additional light on the nature of the disorder. The assumption underlying this procedure is that, once the relevant facts are established, the physician can make a specific diagnosis and prescribe the appropriate treatment which will cure the disease.

The ultimate objective of the diagnostician is very much like that of a taxonomist. He attempts to learn as much as possible about the single individual in order to be able to classify him in some particular group. A biologist who discovers a new animal and classifies it as an insect can infer a great deal about the particular specimen from what he knows about Insecta as a class. Similarly, the ontogenic diagnosis of schizophrenia should enable the psychiatrist to say something about the nature of the patient's illness, based on his knowledge of schizophrenia in general. Hollis, for example, feels that "there are two major parts in any diagnostic study. One is our knowledge of the individual, the other is our background of knowledge about patterns of human behaviour". The premise underlying diagnosis is that what we learn about one individual will shed light on how to help another.

How much of this thinking can be validly applied to vocational guidance cannot be stated categorically but requires further consideration and verification. Daily contacts with clients suggest that an objective evaluation of a client's potentialities or a classification of his problems into certain groupings does not in itself constitute vocational help. Some of the dynamics that enter into the professional helping relationship have already been considered—the ambivalence the client may have about asking for vocational assistance, the anxieties that are likely to accompany his desire to bring about a change, and finally the emergence of a new client-counsellor relationship. It has also been pointed with that vocational guidance is a process in which the client is helped to assume the responsibility for asking for vocational guidance and the counsellor makes it upon himself to provide the helping experience.

Dawley makes a valuable point when she says, "Casework diagnosis lies in the area of clarification of exactly what a person is asking of an agency, discussion with him what the agency has to offer and the way in which it can be offered, and determining with him whether this is what he wants and is ready to take at the time." This concept of diagnosis appears to be particularly applicable to the field of vocational guidance, for there seems to be a great deal of misconception among the lay public and vocational counsellors alike as to what constitutes the proper area of vocational guidance and what it has to offer the client. At the two extremes we have counsellors who see vocational guidance as an experience in total emotional readjustment and those who perceive occupational planning chiefly as a fact-finding process. In the light of the complexity of the counselling situation, it would be sheer folly for the counsellor to assume that a comprehensive case history or a battery of tests can in themselves assist the client with his vocational choice.

Perhaps, at this juncture, some counsellors may feel that I am erecting a straw man in order to knock him down; that even a neophyte knows that a psychological test is never the ultimate objective in vocational guidance, but merely a steppingstone toward a total occupational programme. Very well. Then, once again, as vocational counsellors we are justified in asking, What is the actual role of diagnostic findings in vocational guidance?

Some caseworkers, for example, feel that diagnosis is in order when it is desirable to ascertain the presence or, extent of pathology or the client's willingness and ability to use help. In a vocational setting such a diagnosis may precede the counselling process, or it may be integrated into it as a part of the total helping experience. The latter procedure is decidedly preferable.

Diagnosis is sometimes extended to include not only the client as an individual but also these members of his family who may exert considerable influence on his vocational thinking and freedom of action. When the client meets the counsellor, the fanner is never a psychologically completely isolated entity. Quite the contrary, the client probably has relatives, friends, and other ties which make him a social being and also determine his vocational drives and aspirations. Those individuals particularly close to the client are likely to exert the greatest influence on vocational choice and his ability to progress in a particular direction.

Gomberg and Levinson speak of "family diagnosis" for they feel that "the nature and quality of interaction between significant members of a family are vital factors in the prognosis for anyone of the members seeking a more effective personal or family adjustment." This is particularly true in working with adolescents, who because of their age and immaturity are more likely to depend on their parents for guidance. The counsellor who can integrate the familial influence with the vocational dilemma can frequently be of greater service to the client than the one who limits himself exclusively to the treatment of the vocational problems as if they existed in a vacuum.

But diagnosis, useful as it may be in certain situation, is not a static entity. The very fact that the counsellor is endowed with the power to diagnose does something to the client-counsellor inter-relationship. We have already spoken of the fact that many clients tend to regard the counsellor as an authority figure, as one who is going to solve their occupational problems for them. An undue emphasis on the diagnostic aspects of the service is likely to strengthen that belief and possibly actually to block self-expression and self-direction. In the words of Pray, diagnose is "tends to place responsibility upon the worker not only for the relationship and helping process, but for the specific outcome of that process."

Two aspects of the diagnostic orientation will be discussed in somewhat greater detail: *genesis,* which deals with the origin and development of the occupational problem, as revealed through the vocational case history; and *measurement,* which concerns itself with the quantification of psychological data.

The Case History

Among many vocational agencies it is not an uncommon practice to devote a large portion of the initial interview to the gathering of factual information about the client's past and present. Printed forms are sometimes employed, and the desired information is either checked off or filled out. Some textbooks on guidance actually recommended that the questionnaire be subdivided into such specific areas as personal data, family, composition, employment history, hobbies, etc.

Anamnesis and psychological tests are by no means the only diagnostic tools at the disposal of the psychologist. They are considered somewhat in detail because they tend to play such an important role in vocational guidance. Other devices for obtaining information about the client are the interview, the questionnaire, rating, scales, anecdotal records, personnel records, and essays and autobiographies. Other workers extent the survey of personality by including such methods as study of cultural setting (analysis of social norms and ethology), physical records (heredity, endocrinology, etc.), social records (documentary sources, work analyses, etc.), personal records (diaries, correspondence, etc.), expressive movement (first impression, graphology, etc.), miniature life situations (time sample, vocational miniature etc.), laboratory experiments, depth analyses (psychiatric interview, free association, dream analyses, automatic writing, etc.), and ideal type (literary characterology, etc.).

For one interested in research, data sheets may be of considerable value, from a helping standpoint, their usefulness may be questioned. In passing, attention may be called to the fact that the term "case history" was originally coined by the social-work profession, which has traditionally considered the personal historical approach as a significant feature of its service. Social work, as perhaps no other field, has developed the concept of case history to the point where today it is considered as one of the major tools of the profession. Social work has also set up what is known among the workers in the field as the Social Service Exchange, an organisation whose chief function is to "clear" information about a client. When a client applies to a social agency for a service, his name, with other identifying data, may be sent to the Social Service Exchange, which files it and simultaneously provides the referring agency with certain information about the client. Thus the agency can tell whether the client is "active" elsewhere, whether it is his first contact with any agency within the community, or whether the individual and his family have been known to several institutions for a long period of time.

It should also be noted that, although the value of the Social Service Exchange is rarely questioned by the majority of workers in the field, there are some professionally trained individuals who "have very serious reservations about the continued existence of the Exchange" and are "prepared to suggest that it be abolished." The basis for such thinking may be attributed to the realisation on the part of some workers that knowing a great deal about the client's past is not essential in helping him to effect an adjustment in a particular area. Sometimes such knowledge may act as a prejudicial force against the client and interfere with the spontaneous development of the relationship.

For example, the vocational counsellor finds himself face to face with a client seeking work. The employment history reveals that the man has held ten different jobs in the past two years. It would take a great deal of professional discipline to abstain from generalisation and inference. The counsellor is likely to conclude, and perhaps correctly so, that the client is not going to keep his next job either. On the other hand, the counsellor has no right to make such an a priori assumption, since he cannot know all the forces that contributed to the previous behaviour, nor is he aware of possible new factors which might change the hitherto existing pattern. This situation confronts the counsellor with a neat dilemma; should he blissfully ignore all the evidence that points away from the probability of the client's holding onto the next job, or should he deny the client the placement service on the grounds that he would not stay on a job for long anyway? The answer to this quandary lies not in the actual act of referring or not referring the client to the new job but in the counsellor and the client working jointly on what a job may mean to the client, what leaving a job may signify, and what future employment may hold, psychologically, for the applicant.

A vocational case history may very easily become a mixed blessing. Whereas in some ways it may help the counsellor assuage some of his anxieties, it may also saddle him with a need to exercise great self-discipline in dealing with the client, lest he fall a victim to prejudice or a priori assumptions.

We have already discussed the significance of the first interview as a starting point for the vocational process. To spend the precious first hour in taking a case history is to deny the meaningfulness of the client-counsellor relationship and the importance of the feelings the client may have about getting help. But this is not all. Delving into the client's past simplicity presupposes that such information will help to solve the present difficulty. This need not be so. No amount of factual information, as such, whether it pertain to the past or the present, will enable the client to progress one iota. Direct questions, furthermore, structures the client-counsellor relationship in a manner which will make it more difficult for the client to progress in the direction of his own choice. Such a procedure may block the client's impulse to follow any course except the one leading to a static past.

It may be necessary for the physician to ask the patient questions in order to prescribe a medicine for the ailment. The patient's psychological self need not be involved. Under ordinary conditions a given medicine will have a specific effect on the pathogenic organism without the client's active psychological participation in the cure. In other words, the entire experience is externalised, with the physician taking on the sole responsibility for the treatment. Viewed psychologically, the doctor says, "Tell me what hurts you, tell me how it happened, and I will heal it for you." The counsellor who probes into the client's past is unwittingly setting up a trap for himself and for the client. Whereas the physician can, by asking questions, come to certain conclusions which will enable him to do something to the patient that will relieve the complaint, the counsellor has no such power. Helping a client with his vocational problem is a process. That means that the client himself must share fully in what transpires during the counselling session. He cannot remain indifferent or aloof, hoping that the counsellor or the tests will provide an answer to the occupational dilemma. The counsellor can, indeed, bring into focus the pros and cons of the client's plans. He can provide specific occupational information, or appraise objectively the client's various abilities and attributes. Above all, he can attempt to clarify the client's feeling about his vocational conflict and thus help him reach a decision. But such activity cannot proceed without the client's taking responsibility for his part in the process. This, too, is frequently difficult. Considerable time and effort may have to be spent in assisting the client to reach the level at which he will begin to realise that it is he himself, rather than the counsellor, who holds the key to his occupational dilemma.

It is the cooperating or sharing nature of the vocational guidance process that distinguishes it significantly from physical medicine. Physical therapy can be applied unilaterally, in the sense that the physician is the central figure, with the patient playing a minor role or none at all. (An unconscious person can be revived with no participation on his part whatsoever.) Vocational guidance, in contrast, is a bilateral process in which the client and the counsellor have definite roles.

The purpose of the present discussion is not to minimise the importance of diagnosis in vocational guidance but rather to assign it its proper place. As previously indicated, help-centered guidance does not deny the value of objective appraisal.

But diagnosis as a necessary steppingstone to treatment derives its meaning from the total discipline in which it is employed. It may be the *sine qua non* in medicine, where the physician assumes the full responsibility for helping (or healing) the patient. It may be a serious hindrance in vocational guidance, which is predicated on collaboration between client and counsellor.

For illustrative purposes two cases are cited to show how a nondiagnostically oriented counsellor may employ psychometric testing. The first case is that of a young man who initially, at least, perceived the vocational service strictly in psychometric terms.

Mr. Frank is a twenty-four-year-old Korean veteran who heard of our service through a friend of his. He requested that he be given "the aptitude test" to help him decide whether he should enter the school of engineering in the fall.

I asked him what his vocational plans were, and he told me that he would like to matriculate for a four-year programme leading to a degree in engineering. However, he had some doubts regarding his ability to do the schoolwork, especially in view of his mediocre high school record and rather low grades in algebra. I asked Mr. Frank how he happened to choose engineering, and he told me that from what he knew about that profession it was a good field in terms of salary, promotional opportunities, and prestige. Mr. Frank continued that at present he was employed as a bricklayer's helper in a steel plant. His job was to repair and to maintain in good condition kilns used in the steel-manufacturing process. He also added that the' engineers at the plants were the "big shots" and that unless you were an engineer "you were nobody." I reflected the sentiment that he wanted to be important, too, and that without formal schooling he felt he could not advance himself. Rather sheepishly, Mr. Frank admitted that becoming "somebody" was the primary reason for his applying to college. I wondered how much it was worth to him and if he had considered carefully the various aspects of the present undertaking. Mr. Frank replied that he had given going to college some thought and that since he could get his education free he would like to try it. I raised the question whether education was really free, considering the fact he was now earning $3,500 a year and that going to school would mean a loss of income of about $14,000, exclusive of his GI allowance. Mr. Frank said that he had never considered it from that standpoint.

We continued to talk about other implications inherent in his going to college. Mr. Frank had been out of school for five years. He had worked in a plant even prior to his induction into the armed forces. Originally he never thought of going to college. None of his relatives as much as graduated from high school. I raised the question of how it would feel to return to the classroom, do homework, write term papers, and study for examinations. Mr. Frank said that there was a lot of "chicken" in school and in the Army but that he was used to taking "chicken." I commented that he thought our educational system, like the Army, was full of unpleasant details but that he felt strong enough to "take it." Mr. Frank believed that once he made up his mind he could carry on with his schoolwork.

After a brief pause Mr. Frank commented that he had never viewed going to college in the new light. He was told that taking the tests would suggest to him what he should do but that, as he was beginning to realise, tests alone could not provide all the answers. I wondered whether Mr. FranK felt that I was attempting to dissuade him from entering college. Mr. Frank said that he understood I had no personal stake in the matter and that he was grateful for my contribution. He would not want to start something "half-cocked." I said I thought I knew how he felt, that going to school represented a major step to him, and that he wanted to be pretty certain that he was not making a mistake.

A silence ensued. Mr. Frank asked me what I thought he should do if he did not enter college. I replied that he was beginning to doubt the advisability of his going to college and was looking for some suggestions. Mr. Frank said that now he was "all mixed up" and that I had raised a number of points he had never thought of before. I indicated to Mr. Frank that the final decision was up to him and that I was merely trying to help him evaluate the pros and cons in the situation.

We then talked about the positive aspects of his going to college and what being an engineer may mean to him. He thought he would like very much to begin school in the fall, realising that it might prove to be a big undertaking. It would mean a substantial reduction in income and less time for pleasure and social activities, but going to school would also signify moving toward a worthwhile objective, working toward a degree, and abandoning the present dull and at times hazardous job. Understandably, Mr. Frank felt conflict about the entire matter.

Toward the end of this interview I raised the question of psychometric testing. Since that was what he came in for originally, I wondered if he still wanted to take the tests and how he thought they might contribute to his occupational planning. Mr. Frank replied that tests might show him whether he was likely to succeed in the engineering curriculum. I agreed with him entirely, stressing simultaneously that we knew nothing about his intellectual abilities, aptitudes, or pattern of interest. Thus far we had talked about his college plans with the tacit assumption that he could compete successfully with other engineering students. What would he do if the test findings should suggest that he was likely to fail in school? Mr. Frank thought he would register anyway and "give it a try." I pointed out to him that he was going to use test evidence only if the findings were positive but would disregard it if it did not substantiafe his own ideas. Mr. Frank agreed to that, but I could see he was not happy about it. I remarked that deciding on one's occupational future was a big thing and that he probably wished it could be solved more easily by taking a few tests. Mr. Frank said he certainly wished it were so, shaking his head as if to indicate perplexity and dismay.

I asked Mr. Frank if he still wanted to take the tests considering the limited influence they would have on his vocational planning. It was possible that the findings might complicate rather than simplify the situation—was he quite certain that he wanted to go through with the testing? Mr. Frank replied rather warmly that he was determined to find out the truth. I reminded Mr. Frank that, whatever the tests show, test results are but one aspect of the total situation. Mr. Frank replied that now he understood it perfectly well.

We then talked about tests that might be helpful in appraising his potentialities as an engineering student. Mr. Frank seemed to be getting quite anxious. He asked me to bear in mind that he had been out of school for many years, that he was never too good in "math" and probably had forgotten most of what he did know. I verbalised the feeling tone for Mr. Frank by saying that in effect he was asking me to "go easy on him" and to give him the benefit of the doubt. I Mr. Frank accepted that point, and I continued by saying that I understood how he felt about taking tests after having been away from a school situation for such a long time. I assured him that I would share with him the test results and that together we would decide what their implication was. Mr. Frank switched the discussion to a more general topic, and after a few minutes of unfocused conversation I asked him if there is anything immediate he could like to talk about. He "guessed that was about all." I then asked Mr. Frank if he wanted to start with the test right now, to which he replied in the affirmative.

Schematically the first interview may be broken up into the following components: *(a)* client asks that aptitude tests be administered to him; *(b)* client is offered an opportunity to discuss his vocational objective; *(c)* client does so, simultaneously expressing considerable doubts about his fitness for the particular choice; *(d)* client is helped to see what going to college actually signifies to him; *(e)* client is helped to evaluate going to college in terms of sacrifices he would have to make; *(f)* client begins to see some implications in going to college which have not occurred to him previously; (*g*) client begins to realise that test results alone cannot possibly provide all the answers; *(h)* client is given a chance to verbalise his intensified confusion, with the result that he assumes the responsibility for the continuance of the interview; *(i)* client and counsellor dwell on the positive aspects of his plan; *(j)* counsellor reintroduces the question of psychometric testing; *(k)* client is still interested in the tests, but now he perceives them chiefly as a device that will estimate his success in college, rather than a panacea for his vocational conflicts; *(l)* counsellor helps client to realise the one-sided use he would make of the test findings; *(m)* client begins to see the limited usefulness of tests in general; *(n)* the hitherto latent anxieties regarding the testing situation are coming to the fore; *(o)* counsellor invites client to share in test interpretation rather than doing it for him.

From the above it can be seen that a large portion of the interview was employed in helping the client overcome some of the misconceptions he may have had about psychological testing. However, in so doing the client was brought dynamically face to face with his actual vocational dilemma. It should be noted that the counsellor abstained from delivering an introductory lecture on tests and measurements but handled the question of testing within the client's phenomenological frame of reference.

One cannot help speculating on how much more meaningful the entire vocational counselling experience could be generally if psychometric testing had never been invented. Both the client and the counsellor would then be thrown on their own resources with no magic instruments to dry upon to solve the occupational difficulties for them. The immaturity client could no longer ask for an aptitude test as a substitute for self-direction nor could the counsellor provide him with a simple numerical score which would incidentally obviate the need for a difficult counselling relationship. Whatever value exact measurements may have in vocational guidance, their benefits are often vitiated, if not completely nullified, by an excessive dependence on them.

But psychological tests are a part of reality to every counsellor irrespective of his personal philosophy. Tests are, also real to many clients. One cannot simply wish them out of existence. What a professional counsellor can do, however, is to attempt to restore tests and test results to their proper perspective. The situation may be likened to that in which a pharmacist is asked for a bottle of aspirin. As a pharmacist he has no other obligation to the customer than to sell the merchandise. A sensitive counsellor, however, observing such a sale, would immediately recognise that, although the customer merely asked for aspirins, he did so in order to relieve a headache. Headache, therefore, is the primary reason for his buying aspirin. A client who naively asks for a test is also in a sense suffering from a headache. He is not interested in the tests from the scientific standpoint any more than the aforementioned customer is interested in the chemical formula of acetylsalicylic acid. Both the hypothetical customer and client ask for a specific remedy which they believe may relieve a painful condition.

A physician, unlike a pharmacist, is not likely to dispense a medicine merely because his patient has asked for it. Instead he will probably try to find out why the patient wants a particular prescription and then decide whether to comply with the patient's request, write a different prescription, or select an entirely different course of treatment. The professional counsellor, too, will not administer tests simply because the client has asked for them. He will explore with the client what testing means to the latter, how he can use test results, and finally whether testing is really indicated in the particular situation.

The second case is presented as an illustration of another use of diagnostic testing by a help-centred counsellor. Whereas in the first illustration Mr. Frank was essentially a normal person with a vocational problem, the case that follows discusses counselling and the place of diagnosis with a mentally defective and possibly psychotic individual:

Jane is a twenty-five-year-old single girl. She came with her sister-in-law, who had learned of our service through a newspaper column. The sister-in-law appeared to be an energetic and intelligent woman who, despite very limited formal schooling, had used herself successfully in life. Jane, in sharp contrast, had always perceived herself as a failure. She was slow in school but managed to complete the eighth grade at sixteen. Subsequently she had several domestic jobs which she did not like. Jane did hold one job in industry, where she did simple assembly work. She was genuinely fond of her work and the other girls in the room. Unfortunately she was laid off because of general business conditions.

The first interview was held with Jane and her sister-in-law. The latter asked me if she could come in, too. I let Jane decide that, and she informed me that she "didn't mind." The initial interview was monopolised by the sister-in-law, who did most of the talking. Jane preferred to answer in monosyllables only when addressed. Before replying she would invariably look at her sister-in-law as if asking her for support.

The problem as the sister-in-law saw it lay in the fact that Jane was "backward," had no friends, was vocationally untrained and at present unemployed. As the sister-in-law spoke, Jane nodded in agreement. I asked Jane how she felt about getting a job. Jane wanted it very much. She had not looked for one yet but would start "soon." I asked Jane how she would go about looking for work. She replied that she would "dress real nice and then take a bus." Regarding her friends Jane complained that she had practically none, that nobody cared for her, that most of her friends were married, and that she was all alone. She hoped to get married, too, some day, but "you can't trust men these days." Jane had a very vague idea as to how we could help her, except perhaps we could tell her where she could get a job. I explained our service to Jane in simple terms, but I don't believe she understood me. Toward the end of the first interview I asked her if she would like to return, and she told me emphatically that she would.

Jane came alone for the second interview. She talked much more freely. She again restated her problems, dwelling on her loneliness, unacceptance by others, and desire to get married. I indicated to Jane that I could not help her directly with marriage but that we could work together on trying to find her a job by helping her develop some self-confidence in relation to others. Jane saw her problem as being always "cooped up all alone." This situation, she believed, made her unduly timid, which in turn prevented her from seeking employment. Jane and I discussed concrete plans which would enable her to socialise, such as joining girls' clubs, religious organisations, etc. Jane told me she had a couple of girl friends whom she could visit and who could conceivably take her out on a "blind date." Jane terminated her second interview with a feeling that "you helped me so much."

The third session was rather uneventful. Jane reiterated much that she had told me previously except that now she seemed to have so little feeling about it. The specific plans we had discussed did not turn out too well, although she did make several attempts to carry out her intentions of meeting more people.

Throughout my contact with Jane I had a feeling that I was dealing with an intellectually extremely dull individual. Now I was beginning to wonder if perhaps in addition to intellectual retardation Jane was not seriously disturbed emotionally. At the closing of our session Jane said she would like to see me again.

The fourth session was quite unproductive. Jane appeared to be sullen and listless. She kept on looking idly through the window most of the time, replying to my comments with "I guess so," "You said it," etc. Again I sensed an inordinate lack of affect. I then asked Jane if she would be interested in taking some tests that might give her an idea of what type of work she might be expected to do and what we could hope to accomplish. Jane showed no curiosity or anxiety about the tests but merely told me that she was ready whenever I was. The Wechsler-Bellevue Scale and the Rorschach were administered to Jane. Verbal IQ was 78, performance IQ 60, total IQ 67. Qualitatively there were some suggestions of psychopathology. The Rorschach findings pointed to a schizophrenic process with marked paranoid tendencies.

Several days later Jane's sister-in-law called me saying that she had managed to find a job for Jane in some plant. She also wanted to know what I "found out" about Jane and whether the latter was coming in to see me again. Indicated to the sister-in-law that I could not discuss it with her over the telephone but that she was welcome to make an appointment. The sister-in-law said she was unable to see me at this time but would call me again.

The significant features of the above case appear to be: *(a)* Jane came for help in several areas (vocational, placement, social, marital, and personality) but was able to accept the limitations set by the agency in the sense that it was prepared to offer her help only in the vocational and placement areas. *(b)* Although Jane appeared to be overdependent on her sister-in-law and gave all the indications of being intellectually retarded, she was given an opportunity to take the fullest advantage of the counselling service. *(c)* Jane seemed to show some movement during the first two sessions. The impression was that the counsellor and she were working out simple realistic objectives that could lead ultimately to somewhat greater self-assurance and possibly a factory job. *(d)* The third interview showed some regression in relationship and affect. It was questionable that Jane was using either herself or the service. *(e)* The fourth interview showed further regression in the sense that it was becoming fairly evident that for whatever reason no headway was being made. *(f)* The tests were introduced at this point to help ascertain whether or not Jane was capable of further growth (*g*) The test findings suggested that Jane was not likely to benefit from further counselling.

At this point many a counsellor may raise the question whether or not it was necessary to spend four counselling sessions prior to test administration. Would it not have been more practical to administer the test during the first contact and by so doing arrive at both diagnosis and a prognosis? A possible answer to this question lies in the fact that the vocational counsellor is interested in *helping* the client, not in the diagnosis per se. He holds that most individuals (even some psychotics and mental defectives) can make a fuller use of themselves and that counselling is frequently one way of helping them mobilise their strengths. Instead of taking on the power of diagnosing and, by implication, the right to treat correct, or advise, the counsellor merely offers the client an opportunity to become engaged in the self-helping process.

It is undeniable that not all persons can benefit from a counselling relationship. This may apply with equal force to the clinically disturbed as well as to the normal. The reasons why one cannot use a counselling service are numerous and, from the practitioner's standpoint, perhaps of secondary importance. Some persons are not sufficiently pressed by their vocational conflicts to go through counselling; others may be too fearful of effecting a change. Some individuals are too disturbed or too disintegrated to use themselves constructively or to take advantage of the vocational services offered to them. Diagnosis in such situations may be in order to enable the counsellor to understand why the client failed to profit from the vocational experience. Conceivably a better understanding of the difficulty may lead to an appropriate referral.

It may be unorthodox to question the case-history method, which has become almost a *raison d'etre* for some counsellors. Information about the client has always been considered such an important part of the helping process that, in the minds of some, it has become actually synonymous with it. Let us, therefore, pause for a moment and examine the real value of anamnesis. In addition to identifying data, a comprehensive case history may begin with prenatal development and .then proceed in chronological order through delivery, weaning, teething, toilet training, right up to the present. How much of this information is accurate is questionable, but even if it were perfectly reliable, what bearing is it likely to have on occupational planning? Some may object that the illustration is not entirely fair. There are counsellors who will argue that, whereas teething may not be too important in vocational guidance, one certainly ought to know something about the client's family constellation educational background, employment history, leisure-time activities, and hobbies. Traditionally such information is integrated with objective test evidence, and an occupational plan is evolved. Useful as such evidence may be, still more important, from the counselling standpoint, is the manner in which the client perceives the facts about himself and the use he makes of them. The client may be a college graduate and still be unable to utilise his academic training. On the other hand, he may possess only elementary education and still accept himself for what he is and take advantage of his potentialities. Counsellors may encounter time and again individuals who, although very superior as measured by tests, are failures in their daily endeavour and may actually regard themselves as being aver age or dull. Conversely, individuals of mediocre ability sometimes not only aspire above their apparent capabilities but actually succeed at levels beyond expectation. The crucial fact is not the objectively measurable potentialities but the client's *ability to mobilise* the resources in his possession.

This is not Bishop Berkeley's subjective idealism in disguise, Objective reality is of tremendous importance in vocational planning, but no planning can be effective without its subjective, acceptance by the individual. It is precisely because reality is so important that so much attention is paid to the client's feelings, for these constitute the most significant aspect of *his* reality.

The counsellor can never take it upon himself to decide what should or should not be important to another person. It takes a tremendous amount of professional training to be able to diagnose correctly; it takes an equally large amount of professional discipline to allow the client to reach his own decisions. In the words of Taft, "To become willing not to know everything about the patient in advance, to enter into the dynamic interplay of the therapeutic process without trying to predict or control the outcome, is as exacting and responsible a discipline as exists in the world today."

Taking a case history presupposes that the counsellor knows which are the important high lights in a client's development. The counsellor may aver that on the basis of his professional training and experience he has learned to recognise those factors in growth which tend to contribute most to personality structure. For example, a broken home during childhood, current marital discord, unemployment, etc., are some of the forces which might account for the present occupational difficulty. Very true, they might—and they might not! Not all children raised in broken games develop into vocational failures. Similarly, children raised in stable homes may need vocational assistance as adults. What determines the importance of an event is not the event itself but how it is perceived by the individual. Fortunately, the distinction between objective reality and its subjective perception is not a dichotomy but a continuum. A competent counsellor will work with bath as aspects of the client's reality. The counsellor who, because of his professional position, presumes to know what is important to the client leaves the latter outside the pale of selfhelp. Hiltner develops this point even further when he questions the necessity for the counsellor to know more than the client about any particular subject. Knowledge, he holds, may be an unsuccessful substitute far genuine and reciprocal feelings.

In the light of the preceding discussion one cannot help wondering of what significance are the detailed questionnaires, what relevant areas they actually cover, and how much valuable material is lost. Would it not be better to let the client tell his own story, unsystematic and artless as it might be—tell what seems to perturb him, haw he thinks he could be helped, and haw he feels about different matters? It is not only what the client says that is important but how he says it and what he is really trying to convey by his statements as well as by silence.

As the client talks about his plans and aspirations, he may never reveal the fact that he has studied the violin far eight years or owns a photographic darkroom. A comprehensive vocational case history would undoubtedly detect these emissions, to which one could cynically respond, "Sa what?" The fact that the client has not as much as mentioned music or photography is probably no accident. He apparently has certain feelings about his hobbies which he does not care to share with the counsellor. The subject perhaps is too painful or too trivial. At any rate he is not likely to build his vocational future around these particular avocations.

The anamnesis-oriented counsellor, having obtained information about the client's hobbies, may wish to "explore" further their vocational implications. It would be very surprising indeed if he obtained anything more than noncommittal replies. There is usually as good a reason for not discussing a subject as there is for talking about it. Thus ones again we return to the question of the client's right to bring up and to discuss only those matters which he is ready to share with the counsellor.

Does the present discussion deny the importance of facts when they are not related to feelings? It certainly does not. Factual information is essential in vocational planning, but it cannot be artificially separated from the psychological meaning imputed to it in the client's own mind. An objective fact becomes a psychological reality only when the individual begins to own it, or accept it as part of his real self. For that matter, a large portion of the counselling process will proceed from a total rejection of the actual problem by the client, to its intellectual understanding, and finally to a psychological acceptance. This aspect of counselling will be discussed more fully in the section on Interpretation.

The purpose of the present discussion is to differentiate between objective data, as they may be revealed through the case history, and dynamic data, as brought out in counselling. Although in content the two may be identical, they are far apart in their psychological significance. Information, highly important from the vocational standpoint, may be intentionally withheld by the client if he is not ready to accept it as part of himself. Such deliberate omissions may take place either during the taking of the case history or in the counselling process itself. In the latter case the lacunae stand a better chance of being handled if they should come to the surface. A case in point is Miss H.

Miss H is a young woman of twenty, a high school graduate, living with her family. She came to the agency to discuss the advisability of taking a secretarial course. Nothing outstanding was revealed during the first interview, with the possible exception of the fact that Miss H had never held a job for any length of time. Miss H told the worker that she had been employed briefly as a salesgirl, had done some baby sitting, and helped her mother at home.

The tests administered to Miss H suggested her to be of high-average ability. She did well on the clerical-aptitude test and according to an interest inventory showed a marked preference for the clerical field.

From the vocational standpoint Miss H's plan to take a secretarial course and then get a job as an office clerk appeared entirely sound. It was not until the latter part of the last interview that Miss H rather timidly informed the worker that she was afflicted with a chronic and disabling condition of the spine. Miss H was unable to remain in a sitting position for more than half an hour without having to get up. She was also compelled to lie down for a few brief moments during the day. It was this condition that had prevented Miss H from taking a job.

The above case illustrates the importance of objective facts in vocational planning. It also shows how difficult it is at times to accept these objective facts. There can be little doubt that Miss H was intellectually aware of her physical limitations throughout her contact with the agency; yet despite this awareness, she proceeded to talk about her future as a clerk, took the various tests, and on the whole behaved as if the disabling condition did not exist. Although it is impossible to know what her actual motives were, it is extremely likely that, at the beginning of the vocational session, she could not bring herself to the point of discussing this extremely painful subject. Perhaps she hoped for some sort of vocational miracle; perhaps she was trying to convince herself that her condition was not serious and that she was really as healthy as other young women. Miss H's unacceptance itself as a semi-invalid probably stemmed from her tremendous need to regard herself as a well girl. The few counselling sessions helped her move from an almost total unacceptance of herself as a handicapped person to a point where she herself wanted to discuss her occupational limitations.

One might argue that she wasted her own and the counsellor's time by going through the motions of planning, knowing all the time that the plans were worthless, whereas comprehensive case history would have detected her ailment at the outset, and whatever vocational planning were to follow would take into account her restricted employability. This is a highly debatable statement. The point is that there has been no waste of time. Miss H had to be repeatedly exposed to the counselling experience in order to translate her intellectual awareness of her difficulty into psychological acceptance. The fact that it was she herself, rather than the counsellor, who raised this emotionally charged issue cannot be overstressed in regard to its therapeutic value. Had the counsellor confronted Miss H with the logic of the situation at the outset of the session, she would probably have assumed a defensive attitude and tried to rationalise the seriousness of her ailment. The fact that she knowingly withheld information about the most important single feature of her occupational plan merely shows how dreadfully threatening reality can be. When Miss II came in for her first appointment, she simply could not cope with the overwhelming situation. Miss H had to live through several interviews in order to move sufficiently to talk about her handicap. It is entirely conceivable that, had the counsellor attempted to handle the question of her marginal employability when he learned about it through the case history, Miss H would not have returned for another interview. It is not the counsellor's but the client's readiness that determines what should be discussed and at what point.

Generany speaking, the past, as revealed by a case history or in any other manner, is important only to the extent that it affects the present. In discussing its value, Gomberg makes a significant comment when he says, ". . . I believe that the true power of the relationship as a possible source of help for the client does not lie in the ability to piece together intellectually the meaning of earlier experiences, so that one understands the genesis of a problem, important and useful as this may be for the *worker*. *Hel*p for the *client* rests in the vitality of the immediate contact as an emotional experience, in which the worker takes full responsibility for his own realness and that of the agency."

The growth and development of personality is a fascinating subject, but like scientific research it cannot be regarded as a part of the helping process. Occasionally the client will come in and insist on relating events that happened to him during his childhood and adolescence. Such a situation may arise out of an honest confusion between vocational guidance and psychoanalysis. A number of people entertain the belief that the only way to solve the problems of the present is to go over the experiences of the part. Thus they think that, by telling the counsllor about their childhood, they are helping him in him professional role.

Other will dwell on the past in order not to face the present. They find it easier to talk about their childhood traumata than about their current vocational plans. Apparently the everyday reality of making a living is even more threatening than the pre-historic beasts of the emotional past.

There are also those to whom bygones are still replete with meaning. When they talk about what happened long ago, it is not so much because they shy away from the present, as because the ghosts of yesterday still haunt them today. Obviously the counsellor cannot summarily dismiss their feelings as unimportant by pointing out that it is the present that matters. As already indicated, the counsellor never decides what is or is not meaningful to the client. The counsellor can, however, aid the client to focus on the present by making it a part of the client's reality. What use the client makes of the past, what it seems to represent to him, and what feeling tones he attempts to convey by removing himself from the present is significant. The competent vocational counsellor can capture the true meaning of the feelings expressed and use it constructively in the helping relationship. This, too, may require several counselling sessions, for the client is not likely to give up too readily the fundamental aspects of self.

Thus far the discussion has concerned itself with the significance of the past as it may be related to current occupational planning. It has been suggested that a full understanding and a critical evaluation of the client's background and the events anteceding his visit to the agency are not essential to the vocational helping process. A few additional, comments on the role of vocational diagnosis may be in order.

The ability to function on a vocational level is not always perfectly correlated with the psychiatric diagnosis of the total personality. Recently a case came to the attention of the agency of a client with a long history of schizophrenic episodes and several hospitalisations. This man, although psychotic from the clinical standpoint, had sufficient strength to find a job and to keep it for an indefinite period of time. He reported to work daily and according to his foreman performed satisfactorily at the plant. Another client, who overtly at least, showed no psychopathology, was completely unable to use himself in relation to employment. He was referred to prospective employers several times but for various reasons "talked himself out of a job." Ultimately he was seen by a psychiatrist, who did not find any psychotic process. In his relation to the vocational counsellor, he always stressed his need and willingness to take a job at once. Simultaneously, while apparently seeking employment, he would present himself in the least favourable light to the employer or invent reasons why he could not accept a particular job offer.

These cases show that from the standpoint of the vocational counsellor it is not always necessary to appraise the total personality of a client in order to help him in his occupational adjustment. One can be severely disturbed clinically and still function adequately in the sense that one is capable of gainful employment. Conversely, some individuals revealing no pathology may find it impossible to use themselves constructively. It may be exceedingly difficult for the counsellor to distinguish between those who can utilise the vocational service and those who cannot. This is especially true since some individuals appear to be sincerely desirous of finding employment, follow up every placement contact, and still are incapable of taking a job when one is offered.

In the course of his professional practice the vocational counsellor will occasionally encounter clients who, although in need of immediate placement, are so disturbed emotionally as to preclude any possibility of their being hired. In such instances the counsellor may have to take it upon himself to decide whether the client is likely to benefit from his contact with the agency. The case of Mr. T illustrates this point.

Mr. T is a graduate electrical engineer. He has worked for a nationally known electrical firm but is unemployed at present. He is thirty-five years old and single.

During his first visit Mr. T talked a great deal and with much feeling about his high professional qualifications and the jobs he has held in the past. He has invariably been dismissed because his superiors proved to be antisemites. Presently, he cannot find employment because, the moment he applies for a position the prospective employer checks with a secret clearinghouse and they discover who he is. There exists an organised conspiracy against him involving large electrical firms and officials in state government. He has attempted to expose these machinations but has never been successful because the electrical concerns wield so much power as to influence some Zionist organisations and make them antisymmetric too. Mr. T knows that despite the conspiracy to keep him out of electrical engineering some concerns have called him at his home to offer him employment. However, the telephone messages were never delivered, for his landlady, who took the calls, is a rabid antisemite.

As I attempted to explain the nature of our placement counselling service, Mr. T quickly assured me that all he wanted was a job and that under no circumstances was I to think that he needed "psychological help." Since I knew of an opening for an electrical engineer, I gave Mr. T a letter to the personnel director of the plant where the vacancy existed. Mr. T left me, saying that he hoped I had profited from talking to him, for now I was better aware of the existing antisemitism.

A day later I received a call from the plant superintendent, who angrily complained to me for having sent Mr. T to him. Instead of discussing the opening for employment, Mr. T attempted to recruit the superintendent in a fight against discrimination. Mr. T attempted twice to see me subsequently, but he did not have an appointment and I was too busy to see him. He refused an appointment, saying that he would make one some other time.

A check with other agencies revealed that the man has been known in the Community as a "troublemaker." He has brought unsubstantiated charges against various individuals and organisations, simultaneously attempting to recruit support for imaginary causes.

Mr. T is probably a classical illustration of paranoia. However, from the placement counselling standpoint, more important than the nosological classification is the fact that Mr. T was totally unable to apply his knowledge and experience as electrical engineer to procuring a position. From the vocational standpoint it matters little what that, psychiatric diagnosis may be. What is relevant to vocational counselling and placement is the client's ability to function realistically. It is only when the client demonstrates his incapacity to use the service that the vocational counsellor may wish to seek causality.

To recapitulate, a vocational case history may be useful to the extent that it provides both the client and the counsellor with a formal framework in which the first interview may be developed. It offers both participants something tangible to discuss and simultaneously sets into motion an interplay of feelings and attitudes. Its primary value lies not so much in the factual information revealed as in the psychological meaning it may have for the client and in the way in which he uses it. An extensive case history also carries within it certain undesirable features, such as a possible undue emphasis on the past and the implication that a fuller knowledge of the client's bygones is likely to help him with his present vocational dilemma and that the counsellor, by accumulating sundry information, is going to assume the responsibility for solving vocational problems for the client.

A vocational case history, by virtue of possessing a certain "face validity,"[1] may help the client, during the initial stages, to sustain his relationship with the agency and thus allow him to take a firmer hold on the problem at hand. This may be especially true for test- or advice-oriented clients, who may have considerable difficulty assuming their share of responsibility at the outset.

The present, rather brief discussion of the merits of a vocational case history has in no way attempted to cover this important and complex question. Proponents of the diagnostic approach could

[1] The term "face validity" has been borrowed from the field of psychological measurements, where it is used to refer to a test that "appears to be valid" because of its content but may or may not be valid in fact. Taking down a vocational case history with particular emphasis on educational and occupational information may lend the procedure some face validity without necessarily contributing, to its actual usefulness. The client because of a previous mental set, may expect something of this sort and may conceivably show greater resistance to a different approach.

without difficulty point out areas which, although relevant to the question under consideration, have not been as much as mentioned. Similarly, those opposed to diagnosis could muster arguments why it should be abolished altogether as a methodological principle. A fair conclusion, at the present, seems to be that vocational case history taking need not be antithetical to help-centred counselling as long as the worker uses his diagnostic skills to aid the client in making a free occupational choice.

Test Evidence

Many vocational counsellors, as well as the lay public, regard psychological testing as the most significant feature of occupational planning. Psychometrics are held in particular esteem by those workers who perceive counselling as a "scientific programme" rather than an aspect of a helping process. To some, mental testing has become virtually synonymous with vocational guidance. For example, one survey of vocational services reveals the fact that 152 different tests are employed in the vocational guidance field at one time or another. Although it would be helpful to know what percentage of total time allocated to guidance is spent in testing and how many tests are administered per client, the large variety of tests in itself is suggestive of the importance attributed to vocational measurements. Such a wide application of quantitative concepts is bound to have both a theoretical and a practical effect on the field of guidance itself.

Psychological tests are essentially instruments intended to measure the quantity or amount of any psychological attribute possessed by the individual. The performance on any one test, in order to have any meaning, is compared with that of a group and is usually expressed in terms of deviation from the average or some other point. In specific situations, such as personnel work, tests may be used for "selection" and "guidance." In the latter instance, the counsellor; implicitly assumes the responsibility for "rounding out a comprehensive picture of the individual counselee". Tests are recommended, for "their data are factual, objective, and relatively precise . . ." Thus once more the counselling experience is reduced to a laboratory diagnosis, where emphasis is placed on the precision of the scientific instruments rather than on the client's ability to make use of the findings.

At this juncture the psychologist may question the whole procedure by raising such issues as: Are the test findings sufficiently reliable for individual prediction? Are the test findings valid in the sense that they correlate highly with actual performance on the job? Are the characteristics tested actually measurable psychological entities? What effect do the immediate and the basic emotional factors have on test results? How good are the norms? These questions, although fundamental to psychological measurement, are only of secondary interest to the counsellor, whose chief aim is to help the client.

The counsellor's primary concerns are: How can the tests contribute to the *client's* ability to handle his problem? What effect will testing have on the counselling process? How is the client going to use the psychometric data? We hear so much about the need for the counsellor to understand the client and his problem, and relatively so little about the client's acceptance of himself and his difficulty. In discussing tests in guidance Shallow suggests that the emphasis be shifted from psychometric to "clinical" thinking, using the term clinical in the "therapeutic" sense of the word. Essentially, the, use of psychological measurement in vocational guidance is predicated on the assumption that, once the counsellor can accumulate a great deal of information about the client, he will be in a better position to assist the latter. Both the case history and the testing programme are basically methods of obtaining pertinent information about the client.

This brings us to the original and broader question of the value of factual data in general. In discussing the use of the case history, it was pointed out that frequently factual information is importance only when of the client employs it toward some end. It was furthermore brought out that a stress on objective evidence, especially when it is evaluated by the counsellor, does not afford the client a full opportunity to come to grips with the real problem with which he wants help. Psychometric evidence can be interpreted and used by the client in any manner he pleases, and here, once more, what the client does with the testing programme is at times more important than the scores themselves.

Psychological tests, however, possess one outstanding characteristic that cannot be duplicated through any other known method. That characteristic is the ability of good tests to measure quickly and reliably those attributes which play such an important role in vocational selection. The fact that a well-standardized test can, with relatively little training on the part of the examiner, determine adequately one's general ability, finger dexterity, or interest patterns makes it a valuable tool in vocational guidance.

Although there exists general agreement as to what types of tests lend themselves to vocational usage, there is considerable controversy regarding the suitability of projective tests in occupational planning. Kaback, for instance, 'holds that the Rorschach is not helpful in preparing for and choosing an occupation or in determining occupational progress. This is indeed so if one conceives of vocational guidance in its narrower sense. The Rorschach is not likely to determine the probable success of a trainee in the mechanical area, nor will it distinguish vocationally between a barber and a chef. (Food responses are not indicative of culinary inclinations!) The Rorschach may prove to be more useful in the selection of students desiring admission to schools of social work and graduate programmes in clinical psychology. The "approach," the number of "human" responses, the use of colour, shading, and movement may be some indications of a person's general ability, attitude toward people, maturity, sensitivity, and inner strength. Stated negatively, a Rorschach that is suggestive of marked emotional imbalance or a pathological state could be employed as one of the criteria for barring the prospective student from entering the helping professions. Considerable research is, however, needed to demonstrate that better adjusted individuals (*i.e.*, those whose Rorschachs are free from undesirable implications) will necessarily develop into better psychologists or caseworkers. The Rorschfch can be employed with considerably greater confidence in vocational situations wherein the client persistently fails to take hold of the process or shows no movement toward resolving his occupational difficulties. A client who cannot be "reached" despite the counsellor's efforts may be so disturbed as not to be accessible at all. Such a client may need psychotherapy rather than vocational guidance. A Rorschach would probably reveal the true nature of the problem.

The ease with which many vocational tests lend themselves to administration and interpretation, yielding at the same time tangible numerical results, may act as a booby trap for the inexperienced counsellor. Super lists four pitfalls in diagnostics testing. As we shall see there are still others. Those mentioned by Super are (1) the neglect of other method, of diagnosis, (2) over-emphasis on diagnosis with the resulting tendency to neglect counselling, (3) failure to take into account the specific validity of the tests used, and (4) the neglect other methods of guidance which should normally accompany diagnosis and counselling." Perhaps the greatest danger inherent in all diagnostic testing is the tendency to confuse the measurement of aptitudes with the actual vocational guidance process.

My own practice, especially during the earlier years of my professional development, has been to fall back on extensive testing whenever I was at a loss as to what to do. Testing to me suggested a safe and easy way out of the difficulty of handling a situation. It is well to remember that it is not only that the counsellor represents a threat to the client; the client may in turn engender a great deal of anxiety in the worker. Testing, in certain situations, may offer a painless escape for both the client and the counsellor, especially when both are unready to come to grips with the real problem. Perhaps's that is what happened to the staff of one of the VA advisement units, who found tests very useful because "many veterans are in no mood to listen to advice and suggestions. . ."— not that the veterans could be blamed for resenting "advice and suggestions." The important issue, however, is not the seemingly highly directive attitude of the counsellors but rather the employment of testing in place of counselling procedure. It is doubtful that testing, in itself, can help the veteran, or anyone else for that matter, reach an acceptable occupational goal.

The case of Paul illustrates how the counsellor may be tempted to resort to extensive testing precisely because he does not know what else to do to help the client.

Paul is a lanky, awkward young man of twenty-one. He has been referred by the social service department of a hospital for aptitude testing" and "vocational recommendations." At present he is receiving psychotherapy through the outpatient department because of general personality problems. He is not subject to draft on account of occasional fainting spells which have been tentatively diagnosed as grand mal. Paul reveals a positive" Wassermann; it is believed that his luetic condition is congenital. Paul was born out of wedlock into a large family. He has six half brothers and half sisters. Paul is living away from home on the recommendation of his psychiatrist. As a child he was rejected and unhappy. Despite many obstacles he graduated from a small town high school, where he took a business course. He failed typing twice and dropped shorthand before completing the term because it was "too hard." The school psychologist administered a Stanford Binet when Paul was in the twelfth grade, at which time he attained an IQ score of 104. Although Paul may be considered of average general ability, he is functioning on a below-average level. He has no hobbies, no vocational interests, and no clearly defined plans. At one time he attempted to learn barbering but gave it up because he had "butterfingers" and was fearful of people. Paul tried selling candy at drive-in motion-picture establishments but was dismissed after two days because he was unable to give the right change. He also had an elevator operator's job, which he lost in less than a week because he was slow and did not get along with other employees. Despite the sad work experience Paul does not want to be "just a labourer." He would like to work himself up to a respectable position such as "office manager" or "liquor salesman for some big concern."

During the first counselling session the counsellor was at a loss as to what to do. Industrial employment had been ruled out fairly definitely because of epilepsy. Learning a trade did not seem to be indicated because of Paul's slowness, poor motor coordination, and negative attitude toward manual occupations. Sales and clerical work had to be abandoned because of Paul's personal and intellectual limitations. The counsellor himself was in a quandary, but he felt that it was his responsibility to indicate to Paul what vocational plans he should make. Since the counsellor did not know in what areas Paul could be relatively successful, extensive psychometric testing was undertaken. Approximately twelve tests were administered during three consecutive mornings. The tests revealed nothing that had not been already known or could not have been inferred from the case history and the interviews. A comprehensive summary of the psychometric data was mailed to the hospital that made the original referral, despite the fact that Paul was not helped with his occupational problem.

Perhaps greater assistance could have been rendered if the counsellor had not assumed that it was his obligation to provide Paul with a concrete plan. Had the counsellor allowed Paul to work through his feelings about the various occupations, had the counsellor helped Paul accept his limitations, it is possible that Paul would have evolved some plan and would have chosen some kind of work in keeping with his abilities.

Psychometric testing, however, offered a seemingly easier way out of the dilemma. It provided the counsellor with the impression that he was discharging his professional obligations, it offered the referring agency an opportunity to ponder over the quantitative data. Everyone seemed to be satisfied except Paul.

An important fact that is likely to be overlooked in a test-centred vocational guidance programme is made by Liggett when she states. "Every social agency should accept the fact that help offered to a client. . . creates a problem, a problem now located between the helper and the one who needs help. Asking for help, or needing help is no simple affair. No matter what problem one brings, the experience of asking from someone who is there to give, creates a new dynamic process, which, because of the fact that one does not control it, also creates new fear and resistance." Psychological testing may offer both the vocational counsellor and the client an easy way out of a threatening relationship and simultaneously enable them to go through the motions of helping and being helped.

A situation that conceivably could have developed in almost any vocational guidance agency is the following: A twenty-four year-old man came to a certain agency and requested that he be given "aptitude tests" to help him determine what he was "best fitted for." During the first contact the counsellor learned that the client had graduated from college in business administration. He did not seem to enjoy sales but wondered what other potentialities he might have. In talking about hobbies he indicated that occasionally he liked to work with his hands or paint with water colours. He also spoke with some regret in his voice about the mistake he had made in not becoming a tool-and-die man. He understood that skilled industrial workers earned good money in plants.

The counsellor apparently took the client literally and proceeded to administer tests with the hope that these would help him with his vocational dilemma. A total of twenty tests was administered in the course of the next five contacts, each testing session taking up the entire morning.

First session. American Council on Education (College), Henmon-Nelson Test of Mental Ability, Nelson-Denny Reading.

Second session. Kuder Preference Record, Brainard Occupational Preference Inventory, SRA Mechanical Aptitudes test, Bennett test of mechanical comprehension.

Third session. Minnesota Clerical Test. General Clerical Test; Meier Art Judgment Test, Graves Design Judgment Test.

Fourth session. Wechsler-Bellevue adult, Bell Adjustment In ventory, Minnesota Metaphysical Personality Inventory.

Fifth session. Revised Minnesota Paper Form Board, Minnesota spatial relations boards, Crawford tridimensional spatial relations test, Minnesota rate of manipulation, Purdue peg board, Crawford small-parts dexterity test.

During the seventh (final) visit, the counsellor reviewed carefully the various test scores and explained their individual meanings and implications to the client. Since the client did not reveal any outstanding abilities or, for that matter, occupational interests in either the mechanical or the artistic areas, the counsellor suggested that the client remain in his present field and try to find work that might be more to his liking.

It should be mentioned that the counsellor was genuinely concerned with exploring the client's potentialities in the hope that the tests, plus his own knowledge of occupations, might provide a satisfactory answer to the client's vocational difficulties. Whether the impressive testing programme helped the client make an occupational choice or whether the time devoted exclusively to testing could have been used to better advantage is left for the reader to decide.

Psychological testing plays a dual role in vocational guidance. It helps to establish a diagnosis and prognosis. Under diagnosis fall those attributes which the client possesses at the time he comes or guidance. They represent his mental endowment, interests, aptitudes, special skills, and even his emotional structure and balance. Prognosis deals with the application of the diagnostic data to the probability of success in a selected area. Neither the case history nor the psychometric programme carries within itself the germ of therapy. Neither is a helping process, but each becomes a part of one if incorporated into the affective life of the client.

The client who believes that testing in itself can help him assumes that, once he knows what ails him or what he is "best fitted for," he can go ahead unassisted with his educational or vocational plans. Perhaps some individuals can. Most persons who come to an agency for vocational assistance do so because they are unable to come to a satisfactory solution without outside help. It is extremely unlikely that knowing the results of tests will help them significantly with their difficulties.

Many clients place an undue emphasis on psychometrics because they themselves are not ready to share in the counselling process. Testing to the client represents an externalisation of his difficulty. Whatever the outcome of the testing programme may be, it is the tests, not the client himself, which suggest what his abilities are, where his interests lie, and what course of action should be undertaken. In short, testing absolves the client of the responsibility of participating actively in the helping process and frees him from having to accept the consequences.

Rogers, in discussing the role of testing feels that "they [tests] tend to increase defensiveness on the part of the client, to lessen his acceptance of self, to decrease his sense of responsibility, to create an attitude of dependence upon the expert." The meaning psychological tests may have for adults is probably quite different from what testing may signify for adolescents, many of whom are constantly exposed to various examinations within the school system. Adults, especially those with limited education or far removed from the academic milieu, are likely to react with greater apprehension toward the test situation. The client's reactions prior to and during the administration proper are important, for they not only are indicative of his attitudes toward himself and the counsellor but also provide the worker with a rich opportunity to help the client clarify some of his feelings. Test taking frequently possesses meaning apart from test results. It is the responsibility of the counsellor to handle the client's feelings of insecurity, hostility, and anxiety, whether they centre in the test results or arise out of the very counselling relationship. To be effective, the counsellor must work with the client's feelings rather than with content alone. It matters little whether the client's defensiveness is revealed before or after the administration of the test. In either case the counsellor has to work with it as part of the helping process.

Some workers feel that letting the client participate in the selection of tests to be administered tends to allay some of his anxieties about testing and also offers him an opportunity for fuller participation. This seems a rather mechanical way of handling the problem of the role of diagnosis in counselling and the place of the counsellor. The client cannot be presumed to be an expert in psychometric measurement. One would not expect a patient to write his own prescription, nor can one leave test selection to client. If testing has a place in vocational guidance, and I believe it has, then it is the responsibility of the counsellor to make the appropriate choice. It is entirely possible that the client may want to take those tests which appear to be least threatening rather than those which would be most effective in vocational diagnosis. How the client perceives the counsellor: and the tests is not likely to be affected seriously by his taking the tests α la carte, not can such a procedure be claimed as a valid substitute for a professional and yet meaningful interrelationship.

As diagnostic instruments, tests can tell the counsellor a great deal about the client and the soundness of his vocational plans. There can be little doubt that in the course of his practice every counsellor has come across numerous clients whose endowment was considerably below their occupational aspirations. Through psychological measurement it is possible to establish a fairly accurate diagnosis and prognosis, but the tests per se in no way help such clients accept reality or formulate a more attainable goal. An excerpt from an actual case summary is presented immediate below in ordain to illustrate how, by virtue of his professional obligations, a counsellor may be forced into a position which he cannot stop at mere test interpretation.

Mr. L is a twenty-two-year-old high school graduate. At present he is working for his father as a clothing salesman.

Although his father wants him to remain in the business, Mr. L is not pleased with the prospect. In the beginning of the first interview he announced that he would like to enter college and become "a doctor, a lawyer, or a dentist—any kind of a profession people look up to." Mr. L wanted "to take an aptitude test which would show me what I am best suited for."

The counsellor, at that time a new worker himself, agreed with the client that some testing might be useful to verify the latter's interests and abilities. The Kuder Preference Record, the American Council on Education Psychological Examination for College Freshmen (ACE), the Henmon-Nelson Test of Mental Ability, and the Nelson-Denny Reading test were administered, revealing the following: Kuder, high persuasive, social service, and clerical. ACE, Q score 22d percentile, L score 14th percentile, total 12th percentile. Henmon-Nelson, IQ 106. Nelson-Denny, vocabulary 30th percentile, paragraph 20th percentile, total 24th percentile (high school senior norms).

It was fairly obvious to the counsellor that Mr. L's levels of aspiration by far exceeded his abilities. It was also quite evident that the occupational choice did not originate from an interest in the work itself but was dominated almost exclusively by its prestige value ("any kind of a profession people look up to"). A factual explanation of the test results certainly would not help the client give up his unrealistic daydreams, nor would it help him accept himself as a clothing salesman. The counsellor found himself in an awkward position. Implicitly he had taken it upon himself to "tell" the client where his strongest vocational attributes lay and had administered tests to enhance the validity of his judgement and recommendations. Now he was confronted with the task of informing the client of the unfavourable outcome of the testing programme.

More serious, however, than the counsellor's discomfort is the fact that the client, who originally came for professional vocational assistance, was about to terminate his contact with the agency without having been helped one iota. Still worse, he was going away with possibly greater conflicts and doubts than he had at the outset. What could have been a genuine helping experience became metamorphosed almost overnight into an emotionally painful predicament. The original vocational ambivalence, which compelled the client to seek occupational assistance in the first place, may actually have been accentuated. Now the client was confronted with two alternatives: to reject the test findings *in toto* and attempt to gain admission into college, or to accept the test results and try to adjust to what he considered to be a vocationally unhappy existence.

Actually, and this is mere conjecture, for the client never returned, he probably, did neither. He may have rationalised a great deal about the tests; he may even have gone elsewhere to verify (really to disprove) the original psychometric findings. He may have applied to some college, or possibly he decided to leave his father's business for a different job elsewhere.

It is at the point where test results are in opposition to the client's occupational goals that the counsellor may be called upon to exercise his professional abilities to the utmost degree. In practice, because so many clients come in with a definite preconceived, idea about testing, it is often necessary to help them see the value of psychometrics in vocational planning in its true perspective. But a brief and elementary lecture on the role of psychological measurements in vocational guidance is not what is likely to help the client at the moment. He may listen carefully to what is being said, nod in approval, and still retain his psychometric orientation. To be effective, the counsellor has to transcend the intellectual level of understanding and come to grips with the inner meaning of the problem. Why does a particular adult client place so much emphasis on tests? What does testing signify to him? Does he really believe that a test can tell him what vocational choice to make, or is he merely rationalising for his inability to assume responsibility for his action? Test results, especially if they are contrary to the expectations and wishes of the client, are not likely to change his original plans. A detailed factual statement as to what the tests suggest does not necessarily help the client accept the vocational implications; quite the contrary, such a presentation is likely to evoke defensiveness and actual block a free expression of feelings. The confusion between diagnosis and therapy, or vocational assistance in the present instance, is not restricted to the lay public alone. Counsellors have been heard to say about obviously disturbed clients, "He needs a Rorschach," as if the Rorschach were a therapeutic measure of some kind.

The last aspect of testing in a counselling situation to be considered deals with the anxiety which may be engendered by the tests themselves. Comparatively little is known about the psychological effect of a test on the individual. Textbooks on psychology usually recommend that, in order to attain optimal results, the subject should be put at ease and a generally good rapport should be established. What the test does to the client in terms of his inner dynamics is an open question. There is empirical evidence to support the contention that psychological tests do have an effect on the person taking them. Less stable individuals will sometimes break off in the middle of the programme. Those who, for whatever reason, are led to believe that their emotional soundness is questioned will often react to the tests negatively or actually refuse to take them. There seems to be an element of threat in every test for every individual. The extent of the anxiety aroused will vary with the purpose for which the test is administered, the person taking it, and the test itself. How the client apperceives testing in relation to his total vocational problem will further influence his attitude toward measurement. Although most clients probably assume that tests are administered to them in order to facilitate the resolution of their occupational problem, they cannot help experiencing certain feelings that accompany test taking itself. For example, they may say defensively in jest, "Now you will know how dumb I am," "I never learned to read properly," or, with respect to a personality inventory, "This is like being psychoanalysed." When the relationship between the counsellor and the client has been meaningful, the latter may be particularly anxious that the tests reveal him in a favourable light. At times the client may distort a paper-and-pencil questionnaire, presenting himself not as he actually is but as he would like the counsellor to see him. It is perhaps reasonable to assume that vocational tests which are intended to measure suitability for an occupation probably engender less fear than those whose specific purpose is not known. But even vocational tests may become anxiety-arousing if an important issue, such as getting a job, should depend on their outcome.

Psychological diagnostic tests that do not carry a direct vocational implication are likely to appear more threatening. It is probably not an accident that in many psychiatric clinics these tests are referred to as "bug tests" and the psychologists as "bug doctors." Tests that quite obviously probe into the basic aspects of personality, such as the projective tests in particular, are probably the most menacing of all. The very fact that they lend themselves to unconscious manipulation and at times thinly disguised symbolism cannot be unnoticed by the subject. A tense or disturbed client can become very seriously upset by relatively indiscriminate use of psychological tests of different kinds. Institutions that practice psychological testing as something apart from the counselling process may lay themselves open to the criticism that anxieties thus aroused may not be handled constructively by the counsellor.

Counselling and testing must be integrated into an experience which is meaningful to the client. Fears, doubts, and conflicting feelings that emerge during the vocational contact, whether they be engendered by testing or by the face-to-face relationship itself, are the very substance that make vocational counselling real. Dynamic psychological testing is perhaps the term that may be applied to the theory and practice that perceives test administration not as a static quantification of various "aptitudes" but as a part of a total vocational, experience. Considering the value so many clients tend to attribute to test evidence, it cannot be entirely devoid of emotional significance. The counsellor, therefore, cannot disregard the possible affective realness of tests without also disregarding that which is important to the client.

It is unfortunate indeed that, in some vocational circles at least, one encounters such expressions as "human engineering," "work tolerance," etc., as if one were dealing with electric motors instead of human beings. Perhaps some counsellors do see themselves as engineers and their clients as so many automatons. Such an attitude even if justifiable in the eyes of the less enlightened industrialists or efficiency experts, has no place in a helping relationship. The responsible vocational counsellor who is concerned with the welfare of his client will take psychometric testing seriously, for he knows that it may mean a great deal to the client and, if mishandled, may arouse considerable untoward anxiety. °

A brief restatement of some of the ideas outlined thus far may be useful, particularly since psychometric measurement plays such an important role in occupational planning and so many divergent opinions as to its role and value exist.

Testing, in vocational guidance, has become so much the stock in trade of the counsellor that many workers would be at a loss how to proceed if for some reason they were prevented from administering tests. This is a serious indictment of the profession and demands further examination. If this situation were the rule, the counsellor would lose his status as a professional worker whose function is to assist people with their occupational adjustment. Instead, he would become a technician who specialises in the administration and interpretation of various educational and trade tests. Some counsellors are precisely that. Others, however, see their roles as that of a helper and refuse to bow to the limitations imposed upon them by the tradition of occupational measurements. The indisputable fact remains that it is possible to do a comprehensive vocational guidance job without the employment of any vocational tests whatsoever.

Psychometric tests, in the generic sense of the word, are essentially an expedient. Valid tests are not only timesaving devices but also instruments which are capable of measuring fairly reliably many human attributes that lend themselves to quantification.

Super seems to hold this view in his extremely comprehensive volume on vocational testing when he says, "When a suitable test is available, its use will generally save time and obtain the information in a more objective, valid, and usable form than would otherwise be the case". The usefulness of such tests varies from problem to problem and from client to client. No blanket condonance or condemnation is called for. Conversely, there is nothing supernatural about psychometrics, either. Tests will rarely, if ever, reveal anything about a client that a competent counsellor cannot ascertain without their use. Tests can, however, do the job more quickly and more reliably. Psychologists recognise that not all human characteristics lend themselves equally, to measurement and that some of the dynamics in the counselling relationship are probably not subject to quantification at all. As the client and the counsel or come together, the counsellor may realise that the area which he is able to measure with his psychometric tools is small and at times relatively unimportant. For that matter, the uncharted seas of total adjustment and total behaviour are far faster than the small and better known islands that constitute the measurable characteristics. To attempt to infer the whole from the meager measurable sample is an indefensible procedure. And yet some vocational counsellors will venture to suggest a comprehensive occupational plan almost solely on the basis of relatively minute and at times inconclusive psychometric evidence.

In practice, situations may arise wherein and intelligent and educated adult may be as much in need of vocational assistance, as a physically handicapped and intellectually limited person. Whereas motor-coordination and general-ability tests may be helpful in the latter case, they may be entirely superfluous when dealing with the superiorly endowed individual. But the better equipped client may need and want occupational assistance badly even if his difficulty cannot be expressed numerically.

Since most vocational counsellors would probably agree that tests actually contribute but a small portion to broad occupational planning, one might ask, Why then do they loom so large in the eyes of the professional worker and the layman alike? Some of the possible reasons have been mentioned previously. It has been stated that: (*a*) Some tests are capable of providing the wanted information quickly and reliably. (*b*) Viewed psychologically, tests may appear to be less threatening to the client because they tend to absolve him of many responsibilities. (*c*) Tests may provide an opportunity for externalising the vocational counselling experience. (The client may take the tests, reject their findings, and still remain largely emotionally intact.) (*d*) Tests may possess considerable face validity in terms of what the client expects to happen (*e*) Psychometric testing is socially more acceptable to some than any other kind of personal assistance. (*f*) Last, but by no means least, is the fact that most vocational they deal with counsellors feel comfortable and at home when "aptitude" testing.

The above brief listing does not completely explain why psychological measurement has taken such a hold on the American imagination. European psychologists, for example, seem to pay less attention to psychometrics, and in the Soviet Union, "testology" is actually held in disdain. Additional reasons why tests appear to be so popular among vocational and educational counsellors may be mentioned. (*a*) Test administration is easy to learn and requires no special professional skills. This is an important consideration if one bears in mind that the majority of educational counsellors are schoolteachers some of whom may have had but minimal training in guidance. (*b*) Test scores are relatively simple to understand and provide the teacher-counsellor with a ready index for classification and comparison. (*c*) Commercial test-development and test-distributing concerns maintain round-the-clock advertising campaigns addressed to the school systems. Well-meaning but uninformed principals frequently assume that a self-administering, self-scoring, and self-interpreting test battery is an adequate substitute for individual educational guidance. Thorndike's often-quoted dictum, "Whatever exists, exists to some extent and can be measured," may have contributed its share for the quantification of human activities and indirectly to the position testing occupies in vocational guidance circles.

It is a human characteristic to derive security from that which is thoroughly familiar and known. As a corollary, that which is unfamiliar or unknown carries within it an element of threat or danger. The vocational counsellor, by virtue of his academic training and professional upbringing, is more intimate with tests and measurements than, perhaps, with any other phase of the helping process. It is relatively recently that some universities began to stress the nonpsychometric aspects of the vocational guidance curriculum. The majority of workers in the field, if judged by the contributions that appear in occupational literature, still seem to feel that psychological testing constitutes the major tool of the vocational or educational counsellor.

Professional interest in psychometric measurements is also reflected in currently conducted graduate research in guidance and personnel. Thus in a two-year study of theses, projects, and dissertations in guidance and personnel work, the largest number of topics chosen dealt directly with Tests and Measurements. Significantly, the lowest topic frequency fell to Philosophy and Principles of Guidance (less than 1 per cent).

The present difficulty, however, does not stem from excessive competence in measurement, or even from the conceivable onesidedness of the professional armamentarium of the vocational counsellor, but rather from his limited conversance with other helping techniques. Perhaps because some counsellors may feel less secure in a helping role and more comfortable in a situation that calls for testing, the vocational guidance experience tends to confine itself frequently to fact finding, test analyses, and occupational information. Some workers, because of their individual backgrounds, may reject the concept of vocational guidance as a helping phenomenon and will see the vocational counsellor as one who "examines, diagnoses, prescribes, and follows up." Thus, in no small measure the vocational counsellor himself may be contributing unwittingly to the prevalent tendency to equate vocational guidance with vocational measurements.

In conclusion it may be desirable to emphasise the fact that, although psychological measurements play an important part in the practice of vocational guidance, the amount of testing in itself cannot be employed as a satisfactory criterion for the evaluation of a guidance programme. It is not the use of tests or, for that matter, any single technique that determines the vitality and meaningfulness of the vocational guidance process. Assistance with occupational problems, as envisioned in the present work, transcends the boundaries set by specific techniques; instead it attempts to encompass the broader aspects of the vocational process itself.

Interpretation

In psychotherapy the term interpretation has been used to describe different processes such as the bringing of unconscious material into consciousness, the translation of symbols into everyday language, or the establishment of a causal relationship between various event. In the latter instance interpretation may be considered as an outgrowth of diagnosis for in a sense, one set of phenomena is explained in terms of another set of data. For example, an apprentice's difficulty in learning watch repairing may be directly attributed to his low finger-dexterity scores and poor hand-eye coordination. In vocational guidance, interpretation almost invariably concerns itself with an explanation of objective facts in relation to a particular occupational or educational plan. The counsellor assembles and integrates various test results and information obtained from the case history and remarks made by the client during the interviews and explains or interprets to the latter their meaning or implications as applied to the problem at hand.

From the present standpoint interpretation is considered chiefly as a counsellor-initiated activity. It is the logical outgrowth of the process already discussed, viz.: the client brings his problem to the counsellor; the counsellor attempts to solve the problem through diagnostic means; the counsellor interprets the vocational implications of his findings. Some counsellors consider it as their primary responsibility to accumulate as much knowledge about the client as possible, to integrate this information into a unified whole, and then to apprise the client of the over-all findings. It is presumed that the client, thus equipped with objective evidence and the expert opinion, is ready to make a wise and lasting vocational choice. Nothing can be further from the truth.

The explanatory character of interpretation is revealed when the counsellor apprises the client of a particular score on a test. For example, the counsellor says, "You attained the 80th percentile on your vocabulary test, which means that you did better than 80 per cent of college seniors, or that 20 per cent of college seniors have a better vocabulary than you." The causative aspects of interpretation are implied when the counsellor traces the client's rejection of all authority and the plant foreman in particular to his childhood dislike for his father.

A subtler concept of interpretation is conveyed in Aptekar's definition when he perceives it as "the worker's purposive projection of his own thoughts into the discussion with the client." In this instance interpretation is neither explanatory nor causative. Its presence may be felt, nevertheless. in the counsellor's purposeful remarks. A brief excerpt from an interview with an unemployed client follows:

C. Do you ever follow the help-wanted ads in the paper?

c. Once in a while.

C. Do you think it might help if you did it every day?

c. I guess it might.

C. And yet you don't feel like doing it.

c. I suppose you are right.

(*Pause*)

c. Then you think if I followed the ads it would help me find a job quicker?

C. What do you think?

c. What you are saying is that I don't look for work hard enough.

C. Do you?

c. (*Grins sheepishly*)

This passage illustrates the counsellor's interpretation of an event with the client doing the actual interpretation. It would be much simpler for the counsellor to say, "The trouble with you is that you don't look for work hard enough," which would probably put the client on the defensive and might actually have a blocking effect on future efforts to find employment. Looking for work might signify a surrender to the counsellor's wishes.

In the present work; interpretation is used to designate a process which enables the client to accept an idea on an emotional level. It has little in common with the formal and intellectual definition of a concept or an academic presentation of some phase of personality development. This distinction in definitions goes right back to the basic difference between the process in which the counsellor assumes the dominant role and the one where both the client and the counsellor participate actively in the planning. In the former, the counsellor utilises his professional knowledge to explain the objective findings with all their implications to the client; in the latter instance, both the client and the counsellor grapple with the subjective meaning of the factual evidence before them. The chief goal of the vocational process is not to explain the technical meaning of a score but to help the client use the facts in a constructive manner, Actually interpretation is something that the client always does himself in accordance with his needs. Even when the counsellor explains painstakingly the significance of every test result or fact revealed in the case history, the client is going to mold the explanation to suit his inner purpose. When the evidence produced by the counsellor is so threatening that the client cannot modify it or mitigate it in any way, he is likely to reject it *in toto*. This may also mean the end of the vocational sessions, for the client is not likely longer to expose himself to an experience that is so damaging to his ego.

What does it mean to accept an idea on an emotional level? We are constantly surrounded by facts which intellectually we know to be true but nevertheless cannot bear with. The mother who wants her dull child to become a professional is aware of his intellectual limitations but nevertheless emotionally rejects the idea of his not being able to reach her objective. She may rationalise a great deal by saying that the tests are at fault, that the teachers are prejudiced, that the curriculum is obsolete, or that her boy does not "apply himself." Even if each and every argument were refuted, she would invent new pretexts for her son's not progressing in his work. No amount of convincing on the part of the counsellor would help her accept an idea which is so fundamentally incompatible with her total needs. This concept is akin to Roger's "reality-as-perceived" and is related in general to the phenomenological interpretation of reality and "apperception" of the objective world mentioned previously. Many other illustrations can be cited which support the observation that logic and common sense have little meaning to a person who feels strongly about some issue. From a practical standpoint, the more insistent the counsellor is, the less receptive will the client become. The client is put on the defensive and will use every device to preserve his original position. The interview then degenerates into a "battle of wills" and is of no therapeutic value.

An idea is accepted emotionally when it is incorporated into the total psychic life of the client, when the person actually "owns it" and can live with it comfortably. This is not synonymous with resignation but rather with self-acceptance. It is a genuine reconciliation between what is (*i.e.*, reality) and the individual's perception of a particular situation or of himself. The process of emotional acceptance is of necessity slow and not always total. There are degrees of owning just as there are degrees of rejecting. The counsellor who allows the client to struggle with himself in trying to reach his goals is helping the latter to move in the direction of his choice, at his own rate. It has been said that nothing is as therapeutic as living through the experience of therapy itself. The client who becomes aware of his own movement is gaining tremendously from the very experience of moving. Movement is a phenomenon in the realm of feelings and cannot be brought about through purely ideational understanding.

Interpretation, if it is to be psychologically effective, must be conveyed in such a manner as to involve the affective life of the client. In the light of the present discussion, interpretation is not something that is done to the client, any more than test administration is. The client does not come in to be measured, as he might if he were buying a suit, and the interpretations made to him do not consist of a recitation of numerical data, no matter how carefully explained. Both psychological testing and interpretation of the findings are a part of the total and larger relationship process. We have already touched upon the feelings the client may have about taking the tests—his fears as well as his hopes. The anxieties are probably intensified when he is about to hear the "verdict." Here again the counsellor is face to face with a multitude of feelings which will not lend themselves to intellectual interpretation.

Whatever the numerical scores may be, irrespective of their vocational implication, they may have a profound psychological meaning to the client. It is this subjective meaning, as expressed in feeling tone, that demands handling. The difference between the 50th and 80th percentile is not only 30 points; it is not even the difference between going or not going to college; it is the difference between all the feelings that accompany one plan as against the feelings that go with the acceptance of an alternate objective. For example, going to college may be a rather unimportant matter to some, in which case there is little emotional investment in having to make a choice. The client is not too concerned with the outcome of the vocational guidance programme. On the other hand, entering college may be vested with a tremendous amount of feeling—college may symbolise success in life, attainment of status, and self-acceptance An unfavorable academic prognosis may indicate failure and frustration for the rest of one's life. In making an interpretation of psychometric evidence the counsellor is charged with the responsibility of helping the client to assimilate on an emotional level the meaning of the factual evidence. The purpose of the vocational interview is to help the client with his vocational problems, rather than to teach him the fundamentals of psychological measurements.

❑❑❑

7

The Vocational Counsellor in Relation to the Guidance Process

The Vocational Counsellor

Thus far a great deal of attention has been given to the client, his desires, his doubts and fears. That it should be so is understandable if one considers that the client is the central figure in the vocational guidance process. It is because of the client's inability to arrive independently at a satisfactory resolution of his problems that a helping vocational service has been organised. Irrespective of the agency's theoretical approach, the primary objective of vocational guidance is to help the client with his occupational and educational adjustment. The vocational counsellor, as a member of the staff, becomes the medium through which the agency can function. In the eyes of the client the counsellor becomes virtually synonymous with the agency.

But a counsellor is a human being too. All attempts on the part of the counsellor to deny his own significance in the vocational process are not only futile but actually harmful to the client-counsellor relationship. The artificial objectivity by which the counsellor tries earnestly to become a psychological robot is a farce and an impossibility. The harder he tries to remain objective, in the sense of being impersonal, the colder he will appear to the client, and the less fruitful will be the outcome of his contacts. The situation is analogous to the vogue in infant training in the early thirties when parents attempted to deny their own feelings in relation to their children and tried to rear the latter in a sterile atmosphere of impersonal objectivity. It took some time to discover that "babies are human beings" and that a growing child needs a human, loving, and occasionally erring parent rather than a milk dispensing automaton. The counsellor who believes that he can remain "objective" toward the client has, indeed, much to learn. An artificially warm attitude created to foster rapport is a poor substitute for a genuine interest in the client and a desire to help him.

Some attention has already been given to the client's perception of the counsellor and the counselling situation, but little space has been devoted to a critical examination of the counsellor and his perception of himself. As previously suggested, perhaps because of the newness of vocational guidance as a profession the counsellor has not had an opportunity to evaluate his own psychological role but has accepted, somewhat naively, some of the techniques and principles practiced in psychology. In the influence of psychology it was pointed out that psychology, perhaps more than any other profession, has left indelible marks on vocational guidance. It was also noted that psychology, although quite competent in research and psychometrics, is itself relatively inexperienced in helping people with their problems. This may at least partially account for the prevalent idea that a vocational counsellor should remain essentially aloof in the counselling process lest his subjective participation "contaminate" the scientific atmosphere that supposedly prevails.

Those professions which for a long time have made help the central theme in their thinking not only have recognised the dynamic role of the therapist but have in some instances focused. On the relationship itself as the crux of the entire therapeutic process. Freud's concept of transference as a phase in the psychotherapeutic development in a sense laid the foundation of what became known among caseworkers much later as "relationship therapy." Both disciplines, although with varying contents, recognise the importance of the therapist as the other person in the relationship. Reik, who studied personally under Freud, goes so far as to assert, "Psychology makes the presence of two persons necessary—even if it is introspection done by a researcher in a lonely study. There is always a second person who observes the *Me*." How much more vital is that second person when two real people meet face to face!

Since the counsellor is such an important figure in the vocational process, it is imperative to know more about him and to examine some of his attributes as they are related to the client and the agency. The term counsellor, quite obviously, is an occupational classification, not a psychological type. The range of personality variations among counsellors is as great as among the rest of the population. Consequently, no attempt will be made to analyse the counsellor as a psychological entity—if indeed such an entity exists.

However, it may be possible to learn something about counsellors as a group in terms of their interests, training, and, above all, their suitability to assume the professional role. Theoretically, once norms are established for the "good" counsellor, others can be classified and evaluated accordingly. But no such norms exist, nor are there, for that matter, norms for "good" physicians or "good" social workers. At best, certain tentative criteria have been set up to guide the respective schools in their admission policies. Apparently there have been no major follow-up studies of those admitted to the universities as contrasted with applicants who were denied admission as unsuitable material. The difficulty of the problem, however, need not deter one from considering some of its aspects, especially as related to the counselling situation. A few of these characteristics will be considered presently.

The majority of counsellors are employed by school systems and consequently deal primarily with adolescents. A sizable number, however, work with young adults as college personnel workers. Still other counsellors are employed by the various state employment services and state commissions of vocational rehabilitation, the Red Cross, YMCA, Jewish Federations, Veterans Administration, private and public community agencies, commercial enterprises, and finally industrial concerns. This does not exhaust the list of places that utilise the skills of vocational counsellors, for some are employed by hospitals, prisons, and similar institutions.

The tremendous diversity of employment sources is bound to pose real problems to vocational guidance as a professional field. Unlike some of the older professions, such as medicine for instance, vocational guidance has not defined its function and its objectives in a manner acceptable to most counsellors, nor has it developed uniform standards for training, qualifications for the counsellor's position, or certification. The survey conducted by Yeo, as an illustration, is quite breathtaking in revealing that out of forty-two schools employing counsellors only one required previous experience in counselling as necessary for appointment. "Seven cities do not consider counselling experience a determining factor in appointment to a counselling position." Even a matter seemingly as simple as giving the counsel or an appropriate occupational designation has caused some difficulty and confusion. Thus, a study conducted by Polmantier reveals that school guidance workers alone bear as many as fifty-three different titles. What the number of titles would be if all the counsellors working for organisations other than schools were also included appears to be a problem in higher mathematics.

It is extremely difficult to find a definition of the concept "vocational counsellor" that is sufficiently broad to include the different philosophies, objectives, and functions and still be specific enough to differentiate it from related professions. And yet vocational counsellors do exist. Furthermore, they exist not merely as "operational definitions" but as human beings made of flesh and blood and endowed with their share of personal drives, needs, and neuroses. It is these aspects of the counsellor's personality which concern us most in discussing the counsellor-client relationship.

The personal history of the counsellor probably has a great deal to do with his proficiency and competence as a worker. Aside from the ontogenetic intrapsychic make-up that is peculiar to the counsellor as an individual, other important factors enter into professional configuration. For instance, it may be of interest to examine how a particular counsellor happened to choose vocational guidance as his career. Did he choose it because he was denied admission to graduate clinical training in psychology, or was he assigned his duties by the school principal because someone had to do the job? The possibilities that determine occupational choice are almost infinite. Some counsellors choose the field out of negative considerations: others select vocational guidance as their life's work because of a genuine interest in people and their struggles in effecting a satisfactory vocational adjustment. Frequently both negative and positive forces are at work simultaneously.

The counsellor's academic training and field-work supervision are some of the other components that in a general sense will affect his competence as a worker. Curricula and standards of training vary from school to school; some counsellors enter the field of guidance with a background of education, psychology, social work, and sometimes such unrelated subjects as pharmacy and engineering. The professional backgrounds of vocational guidance counsellors vary not only in areas of specialisation but in the intensity and extent of training; thus one finds among guidance workers a gamut of academic preparation ranging from a high school diploma to a Ph.D.

Supervised practice, which is considered by some as the most significant single aspect of a counsellor's training, varies from a perfect zero for some workers to several months for others. When one attempts to integrate these multiple variables that enter into the total make-up of a counsellor, one cannot help being impressed by the tremendous differences in individual professional caliber which one encounters in the field as a whole.

The Counsellor's Need

The present discussion is founded on the fact that counsellors are human beings. Counsellors are not Olympian gods who by virtue of their professional training have attained a status of impracticality and objectivity which places them beyond good or evil. Quite the contrary, their professional development, if it extended at all beyond the intellectual absorption of factual information, has made them more human in the sense that they have become more keenly attuned to the attitudes and feelings of others. We have already spoken of the counsellor's learning process, not as a matter of formal knowledge and skills, but as an internalised experience. It is a growth process which enables the counsellor to mature as a person, to control his own impulses and needs, and to offer the client an opportunity to establish a meaningful and warm relationship.

The strength of the vocational counsellor lies not so much in his diagnostic skills or in his knowledge of occupational trends as in his capacity for understanding people and his ability to allow them to begin at a level where they are (not where he is). His strength also lies in self-discipline, which enables him to withhold his own impulses in a manner which will promote optimum expression and movement in the client.

Some counsellors speak only too readily of the client's "lack of readiness" or "resistance." A more careful examination of the dynamics may reveal that failure to make any significant headway is due to the counsellor's insensitivity to the client's frame of mind. Sometimes, quite unwittingly, the counsellor places his own psychological needs before those of the client. When this happens, the client is not likely to derive much benefit from the counselling experience. Considering the importance of the counsellor's needs in the relationship process, some aspects of this subject will be discussed in somewhat greater detail.

The Need to be Helpful

The counsellor, like the client, has certain needs, which may be considered as a manifestation of his total personality. Unlike the client, however, he is not free to give vent to his feelings, for an uncontrolled expression of his own emotional needs may upset the delicately poised relationship. An unrestrained attitude on the part of the counsellor may very easily block the client to the point where he cannot express himself or where he begins to feel so frightened and rejected as to withdraw completely into his shell. This may hold true for an unbridled positive expression as well. The counsellor who beams with benign self-assurance, encouragement, and uncritical good will is probably responding to his own inner needs to appear omnipotent and jovial at the expense of the client.

The need to be helpful is probably present in all of us in varying degrees. The counsellor who perceives himself as a person who is expected to render concrete assistance is tried sorely if he cannot show definite and positive results. Much of his activity may centre in reassurance, giving advice, interpreting tests, or imparting information. He does so not so much because he necessarily believes in the superior efficacy of his methods as became he finds it difficult to use himself in a different capacity. The need to help may be so strong as to throw a counsellor into a panic unless be can point out, for himself, the concrete ways and means he has employed to assist the client with his problem. Such a counsellor is hurt if the client implies that he has not received much help. He is also personally pained if the client breaks off his visits to the vocational agency.

The Need to Take the Problem Away

Closely related to the need to be helpful is the counsellor's tendency to take the problem over and hopefully relieve the client of his self-imposed burden. The counsellor may feel sorry for the client and try to relieve the latter's load by taking some of it over upon himself. But anxiety is not like a heavy parcel; its weight cannot be lessened by the counsellor's giving a helping hand. Many counsellors find it painful to watch a client struggle with his fears and indecisions. They are impelled to "do something" to attenuate, the pain, but it is at this point that one is tempted to ask, "Attenuate whose pain?"

Can a problem be assuaged by the counsellor's taking away its meaning to the client? Can it be wished out of existence by denying its reality? Unfortunately painless therapy does not exist. The counsellor has to respect the client's right to feel about a situation as he does. By being allowed to verbalise his inner conflicts more freely, the client may resolve some of his ambivalence and arrive at decisions which will be his own. The process of beginning to own a problem, grappling with it, and finally arriving, at least partially, at a final solution is perhaps the most significant aspect of the counselling situation. The counsellor who, because of his inner urges, tends to deny the client's prerogative to struggle with himself is also hampering the latter's attempts at self-help.

The Need to Win the Client's Approval

Much of the counsellor's behaviour during the interview may be guided by an unconscious desire to win the approval of the client. Those less secure in their relationship with the client are more likely to behave in a manner that will tend to dispose the latter more favourably toward them. They "bribe" the client by telling him things he wants to hear. Such acts are sometimes rationalised as "establishing a rapport," "putting the client at ease," etc.; actually they represent the counsellor's drive for acceptance and love. Whether the counsellor succeeds in his attempts is of little consequence from the counselling standpoint, for the success of a guidance programme rarely hinges on the fleeting feelings the client may have about the counsellor. What is important in the counselling process is the client's attitude toward the counsellor as it is related to himself. In other words, how does the client perceive the counsellor in relation to his own problems, and what is the client going to make of their relationship?

The client may genuinely dislike the counsellor and consider him an obstacle to success, and yet, as if to spite the counsellor, he may evince much movement and ability to mobilise his own resourcefulness. It is as if the client were saying angrily to the counsellor, "If you don't do it for me, I'll do it myself, so there!"

Negative feelings toward the counsellor play a definite role in therapy and counselling. It would be un-realistic to expect the client always to feel positively toward the counsellor. If the interpersonal relationship is to have any meaning, the client will use the counsellor as someone on whom he can project both his positive and his negative feelings. From the present standpoint it matters little whether or not the expression of hostility toward the worker is a phase of "transference" and signifies a release of repressed childhood impulses toward the father. Hostility may also be engendered as a result of immediate frustration, as when certain limits are set, or it may be the client's way of testing whether or not the counsellor is genuinely interested in him.

Whatever the interpretation of the hostile feelings may be, they constitute a significant aspect of the process. The counsellor who flinches under the client's nonacceptance or the impact of negative feelings may be, again, placing his own emotional needs ahead of the client's. The need to be loved, as the need to love, has to be curbed in order to enable the client to make a fuller use of the counselling experience.

The Need to Control

This particular need, like the need to win the client's approval, probably stems from the deeper, total aspects of personality. As in the preceding instance, it is of interest to us to the extent that it may influence the progress of counselling. The all-important significance of the client's making a free choice and assuming the responsibility for his action has been emphasised on several occasions. A counsellor who has a need to control is actively projecting his own ideas into the situation.

Such a counsellor does not limit himself to mild approval or disapproval, nor does he stop at suggestions which he may submit for the client's consideration. By implication, he *knows* what the client should or should not do. The counsellor who is almost compulsively controlling not only arrogates to himself the client's rights to his feelings and occupational choice but practically insists that the client follow his advice and recommendations. It makes little difference whether the controlling attitude is expressed as direct admonitions or is subtly disguised. In either case the client is likely to respond by noncompliance and general negativism. We have already spoken of how difficult it is for some people to accept help. It may be doubly difficult to accept a process that is replete with someone else's ideas and suggestions.

The Need to Diagnose

Psychologically oriented, counsellors sometimes discover that the centre of several days' activity has been not the client or the problem with which he wanted help but rather a scientific diagnosis. Driven on by his need to classify and to label, the counsellor may have accumulated an impressive stack of letters and reports about the client, a comprehensive anamnesis dating from Day One, and, of course, a formidable array of psychological test data. The value of such information has been discussed in connection with diagnosis, where it was pointed out that diagnosis, no matter how valid, is no substitute for treatment. The counsellor who is more concerned with finding out facts about the client than helping him not only taking up the latter's time needlessly but is actually misleading him. Without positively saying so, he is fostering the belief that tests and other objective evidence will in some magic manner take away the problem and its inevitable pain.

Many counsellors hold the belief that, in order to be in a position to assist the client, they must know a great deal about him. Some workers insist that a comprehensive diagnosis is essential before congesting can begin. It is not inconceivable that an examination of such an attitude may reveal that much of it is due to the counsellor's own needs. The need to diagnose may be indicative of the counsellor's feelings about entering into an intimate relationship with the client. Just as some clients may want tests to be administered to them in order to escape the pain and responsibility that are frequently associated with the helping process, so may some workers insist on diagnosis as a means of avoiding a threatening relationship. We have spoken of the fact that the client is not the only one who may have difficulties in establishing an interpersonal relationship. The counsellor, too, may shy away from a relationship that may prove to be emotionally too taxing and in a sense frightening. A diagnostically oriented vocational guidance programme may provide both the client and the counsellor with a feeling that something is being done about the vocational problem without either one becoming much involved personally.

Stated negatively, the need to diagnose may be viewed as the worker's rejection of the counselling situation and as an unconscious desire to shift the responsibility for the vocational programme onto psychometric evidence. As a corollary, the less comfortable the worker feels in counselling, the more likely he is to depend on genetic information and to resort to diagnostic testing.

The Need to Test a Hypothesis

A diagnostically oriented counsellor, having reached a tentative conclusion, may wish to verify it (for his own edification) by asking the client certain pertinent questions or by administering additional tests to substantiate his diagnosis. Praiseworthy as scientific curiosity may be, it is likely to detract from the helping experience. Perhaps it would be best to relegate research and experimentation to those whose function it is to establish scientific principles and let vocational counsellors concern themselves with the helping process. As it is, rendering assistance to others will tax all the skills and abilities of most mortals.

Without running the risk of exhausting the list of personal needs the counsellor may possess, one can mention several additional needs that may imperil the counselling process. Among these is the need to be *omniscient*. This need may stem from the counsellor's inner fear of admitting to the client that he does not have a ready answer to every possible specific question. A counsellor who so feels perhaps does perceive himself as an all-knowing vocational expert. If that be so, he will probably find it extremely difficult, if not impossible, to convince the client to the contrary. We have discussed the implications of the client viewing the counsellor as someone who can provide him with a ready answer. How much less helpful is the counselling experience likely to be when both the client and the counsellor labour under the same misconception.

The Need to Talk

This is another need that may compel the counsellor to act against the best interests of the client. Silence is indeed often embarrassing and even painful; but it may also be highly productive. The counsellor who cannot bear prolonged lapses in conversation may be interfering with the client's ability to move. The client may be blocked or may find it difficult to express his feelings in words. It takes his time to fight it out with himself—hence the painful silence. The counsellor who has a need to keep up a lively chatter at all costs may be seriously hampering the client's attempts at self-expression and self-direction.

The Need to Practice other Professions

This is another need that deserves mention. Some workers find it quite difficult to limit their functions to those of a vocational counsellor. The reason for this condition are quite complex and at times obscure. They may originate in the counsellor's unacceptance of his own field of work or in his personality make-up which prompts him to handle every problem the client may mention, even if it lies outside of the vocational guidance field. Frequently meddling in other professional areas stems from a failure to understand the role and function of a vocational counsellor. The counsellor who has a need to practice psychiatry or social work is likely to do more harm than good by offering help which he is not qualified to render. A straightforward referral to the appropriate resource is probably a much wiser and safer procedure.

Momentary Needs

A counsellor, like any other mortal, is endowed with fundamental needs which spring from his very personality make-up and other needs which are temporal or situational in nature. The latter may be considered as moods of brief duration which, although of no particular significance to the worker, may have their effect on the counselling situation. In the course of the working day the counsellor is likely to feel somewhat elated at one time or perhaps depressed at another. What happened at the preceding interview may influence his attitude during the session that follows. Anxieties aroused in the morning may become "displaced" in the afternoon, just as a feeling of self-assurance and satisfaction felt in working with one client may be carried over to the counsellor's activity with another applicant.

These fluctuations in mood are essentially an expression of the counsellor's momentary needs. The fact that they may be transitory in nature does not reduce their possible importance in the counsellor-client relationship. Their significance lies in the fact that they represent the counsellor's needs, rather than those of the client. We have already seen that a free expression on the part of the counsellor, although, probably beneficial to the worker, is of no value to the client and may actually retard his progress.

Emotional Blocking

The term blocking unfortunately carries with it a static connotation. We speak of a road block or of blocking a stream where a stationary object is used to stem the rushing water. Viewed psychologically, blocking is a dynamic force which tends to repress or to inhibit other forces which for whatever reason must not come to the force. Pavlov recognised the fluid nature of the inhibitory impulses, with Freud contributing further to their understanding by ascribing to them a definite purpose-fulness

In other words, blocking is not accidental but performs a useful function in the life of the individual. We speak of a person as being blocked when he cannot express himself freely or give vent to his feelings. Apparently he fears that what he may say or want to do will be more than he can cope with. Consequently there arises a need to control, or to block, one's impulses. This need, not to reveal oneself, is as real as some of the other needs just discussed. What effect it may have on the counselling situation will be considered presently.

The counsellor who psychologically speaking is preoccupied with his own inner struggles and efforts to repress his inner promptings is not likely to be particularly attuned to the problems of others. He may find it difficult to enter into a warm and understanding relationship with the client, and he may be too fearful to assume his responsibilities as a counsellor. For example, if an awkward silence should ensue because the client is blocked in his emotional struggles, the counsellor who habitually finds it not easy, to express himself may not be able to assist the client with the immediate difficulty. A recognition of how the client may feel at the moment not only can help the latter in his embarrassment but may actually suggest that the counsellor understands what goes into taking help.

The need to block one's free expression is likely to manifest itself in other ways as well. The counsellor may appear cold and uninterested. His comments may seem dry and studied, lacking the spontaneity that is frequently conducive to a better relationship. A counsellor who is seriously blocked may find it difficult both to give and to receive.

Since a counselling situation is essentially a two-way process, the counsellor who has a "need to block" will probably encounter some trouble in remembering names, faces, scheduled appointments, or even relevant facts. In a sense he may be rejecting the counselling situation and his role in it, for he fears that a face-to-face relationship may place demands upon his own personality which he cannot very well meet. Thus a counsellor who has difficulty controlling his own feelings and needs may be unwitting placing additional obstacles in the client's way by imposing his own demands on the relationship experience.

The Need to Impose Own Values

Encouragement, suggestions, and direct advice are rarely based on objective data exclusively. Almost invariably they carry an element of approbation on the counsellor's part. It is very unlikely that the counsellor would ever say to the client, "I advise you to become a salesman, although I don't approve personally of such a plan." Through approval or disapproval in any of its forms the counsellor therefore projects his own needs and his own set of values upon the client. A vocational plan or a course of action may be entirely acceptable to the client but not in keeping with the counsellor's idea of how the situation should be handled. The counsellor may, indeed, express his opinion on the soundness of the client's undertaking. The counsellor may furthermore differ basically from the client on fundamental issues and actually express his differences during the interview. But at no time should the counsellor reject a plan devised by the client because it does not meet with the former's approval. No matter how serious the difference between the counsellor and the client may be with respect to specific issues, the counsellor must always recognise the client's prerogative to follow his own promptings and to proceed in the direction of his own choice. When the client feels in a certain way about a problem, irrational as the feeling may appear to the counsellor, the counsellor should try to understand *why* the client feels as he does rather than attempting to negate the existence of such feelings. What may appear to be "right" to the client is "right" by definition, even if it should seem to be completely "wrong" from the counsellor's point of view.

This point, however, should not be limited to feelings and attitudes alone. The counsellor's values as opposed to the client's values are equally important. Davis notes that in our society persons vested with the responsibility of helping people frequently differ educationally and culturally from those receiving help. The values of the helper are often not the one being helped. The question of social values is of particular importance in vocational guidance because the choice of a career is frequently determined by the values society and the individual place upon particular occupations.

Counsellors, as individuals, may have strong convictions regarding what constitutes sound vocational planning. For example, some counsellors may hold that high school education is a minimum "must" for every young man or young woman. Others believe that a college degree is an asset in almost any endeavour. Similarly, counsellors may entertain definite views regarding unions, apprenticeship programmes, discriminatory practices, the Gl Bill of Rights, the civil service, and a host of other issues important in choosing a career. It may take considerable professional discipline not to allow one's own sense of values to influence the client's freedom of occupational decision. At no time should the client be urged to continue with high school or to major in chemistry because the counsellor may have an interest in the subject. This does not deny the counsellor's responsibilities to the client, which demand that the counsellor raise certain pertinent issues with the client, help him examine critically the various aspects of the plan under consideration, and point out its assets as well as its liabilities. Perhaps the client has developed a plan which in the counsellor's opinion is unrealistic, the client's levels of aspiration being far in excess of his abilities. The counsellor certainly should discuss with the client the impracticability of such a plan and its possible implications. If after a thorough evaluation of the issue at had the client still wishes to follow his initial inclinations, the counsellor should not insist that the client is "making a mistake" in pursuing his objectives. An examination of the plan, however, should not be restricted to an intellectual evaluation of test scores and a discussion of probability as it applies to success in life. Such an examination must take into account the client's attitudes and feelings toward the plan and toward himself, what it may signify to him subjectively, and what a change in some other direction may mean. During such an exchange of thought and feeling the counsellor must be hypercritical of himself lest he allow his own values to influence his judgement. The need to project one's own set of values upon the client may prove to be a serious obstacle to vocational guidance.

Fatigue

The final need to be considered is different from those mentioned thus far because it does not have a similar dynamic significance nor does it stem necessarily from the counsellor's deeper personality make-up. This is the need to relax, the need to rest during the day, the need to be alone for a brief moment. Intensive counselling is usually an extremely taxing experience for the worker. As we have seen, he not only listens to, the client but attends to every nuance conveyed. Counselling furthermore constitutes an emotional involvement, not only for the client, but for the helper as well. But, unlike the client, the counsellor may not give vent to his feelings, nor may he permit the counselling session to degenerate into an unstructured and purposeless interview. This self-imposed discipline places a severe strain on the counsellor. At times the emotional strain and the accompanying fatigue are so great as to interfere seriously with the quality of service rendered. It has been said, perhaps facetiously, that Freud would ask his patients to lie down on a couch because he could not bear people staring at him the whole day. Even a competent vocational counsellor, *i.e.,* one who can handle relatively well the personal needs discussed previously, may succumb to sheer emotional fatigue.

This poses the practical question of what constitutes an optimum caseload. Specifically, on the average, how many clients can a vocational counsellor see daily without impairing his profession effectiveness? An examination of all professional activities carried on by the worker may provide a tentative answer. Let us assume that the hypothetical counsellor is free of placement duties, group guidance work, meetings centreing around various vocational problems, and similar related activities that fall to the lot of many vocational counsellors. In other words, let us assume that the counsellor is occupied primarily with individual vocational counselling. A great deal of what a counsellor may do in the course of a week depends on his place of employment and on specific functions. Generally, in an agency setting, his work will probably consist in counselling interviews and vocational testing.

Counselling interviews will probably require considerable collateral or supportive activity prior to and after the interview proper. For example, if the client is to be seen for the first time, the counsellor will want to study the referral (if one is available) or possibly talk over the telephone with the person making such a referral. If the case is active, the counsellor may want to review the notes on preceding sessions, examine the test findings, or obtain further information about an occupation that is of interest to the client. He may also wish to study the records more fully in order to be of greater assistance during the forthcoming counselling session. The next step is the counselling period itself, which may last approximately an hour. Following the interview the counsellor will dictate what transpired during that visit.

Testing activity may be subdivided into two general categories: the administration of individual tests that require the counsellor's presence, such as Binet, Wechsler-Bellevue adult, various form boards, etc.; and self-administering tests, such as the Kuder, Otis, etc., which may require timing but do not demand that the examiner be present in the room all the time. It is impossible to estimate how much time is generally devoted to vocational testing, for a great deal depends on the counsellor's individual philosophy with respect to measurements, on the kind of tests he may choose, and on the client's reaction to the testing situation. (Tests like the Kuder Preference Record, for example, may take a half hour to an hour and a half. The Knauber art test may take anywhere from one hour to five hours.) Test scoring and test interpretation may consume an additional indeterminable amount of time. Whereas some paper-and-pencil tests may be scored by a trained clerk, tests like the Wechsler-Bellevue adult and the Rorschach must be scored by the worker. This, as every counsellor knows, is frequently a lengthy and taxing procedure. The integration of test data with each other and with additional evidence consumes more time.

A counsellor working within a vocational agency will probably have one supervisory session a week with his supervisor and an additional staff conference. He furthermore may wish to consult with the psychologist or another member of the staff about a particular case active with him at the time.

In the absence of uniform practices among vocational counsellors it is extremely difficult to estimate the ratio between the amount of time spent in actual interviewing and that devoted to collateral activity, (Under collateral activities fall preparation for interview, test administration, scoring and interpretation of tests, case recording, etc,) It is safe to assume that for every counselling hour the counsellor spends two additional hours on supportive or collateral work. This suggests that on the average the counsellor can be expected to see approximately three clients a day.

In practice the counsellor may learn that his case load demands that he see more than three clients daily. He may also discover that he is expected to fulfil functions of which the aforementioned hypothetical counsellor was so generously relieved. This situation presents a serious dilemma to the professionally conscientious worker. An overambitious vocational guidance programme may produce emotional fatigue which may seriously lower the counsellor's proficiency and the extent of his helpfulness. Thus the rather amorphous need to rest or relax may be as vital a force in the counsellor's performance as the psychological needs discussed in the present section.

Professional Discipline

The relationship between the counsellor's needs and his ability to control them brings up the question of self-discipline. The counsellor cannot help feeling about things the way he does, but what he can attempt to do is not allow his feelings to come to the fore. He can modify his behaviour in such a way as not to let his personal needs interfere with those of the client. This is at times quite difficult, especially when both client and counsellor seem to be struggling with the same problem. A client who bursts into tears, cannot put his troubles into words, or pathetically appeals to the counsellor with the eternal "What should I do?" Frequently taxes the counsellor's discipline to the utmost. It would be easy for the counsellor to put in a word of encouragement or reassurance, to formulate his thoughts for the client, or to provide him with a concrete suggestion. Counselling which is predicated on the client's right to make up his mind is far more difficult than the more traditional directive kind, which allows the worker to assume the responsibility for the direction and outcome of the process.

There seem to be no studies available which analyse the success of a counselling interview in relation to the counsellor's needs. Exactly how damaging the counsellor's drives may become is a moot point. It is quite probable, however, that the client's failure to move at times may be attributed to the counsellor's rather than the client's personality. The Fiedler experiment seems to substantiate the idea that the counsellor's skills and experience as a therapist or helper are more important than the specific techniques employed. This viewpoint is expressed also by Thome, who feels that "the critical factor is not what method is used but rather the skill with which it is used."

Professional self-discipline is probably one important factor in a larger configuration of attributes that are recognised as counselling skills. In discussing the counsellor's emotional needs, an attempt was made to show how his own impulses may damage the relationship and with it the extent of his helpfulness. Merely to recognise intellectually the necessity for professional discipline is not likely to help the counsellor to overcome his shortcomings. We have discussed the ineffectiveness of intellectualisation as a method of bringing about changes in personality. Apparently a more basic approach is required to enable the counsellor to deal with those aspects of his own make-up which tend to interfere with his professional growth and his proficiency as a worker.

Although psychotherapy for, every would-be counsellor may be suggested as a way out of the dilemma, such a procedure is neither feasible nor, necessarily, essential. It is required of the physician training to become a psychoanalyst that he undergo psychoanalysis himself; by the same token, having the student counsellor go through the experience of struggling with his own problems may be considered as one important aspect of his training programme. This opportunity for professional development can be provided through supervision.

Positive use of the Counsellor's Self

The counsellor's needs discussed thus far were described in rather negative terms in the sense that they dealt with attributes harmful to the counselling relationship. Although most counsellors possess some of the undesirable traits in varying degrees, there can be little question that most counsellors attempt sincerely to perform a professionally acceptable job. Some workers may be handicapped in discharging their professional responsibilities because of insufficient training, others because of personality characteristics discussed previously; still other counsellors may fail as practitioners because of a combination of the above factors.

The question then arises how the counsellor can use himself positively in relation to the client. Specific "decalogues" for counsellors are encountered frequently in the literature. Among the more recently published articles one may mention the ethical code compiled by Cluck and the principles set forth by the *ad hoc* Committee on Relations between Psychology and the Medical Profession. Because of the ideological proximity between counselling and psychology many of the tenets promulgated by the committee would probably be acceptable to the majority of vocational counsellors. In more general terms the good vocational counsellor may be characterized by the following attitudes or broad personality traits:

1. A genuine concern for the client's occupational welfare and a desire to assist him with his educational or vocational problems.
2. A respect for the client's right to differ from the counsellor on minor as well as basic issues. This includes the client's prerogative to seek help only in certain areas (determined by the client, *not* the counsellor), to reject the service in part or *in toto,* to begin with the helping process at a level acceptable to him, and to terminate the contact at any time of his choice.
3. An understanding of the difficulties a client may experience in accepting vocational help. This in turn implies the existence of a warm and positive attitude conducive to a continuation of the counselling relationship. (This is in sharp contrast with the "take it or leave it" attitude of some counsellors.)
4. A belief in the client's capacity for positive and constructive expression in the vocational area.
5. A belief in the client's genuine desire to effect a vocational change and a concomitant ability to mobilise his strength toward a resolution of his occupational dilemma.

As a person, the good counsellor may be expected to be essentially positive in his outlook on life, sensitive to the feelings and attitudes of others, and relatively free from neurotic characteristics that would compel him to impose his own needs and values on the client. This is not to imply that the counsellor is to become a paragon of virtue operating in an artificially created situation. Above all the counsellor is a human being. As he offers his professional help to the client, he does so as a trained worker. The relationship that is to ensue is predicated precisely on the human and yet professional qualities of the counsellor. Although it is probably impossible to delineate every aspect of the counselling process, a competent worker can usually distinguish between professional and lay help. Perhaps there is an element of art in every counselling experience. The good counsellor, because of his alertness to the feelings of others, will frequently be able to apply his professional skills in a manner that will help the client overcome his initial fears and will assist him in integrating the forces within. It is well to bear in mind that the vocational helping process depends not only on the client but on the counsellor as well. The extent to which the counsellor can free himself from his own emotional needs and use himself constructively in counselling will frequently determine the helpfulness of the vocational contacts.

Working with Negative Feelings

In dealing with clients, fellow counsellors, or professionals from other areas, the counsellor is bound to encounter, every now and then, essentially unpleasant or negative experience. In the course of his working day the counsellor may have to come in contact with arrogant but nevertheless influential laymen, professionals from other disciplines who have but the vaguest idea of what vocational guidance is but who nevertheless insist that the counsellor conform to their preconceived notions, and clients (and their families) who for whatever reason are angry with the counsellor for what he did or did not do. An adolescent, for example, may unconsciously perceive the counsellor as an authority figure and react with habitual reticence because that is how he usually responds to parental admonitions. The adult client may endow the counsellor with unrealistic powers and then subtly upbraid him for having failed to live up to these expectations. It is only too often that the counsellor is rebuked in such terms as

"You still didn't tell me what I should do," "The tests didn't show me anything new," "I am more confused than ever."

Such feelings of disappointment, dissatisfaction, and hostility are an integral part of helping people with their problems. It is imperative that the counsellor understand them, clarify them to the client, and in short "handle" them as a part of the helping process. The counsellor who because of his own personality is impelled to be everything unto all may be denying the client the valuable experience of expressing his negative feelings as a prerequisite to emotional growth.

In reality the counsellors chief contribution to the client's movement may lie precisely in the fact that the client is allowed to express his hostilities against the counsellor, project his own guilt feelings on the counsellor, and, in short, use him in a negative way. It is entirely possible that throughout the client's lifetime he has been advised, admonished, threatened, and moralised at by well-meaning persons. The professional counselling interview, perhaps for the first time in the client's experience, offers him an opportunity to express his accumulated hostilities and to say what he would like to do about a particular situation. The trained worker will usually encourage such a free expression of feelings even though it create a strain on his own emotions. It is therefore not enough merely to "accept" an expression of negative attitudes. To be of assistance, the counsellor must aid the client to express himself freely and to become aware of his destructiveness and negativism and, through an accepting understanding, must help the client to work out his problems.

Some counsellors, because of their own personality structure, find it extremely difficult to function adequately in situations fraught with hostility and negativism. They have a tremendous need to love and be loved and find it most painful, if not impossible, to work in an atmosphere of mistrust, tension, and anxiety. Quite understandably they will attempt to avoid a head-on clash and will seek ways and means of escaping from what they perceive as intolerable and damaging to their own equilibrium. Sometimes a counsellor avoids meaningful relationships because he feels threatened by them, because he does not know how to help the client with his emotionally charged problems. The counsellor then may perceive the entire experience as negatively charged and may resort to the kind of activities that give him the illusion that he is helping the client without becoming personally involved.

Such a rationalised "make-believe" motion may assume several forms discussed elsewhere in the book. At present mention should be made of the excessive use of comprehensive problem check lists which purportedly provide the counsellor with the kind of information which he can use to help the client vocationally. The more obvious criticisms of such a method are as follows: *(a)* The client has a right to assume that providing the counsellor with detailed information will in some magic manner enable the latter to solve his problems for him. The problem check list may therefore serve to structure the relationship in a way which will tend to place the client in a receptive and passive position. *(b)* The counsellor in turn may imagine that, armed with numerous facts, he is in a better position to assist the client.

From the standpoint of the present discussion the problem check list enables the counsellor to touch on the vital issues, even if they be recorded as mere pencil strokes on a sheet of paper, and still have full control over the situation. The counsellor may scan the check list at his leisure and select for discussion during counselling only those problems which he feels he can handle safely. He may thus avoid becoming involved in painful counselling and forestall a flow of negative feelings. Such questionnaires do provide the counsellor with frequently illuminating information about the client and his past, but they also deny both the client and the counsellor an opportunity to work with the feelings that may accompany a meaningful statement.

A concrete illustration may be in order. In a problem check list used by a certain vocational counselling centre the following questions appear:

1. Your father's main interests and hobbies________
2. Which of his traits or qualities would you like to have?
____
3. Which of his traits or qualities would you not care to have?

The client is expected to reply in writing, in the spaces provided, sometimes prior to the initial interview. During the counselling session proper the counsellor may or may not wish to discuss these particular points, thus denying the client the right to bring up what he deems important and substituting instead a situation in which the counsellor determines what is to be discussed. Perhaps a more serious objection to the use of the problem check list in lieu of a personal discussion is the fact that the client's all-important attitudes and feelings may be lost for both participants. It takes little imagination to see that the above questions may be replete with emotional dynamite and may have a very definite bearing on one's occupational objective or attitude toward a trade. Getting at the bottom of these feelings and attitudes may be the most significant single contribution that the counsellor can make, and yet these feelings may never reach the surface because a problem check list rather than counselling was employed. This poses once more the fundamental question whether factual information or its phenomenal perception is more important in a counselling interview. It seems clear that many counsellors, without quite realising it, utilise a problem check list or similar instruments as a device for avoiding a difficult and consequently anxiety-provoking situation.

Intensive vocational counselling is rarely a smooth, pleasurable experience for either the client or the counsellor. Somewhat earlier it was indicated that the counsel or in the course of his work may encounter considerable hostility and negativism as expressed not only by clients but by professionals in other areas and by the lay public in general. A desire to avoid facing such negative feelings is entirely understandable but not necessarily conducive to the professional development of the counsellor. Two illustrations are provided:

Dr. X, who happened to be influential in the community, was known for his bluntness and direct approach. He was a man of action who tolerated no indecision or vacillation. One day he telephoned the director of the agency very much put out because a patient whom he had referred some time before was still vocationally confused and unemployed. His vociferous complaint sounded somewhat as follows: "I sent my patient to you so you could tell him what he should do; instead your counsellor kept on asking him what he would like to do. If my man knew what he wanted to do, I would not have sent him to you in the first place. I want you people to get off your hands and tell my patient what he is best suited for!" The agency director suggested to the physician that he might wish to talk directly with the counsellor who worked with the case. Rather reluctantly, the physician agreed, although he mentioned something to the effect that he was a busy person and that the director should be sufficiently familiar with the case to know what actually had happened. The counsellor, however, was not ready to talk to the physician. When the director informed him that Dr. X was on the telephone "blowing his top," the counsellor paled and suggested that the director himself handle the situation. The counsellor felt it would be best if the director familiarised himself with the case and called up the doctor later in the day. Had the counsellor been more confident of himself as a professional and more secure in his role, he probably would have had less difficulty discussing the problem with the irate physician. In taking upon himself the responsibility for helping the client, the counsellor also implicitly assumes the responsibility for handling whatever difficulties may arise in connection with his work.

Another case of a counsellor who had great difficulty in facing negative feelings appears below:

Mrs. B referred her fifteen-year-old son for vocational counselling. She made the appointment over the telephone with the secretary and was told in general terms of the nature of the service and the fees charged. Her son came in at the appointed time but after spending an hour with the counsellor decided that some of his questions had been clarified and that there was little to be gained from either testing or further visits. A small bill for service was sent to Mr B. Somewhat later in the week Mrs. B telephoned and in an indignant manner proceeded to upbraid the secretary, who answered the telephone, for having sent the bill. She stormed to the effect: "You did not do anything to my son, you didn't give him any tests or advice—what is the bill for?" The secretary attempted to transfer the call to the counsellor, where it rightly belonged. The counsellor, however, demurred. He was in no mood to become embroiled in the argument. If Mrs. B did not want to pay the bill, he was not going to insist that she do so. He instructed the secretary to tell Mrs. B that he could not talk to her and to handle the question of the bill as she saw fit.

A great number of questions could be asked about this particular case. One may wonder, for instance, whether Mrs. B understood clearly the nature of the service, whether she was asked to participate in the planning process for her son, and whether it was she or the boy who appeared to want help. It is entirely possible that the wrath was caused not so much by the bill itself as by a multitude of accumulated feelings of disappointment and frustration associated with the boy's lack of vocational objective but "triggered" by the bill. By being afraid to talk to Mrs. B the counsellor may have lost an opportunity to be genuinely helpful in what may have been a critical situation.

Parenthetically it should be called to the reader's attention that as a matter of policy appointments made over the telephone should be made by the professional worker, not the secretary, whenever possible. As indicated in the preceding chapter a telephone call may have much in common with the intake interview and must therefore be handled with the greatest skill. Still another point that suggests itself in connection with the above case is whether vocational planning on an agency level should be undertaken with a child without his parent's full participation.

The counsellor's inability to handle negative feelings actively may at times manifest itself in still other ways. One of these may be termed "counselling mutism," a condition in which the counsellor because of his own fears and anxieties prefers to remain silent during most of the interview or to limit himself to an occasional "uh" or "mm." The important issue, of course, is not how much the counsellor says but whether or not his over-all attitude is helpful to the client. An emotional withdrawal in the face of negative feelings is likely to prove to be quite un-productive.

A more obvious rejection of negativism may be expressed in reassurance. Here the counsellor cannot bear to hear the client express destructive feelings either toward himself or toward anyone else. When the client says with a sigh, "I guess I'll never be a good artist," the counsellor brightly reassures him with "You can always make art your hobby." The counsellor who thus responds may be insensitive to the feelings voiced. He may be overlooking the fact that the client is upset over his inability to become a professional artist and is not ready to accept art as an avocation. Furthermore, such a response may block off additional expressions of feelings. Perhaps the client has a need to feel sorry for himself, to "wallow in his misery." It may be necessary for him to tell the counsellor how badly he feels about himself before he can begin to discuss his vocational plans constructively. Unresponsiveness in affect at this point may also be due not so much to a lack of sensitivity as to a fear of having to handle an unhappy and essentially negative situation.

Dynamically closely related to reassurance is an attempt on the part of the counsellor to deny the problem outright. For instance, when the client announces, "All is lost, I'll never be able to go to college again," the counsellor exclaims heartily, "Don't say that! Things cannot be that bad! It's only your imagination" Here, the counsellor apparently is so completely unable to meet the expression of a strong negative feeling that he is compelled to refute its very existence.

The foregoing discussion has attempted to call the reader's attention to the fact that in the course of his professional activities the counsellor will frequently encounter attitudes and feelings which possess a negative valence. Such expressions of negativism may be voiced by the client and directed toward the counsellor. They may be conveyed by other professionals or the general public. The counsellor who because of his own personality needs cannot cope with negativism will often adopt the kind of behavioural response which tends to reduce the impact to the minimum. It must not be inferred that such an avoiding attitude stems from the counsellor's conscious unwillingness to help the client. Rather, it is probable that the counsellor's reluctance or inability to handle negative feelings is a result of his professional unreadiness. As he matures as a worker, presumably he will become better equipped to cope with negative situations as they may arise.

The Vocational Guidance Process

The term process has been employed many times throughout this work, although no attempt has been made to define it. The omission was deliberate, with the hope that through frequent repetition, in varying contexts, the inner meaning of the word would be felt as well as intellectually understood. Process has been used to designate a continuous change within the vocational thinking of the client as a result of his psychological contacts with the vocational agency and the counsellor in particular. Gomberg defines it as, "an individual's movement towards using help, his use of it, and then his separation from it."

Time frequently plays an important role in bringing about noticeable changes. Attitudes, feelings, self-perception, and ideas rarely metamorphose overnight. From the practical standpoint this is one of the reasons why it is advisable to space vocational counselling interviews over a longer period, as opposed to the practice of completing the entire programme in one or two consecutive days. It may take the client some time to readjust his attitudes toward the counsellor; it may require still more time to arrive at a vocational decision or to take definite steps.

This view is not necessarily in opposition to the short-term contact discussed previously. However, although it is the intensity of the process itself, rather than its duration, that usually determines the extent of growth, time does appear to play a part in enabling the client to internalise some of his new experiences. In vocational guidance, where both counselling and testing are frequently indicated, several hours may have to be spent in the two activities in order to help the client assimilate and use the new data. For example, in working with adults, one or two sessions may be "pent in helping the client felloe; on the problem, in assisting him to become aware of his own roll, and in aiding him to overcome some of his disabling fears. An additional several hours may be devoted to psychometric measurements, and finally an hour or two may be spent in helping the client accept and utilise the test evidence thus obtained. It is doubtful that a comprehensive vocational programme consisting of perhaps ten hours could be condensed into one or two consecutive visits. Distributing such a programme over a period of approximately two weeks would contribute to its meaningfulness, from the client's point of view, and conceivably would still meet the criteria for short-term counselling.

The vocational process is essentially a form of psychological growth. It differs from other psychological processes, not in depth, but in its vocational focus. The fact that the client seeks assistance with his vocational (or educational) problem distinguishes it from other types of help, where the focus might be the relationship to other members of the family or some aspect of the total personality structure. It shares, generically, with the other helping professions the fact that comparable dynamics may be involved and similar techniques may be employed.

Not all vocational contacts involve a growth process. Some may be termed vocational consultations, where the client seeks concrete information or an opportunity to discuss some aspect of his plan. Other contacts may be primarily diagnostic in nature; the client appears to be in need of an objective verification of his potentialities as related to some course of action. There are also situations where the client asks for assistance with his vocational dilemma because he feels incapable of arriving at an acceptable plan by himself. It is the hitter situation that concerns us most, not only because of its prevalence, but also because it challenges to the utmost the counsellor's professional skills. The *helping* aspects of the vocational process appear to be the most sadly neglected area in the realm of vocational counselling.

The preceding chapter discussed some of the characteristics of the help-taking and help-giving relationship. It was indicated that adults usually apply for vocational aid because they are aware of the existence of a vocational conflict. They frequently experience some dissatisfaction with their work status, achievement or goals and who to bring about a change It was also indicated that the desire to bring about a modification in existing conditions is almost invariably accompanied by corresponding tendencies to preserve the *status quo*. It is against this background of ambivalence that the client and the counsellor enter into a counselling relationship.

Considering the multitude of contradictory feelings frequently experienced by the client, it would be naive to assume that it is possible to resolve this maze of conflicts at one masterful stroke. Nor could one expect a smooth, goal-directed development to take place as the client and counsellor come to grips with the problem. We have already seen with how much hesitation and fear the client allows himself to become a part of the counselling relationship, how he rationalises his action, how he rejects responsibility. During the opening stages he may actually complain that he is more confused than before. This is entirely understandable, for during the opening phase of the interview many hitherto dormant or semiarticulated anxieties come to the fore. The client may begin to see that psychometrics are not going to solve his problem for him or that changing jobs may not be the answer to his occupational unhappiness. Furthermore, the counselling experience may place new demands on the client. He cannot merely sit down and listen to good advice. He is asked to participate, to relate, and to make independent decisions. Quite obviously, not all individuals will respond in the same way to the new situation. Some will have enough strength to go through the initial stages; others may be thrown into a panic and never return. The counsellor may have to gauge the rate at which the client is becoming personally involved and to estimate the latter's capacity to cope with the new situation.

It should be quite evident by now that the multiplicity of psychological factors that usually enter into a vocational counselling situation cannot be significantly altered in a single step. It may be necessary to modify particular attitudes or ideas in order to allow new thoughts and feelings to emerge to the surface. Some blocking may have to be removed before a freer self-expression can take place In other words, a series of steps has to be taken in order to enable the client to attain his objectives. Such a series of steps may be called process.

Closely related to the concept of process is what has become known in casework literature as movement. Movement should not be confused with progress or success. Movement is a change in the feelings or attitudes of the client caused by his establishing a meaningful relationship with the counsellor. In terms of an arbitrary goal, movement may be expressed as being toward it or away from it. When there are several objectives, or points of reference, movement may be simultaneously abient and adient with respect to the several goals. Movement therefore cannot be thought of as an all-or-none phenomenon but can be viewed with respect to a particular objective. A client moves when he decides to make an appointment; there is additional movement when he keeps that appointment. At the end of the first interview the client may decide whether he wants or does not want to return. This, too, is movement. The more important aspects of movement are revealed in the manner in which and the extent to which the client is able to *change*. This involves a modification in feelings, attitudes, thinking, and behaviour. One can see movement when an excessively dependent individual begins to assume some responsibility for his action. Movement is also present in a changed perception of self in relation to an occupational goal or a job. The client's newly found ability to utilise his vocational potentials, to plan toward some objective, and to proceed later in life unassisted is indicative of movement, if this ability was not discernible at the outset.

Process, however, is more than movement. It is a development that is set into motion as a result of the interaction between the psychologically unfocused and at times amorphous needs of the client and the deliberately structured reality in the person of the counsellor. Although certain stages in the vocational process are quite readily discernible, the process itself does not follow a preordained continuous development. Quite the contrary, it follows a meandering, halting course. The client may move forward, *i.e.*, toward the goal, stop, retreat, and then select an unexpected path. The significant features of such random behaviour are the client's recognition of a vocational problem and his desire to do something about it. At the risk of oversimplification, his activity may be likened to that of a person solving a complex jigsaw puzzle. Puzzle solving is frequently accompanied by trial-and-error, random manipulations, interspersed with flashes of sudden insight, but the total activity is purposeful, or goal-oriented. In the helping process, the client, too, struggles with the emotional problems as they arise, showing progress in some areas and very little or no movement in others. The ultimate objective, however, is to resolve the vocational difficulty with which he wants help.

Viewed psychologically, process may be regarded as a development during which certain objective facts and data become internalized. It is frequently difficult to accept reality for what it is. An elderly person may find it almost impossible to reconcile himself to the thought that he is no longer industrially useful, a recent amputee may have to be completely reeducated vocationally to enable him to find employment, and a failing student may encounter great difficulty in recognising the fact that college is beyond his ability. These and many other examples could be cited to illustrate the fact that reality is not always easy to accept. Nevertheless, despite any major changes in the objective situation, numerous individuals do adjust, in the course of time, to conditions which they may have considered utterly intolerable at first. Such an adjustment process may proceed "spontaneously.," *i.e.*, without any assistance from the counsellor. The counsellor can, however, contribute to the facilitation of such a process and to its completion. Vocational guidance process can therefore be considered as a series of changes within the client that enable him to move psychologically toward an occupational objective.

The Ending Phase

Considerable space has been devoted thus far to the opening stages of the interview and to the dynamics of the vocational process. What happens as the counselling sessions come to an end will be considered now. If the vocational guidance experience has had any meaning at all to the client, its termination cannot be without some significance either. The passing away of a relationship, like its inception, is bound to possess some psychological implications. Once again the client is confronted with a polarity of feelings, for, on the one hand, he is glad to be free of the counsellor and, on the other, he is afraid to lose the latter's understanding and support. It is entirely probable that the client has formed some attachment toward the counsellor in which case he may want to disregard the time limits set originally and continue: with his visits. Concomitantly he is likely to feel rejected and also guilty. The client may feel rejected because he still feels that he needs the counsellor's help, and, although the termination was set in advance, the very fact that the helping process has come to an end may signify that the counsellor no longer is interested in the client. The client may wish to prolong the relationship by suggesting that he and the counsellor meet socially outside the agency, etc. Paradoxical as it may seem on the surface, while feeling rejected, the client may also be rejecting the counsellor. Because of the newly gained ego strength and a successful resolution of some of the conflicts, the client no longer needs the counsellor in the same sense as he did during the beginning of the interviews. In his drive for independence he begins to minimise or deny the usefulness of the counsellor who originally helped him attain this stage of development. This denial is bound to engender some guilt feelings, which will complicate the separation process.

The fact that the client has been able to sustain the often painful and trying relationship and finally to bring it to a conclusion is not likely to be a mere episode in his life. Presumably at least two objectives have been attained: he may have been assisted with his specific vocational problem, and, through working on its solution, he may have learned to make a better use of himself. Perhaps for the first time in his life he has been helped professionally to share his feelings, to participate in planning, and to assume the responsibility for these plans.

Whereas the initial contacts may have been spent in helping the client identify himself with his problem and in clarifying his feelings toward the counsellor, the last session may be devoted to the client's acceptance of the difference between himself and the counsellor. The client-counsellor relationship may have been both pleasant and profitable, but the time has come to end it. Once again the client must accept reality, which dictates that he lead a life separate from that of the counsellor. In the words of Taft "It is not easy for anyone to be consistently sure that the end a vital experience is of his own choosing. Always there comes day when it can be felt as imposed, a death sentence, an attack a rejection a desertion." If on the whole the vocational experience has helped the client to make a fuller use of his inner strengths, the parting is likely to be less painful difficult than the early steps of the vocational process.

The value of the vocational contact need not always lie in concrete formulation of an occupational plan or a definite course of action. Hiltner notes that action must not be substituted for clarification in counselling. Arriving at a quick solution that may lead to direct action is frequently deceptive unless the counsellor and the client have examined carefully the feeling underlying the particular decision. The value of vocational guidance does not necessarily lie in an accurate appraisal of the client's potentialities or in providing him with factual information about the various occupations. A clearer perception of self, a more realistic integration of one's attributes with the existing occupational opportunities, and finally a release of inner strength as related to the occupational goals are some of the objectives in vocational counselling. If the success of a vocational guidance programme were to be evaluated, it would probably have to be appraised in terms of what the client derived inwardly from the vocational contacts rather than what type of information he acquired on an intellectual level.

Some agencies have a policy of giving the client a written summary of tests taken by him, indicating also their vocational implications. Such a procedure appears to be completely out of keeping with the philosophy which perceives vocational guidance as a helping experience. The more obvious objections to giving the client a written statement stem from the danger of his misinterpreting or misusing such information. As the client reads and rereads the typed findings, he is very likely to inject meanings and interpretations that are not there. He is equally likely to fail to see certain implications of the report if these happen to be contradictory to his perception of himself. The client may also misuse the test findings by discussing them with his friends or employer in order to secure further advice or even an increase in salary.

A more serious objection to providing the client with a written report is that such a practice implicitly denies the meaning of the counselling experience. It shifts the emphasis from the client-counsellor relationship to amateur self-guidance. In a sense it is akin to vocational guidance by mail, for in both instances the client is furnished with tangible evidence which he is expected to interpret by himself at home. A client who requests that he be given a statement as to "how he made out" is evidently expressing his feelings that his vocational difficulties have not been satisfactorily resolved, that he is still in need of help with his plans, or that he cannot accept the outcome of the vocational sessions. In such a case he certainly should be offered an opportunity for further counselling. To give him a written summary is to suggest that the vocational counsellor does not have much else to offer and that all the needed information is contained in the written report.

The proponents of the practice which furnishes the client with a written statement reason, at times, that a written summary may help the client remember the important aspects of the vocational contact and will provide him with concrete information as to areas where he may succeed occupationally. This argument is fallacious. Had the counsellor assisted the client with his occupational dilemma in the first place, and had the client arrived at his decisions as a result of his struggles with the issue at hand, there would be no room for forgetting what vocational plans he would like to follow. Forgetting, which is probably a euphemism for unacceptance of an idea, is impossible in situations in which the client has reached his own decisions in the course of the vocational process. It is only in instances where vocational guidance is a superimposed, counsellor-directed activity that the client may need to take with him a written report. It is quite unthinkable for individuals terminating their contact with psychiatrists or caseworkers to be given a specific list of "do's" and "don'ts." If therapy has been effective, the patients need no artificial reminders. If they require written directions, the helping process has been either incomplete or ineffective. In either instance a typewritten sheet is no substitute for therapy or counselling.

To return to the question of the final contact, the last session, precisely because it represents the termination of all preceding contacts, may afford the counsellor and the client an opportunity to recapitulate what transpired in the course of the counselling relationship. By allowing the client to reexamine his original request, by helping him recognise the extent of his movement, and by having him evaluate the helpfulness of the service, the counsellor not only can reduce the anxieties that may be aroused by the termination of the contacts but also may enable the client to proceed unassisted toward his vocational objective.

The client frequently endows the final session with special meaning. He has invested several hours in testing, counselling, review of occupational opportunities, etc. Now he expects the counsellor to provide him with the "answer" or, as some clients express it, to pronounce the "verdict." (The choice of the latter word is probably not accidental. It suggests the client's conception of the vocational process and his part in it. Apparently he feels that he is on trial and that the counsellor is the judge and jury who have the power to acquit or to condemn him.) Simultaneously, because of what has transpired during the counselling sessions, the client has gained a greater degree of independence and has moved from a state of relative confusion to a point where he is able to put some of his vocational plans into action. The skilful counsellor can utilise these conflicting feelings by assisting the client to accept his ambivalence as an ever-present phenomenon. He may thus help the client recognise that, instead of finding a ready solution to his vocational problem, he is leaving the agency somewhat better equipped to deal with his occupational difficulties as they arise in the future.

❑❑❑

8

Supervision of Counsellors and Trainees

General Considerations

The term supervision may convey varying meanings in different areas of work. Sometimes it designates direct overseeing as done, perhaps, by a plant supervisor. Frequently the term carries an administrative connotation and is synonymous with directorship or contains within it didactic implications as encountered in the educational system. In the present instance, supervision denotes a psychological process which enables the student (or the worker) to grow professionally and to assume progressively greater responsibilities toward the client. Its ultimate objective is to render a more effective vocational service to those in need of it, as envisioned by the agency or any other body established to do vocational guidance.

Supervision, as an adjuvant to professional development of the worker, has not been given its due recognition in vocational circles. Several reasons suggest themselves; among these may be the very important fact that supervision, in the present sense of the word, is almost invariably linked with field-work training of students. The fact that only few universities offering courses in vocational guidance require supervised field-work training as a part of their curricula is undoubtedly one of the most important reasons why the concept of supervision has not become integrated, generally, into vocational guidance thinking.

When the term supervision does occur in vocational or for that matter psychological literature, it usually denotes essentially an educational or didactic experience. The correct administration, scoring, and interpretation of tests, for example, may become the central theme in supervision. The role of the supervisor then becomes similar to that of an experienced laboratory technician or perhaps a skimmed turret-lathe operator. It is his duty to see that proper procedures or steps be followed to ensure uniform and valid results. This is intended not to minimise the importance of standardised methods in test administration but rather to emphasise the fact that the supervisor's responsibilities toward the trainee extend considerably beyond technical details.

Other workers (43, 91) see supervision as an integral part of a well-rounded clinical programme, but here again the supervisor's chief function appears to consist in imparting factual information to the student. Emphasis may be placed on occupational information, observation of counselling interviews by the student, critical analysis of counselling sessions conducted by the student and observed by the supervisor, etc. In some instances supervision may be conducted by the different members of the team, *i.e.*, counsellors, psychologists, and psychiatrists, with each member contributing his share of specialised knowledge to the development of the trainee.

The significant feature of such supervision lies in its being fundamentally an intellectual process. It is not likely to contribute significantly to the student's personal and professional growth, even though it may enhance his knowledge of the vocational field. The situation is skin to the client-counsellor relationship, which cannot be very helpful if limited to a statement of diagnostic findings and objective data.

Robinson in her excellent book on supervision perceives it largely as a process that requires the involvement of the self. The student in the course of his lifetime has developed certain patterns of relationship to others. As a professional worker he has to learn to relate on new levels. This he cannot readily do without a supervisor. As Robinson expresses it, "No classroom teaching has the capacity to throw the student back so clearly on her own resources as this discussion process in supervisory conference."

What ensues between the student and the supervisor is not a discussion in the intellectual sense of the word. It is a relationship process that is analogous to what takes place between the client and the counsellor. The learning situation, if it transcends the mere cognitive levels, "represents unknown experience, a threat to the equipment and structure previously acquired." Thus again one witnesses the now familiar struggle between the desire to change and the desire to remain unchanged or whole. The competent supervisor may become a threatening figure who seems to challenge the very foundation of the student as a person, his habitual modes of adjustment, his self-perception, and his attitude toward others. Simultaneously, the supervisor, because of superior knowledge and maturity, offers the student security and support that may enable him to cope with the new aspects of his development.

It is highly questionable whether or not this unique experience of being supervised, of having to grapple with oneself on new levels, of having to relinquish established patterns of adjustment can become meaningful through reading books, attending lectures, or amassing graduate credits. Even introspection is not likely to help a counsellor progress as a helper. Thinking a problem through is essentially an intellectual process. It does not as a rule involve the affective layers of personality and rarely results in an international reorganisation. If it were so, many neurotics or otherwise disturbed individuals could free themselves of their ailments by merely thinking through their conflicts. Experience, however, demonstrates that there is no such thing as self-psychotherapy. Psychotherapy or any other experience that is intended to bring about a change or sets into motion a growth process usually springs from the interrelationship between the two persons who wish to bring about such a change. If one considers counsellor training as a growth process that places demands on the student's participation, it becomes quite apparent that such a process cannot be initiated by the trainee alone. The .supervisor has a definite place in such activity. Without him counsellor training is likely to remain an intellectual experience: Some professions undoubtedly demand more self-participation than others. Vocational counselling, precisely because it is predicated on a vis-a-vis relationship between client and counsellor, probably taxes the counsellor's professional maturity to a greater extent than many nonhelping occupations.

When examined critically, the counsellor has very little else but himself to offer to the client. The counsellor, indeed, possesses certain knowledge and skills. He may know a great deal about occupations and educational trends. He is familiar with test administration and interpretation. But all this diversified knowledge is the counsellor's priceless possession—not the client's. Like a sea of oil underground, it is of no value unless piped to where it is needed and can be used. The counsellor's primary function is to make his superior knowledge available to the client in a form in which he can make use of it. We have already discussed the relative ineffectiveness of factual evaluation. We have also spoken of the guidance process as a condition which brings about self-directed changes in the client. A counsellor who has not freed himself of his own problems in relationship to the client, who has not learned to control his own personality needs is not likely to be able to assume his responsibilities as a helper unless he himself has been helped through personal supervision.

The aspect of supervision which deals with the dynamics of the student-supervisor relationship has been almost completely overlooked in discussions of the training of vocational guidance students. Although the concept of "personal maturity" is undoubtedly important, the supervision process is probably indispensable in the training of all would-be counsellors. It cannot be limited only to those students who are "ready" to take full advantage of the supervisory relationship, any more than vocational counselling can be restricted only to those clients who are prepared to accept unquestioningly the new situation. A certain amount of trepidation, resentment, and over-all "resistance" is bound to crop up in both a counselling and a supervisory relationship. The point is that vocational client counselling and student supervision are genetically related in that both are predicated on the subject's ability to take and use help. They are fundamentally unlike each other in that choosing a career involves a different set of attributes from those involved in being supervised. The latter is primarily a learning or an educational experience. A further elaboration of the nature of supervision, and especially its implications for vocational guidance as a helping profession, demands a more detailed consideration.

The Problem of Field Work

Field work in the general sense of the term may be considered as supervised practice carried out in conjunction with a classroom programme. At a certain stage of his theoretical development, the student may be required to begin to apply, under supervision, some of the skills, techniques, and knowledge acquired in his courses.

Medicine was perhaps among the first professions to recognise the importance of field work, or what is usually called internship. The medical profession has incorporated into its lectures and laboratory periods a system of "on the job" training which enables the intern to come into contact with real patients in an actual hospital setting. Recent graduates of medical schools usually spend additional time as resident physicians in order to acquire further supervised experience before commencing a private practice of their own.

Currently, many universities that offer graduate programmes in clinical psychology require students to devote a certain amount of their time to clinical practice. Such students are usually assigned to psychiatric wards or mental hygiene clinics, where they work under the direct supervision of the chief psychologist. Training in psychotherapy is usually carried aut by the psychiatrist .or the clinical team through staff conferences and consultantian. Usually, the psychology student learning the fundamentals of psycho-therapy is not required to undergo psychotherapy himself, although in same instances group psychotherapy for all the doctoral candidates may be employed.

Field-work training, or internship, as many psychologists prefer to refer to it, is, however, of recent origin. Perhaps because of that lucency, perhaps because of other factors inherent in the practice of clinical psychology, psychologists do not seem to have developed this aspect of their training to a significant extent. Standards, objectives, and definitions still appear to vary from university to university.

The differences in graduate programmes leading to M.A. and Ph.D. degrees are noted by Bell. Perhaps mare significant from the present standpoint is his observation that "a survey of the professional affiliations of the instructors of graduate courses in guidance and counselling indicates that only one third of such instructors belong to any of the national professional guidance organisations." Such a situation would be quite untenable in medicine, nursing, dentistry, or law. It is difficult to comprehend how one so divorced from the practice of a profession can assume the responsibility for training students to enter the fields of counselling and guidance. Membership in a professional organisation would suggest at least minimal identification with the field, not as an academic abstraction, but as social reality.

It has also been noted that much of the in-the-field training that does exist in clinical psychology concerns itself chiefly with the application of knowledge and skills gained in the classroom. The field-work supervisor augments that mass of information by providing the trainee with opportunities to exercise his skills in a professionally acceptable manner. Robinson makes an excellent point in distinguishing between knowledge and skill. Whereas knowledge may remain the possession of the knower, *skill by* necessity is developed in relation to some object. "Most skills grow out of the engagement between a workmana craftsman, a mechanic, or an artistand his object around some point of change initiated by the workman." The counsellor may set into motion a process of change in the client; but such a change does not just happen. The counsellor controls it, by working with, rather than against, the client. Simultaneously he recognises the client's feelings about wanting and not wanting to change and adjusts himself according to the situation at hand. The skilled counsellor will identify himself with the client and his problem but will also differentiate himself from them by maintaining his own professional role and identity in the relationship process. It is only on rare occasions that one meets with a supervisor of psychology interns who takes upon himself the responsibility of assisting the student, not only with factual information and techniques, but also with problems that are bound to arise out of the relationship between the trainee and the client.

The foregoing discussion would suggest that clinical psychology is not particularly qualified to offer vocational guidance the necessary leadership in field-work practice in general and in student supervision in particular. As a profession, psychology has made tremendous strides in the last decade by attempting to standardise doctoral entrant requirements, student selection, and clinical training programmes. The American Psychological Association (APA) has contributed immeasurably toward these objectives, but because of numerous theoretical and practical implications clinical psychology still has to develop considerably before it can define its position among the helping disciplines.

At this point it may be of interest to examine the present status of vocational guidance in relation to field-work training and student supervision. The National Vocational Guidance Association (NVGA), too, has attempted to set up minimum standards and objectives for the profession. But the problems that confront vocational guidance are perhaps even more complex than those encountered in clinical psychology. At least one reason for the professional dilemma is the incredible heterogeneity of composition among vocational guidance counsellors. We have alluded, time and again, to the differences in occupational background, education, professional training, and even basic objectives found among workers in this area. At present, it may seem almost impossible to bring order into a field that is expanding so rapidly in different directions. But the seemingly impossible is being accomplished, and there is every reason to believe that vocational guidance, too, will emerge as a distinct profession.

One may mention a few factors that seem to give both impetus and direction to vocational guidance. The fact that there exists a coordinating professional body that holds annual national conferences and publishes its own periodical is of undeniable importance. The establishment of a professional membership category in the NVGA may be viewed as another step toward higher and more uniform standards. An additional encouraging factor may be seen in the vocational guidance literature. Progressively more workers are becoming concerned with the questions of selection of vocational guidance counsellors, with their training, and with professional standards. The question of field-work training, although mentioned more frequently than formerly, still does not seem to receive the attention it deserves.

In passing it may be of interest to consider the effect World War II may have had on vocational guidance. For the first time in its history vocational guidance has received full recognition and vast monetary support from the government. At the height of "advisement" activity Bell saw in the VA programme a tremendous opportunity for professionalising the field. Whether or not vocational guidance has taken advantage of these opportunities is left to the reader to decide. One could employ, perhaps, such tentative criteria as *(a)* the growth of professional membership in NVGA, *(b)* increase in circulation of the *Personnel and Guidance Journal*, *(c)* publication of new periodicals in vocational guidance, *(d)* establishment of more uniform vocational guidance training programmes at the universities, *(e)* enrollment of students in graduate vocational guidance departments, *(f)* research in vocational guidance and counselling, *(g)* development of new skills, vocational tests, and techniques, *(h)* establishment of supervised field-work programmes, (*i*) progress made toward certification, and (*j*) ethical principles and self-regulating tendencies of the field itself.

The development of a sound field-work programme is the responsibility of the university that prepares students for the vocational guidance field. The questions whether field-work practice should be made optional or mandatory as a prerequisite for the degree, how many hours per semester should be spent in the field, what courses should precede it, and how to evaluate the student's progress during his placement must obviously be answered by the university prior to its launching a field-work programme. It is fairly evident that the various student placement resources will differ from each other, not only in the area in which they can provide training opportunities, but in the quality of supervision as well. By familiarising itself thoroughly with the existing facilities the university can provide the student with the type of experience he is going to need and the kind of supervision he will be able to use. It is encouraging to note that progressively more attention is paid by the guidance field to the development of a sound field-work programme and the specific principles inherent in its realisation.

Pierson, for example, lists twelve general objectives that may serve as a nucleus around which a comprehensive field-work programme could be developed. They are *(a)* Counselling internships must be developed; and they must be developed for a specific training purpose. *(b)* Supervising counsellors must be adequately trained and experienced, and they must be willing to accept the added responsibilities of teaching the intern. *(c)* Supervising counsellors should be operating within a well-organised and effective guidance programme. *(d)* Supervising counsellors should permit their interns to carry real responsibility for their cases. *(e)* Supervising counsellors should take the responsibility for making the internship an educational rather than just a work experience. *(f)* The intern should be assigned to his internship on the basis of his particular needs and the unique training opportunities provided by a particular internship situation. *(g)* The intern should be thoroughly familiar with counselling and testing techniques before he is assigned to his internship. *(h)* The intern should serve in the same internship position long enough to become competent in at least that situation. *(i)* Counsellor trainees should intern first in a general counselling situation. *(j)* Counselling and testing techniques should be used to select students for counsellor training. *(k)* The immediate responsibility for supervising the intern should rest with the supervising counsellor. *(l)* Local school administrators and counsellors should participate in the development of adequate internship positions.

It is at times asserted that a field-work training programme for vocational counsellors is impractical because the majority of graduate students are employed on a full-time basis. Many of them are teachers, counsellors, or personnel workers who cannot leave their positions in order to devote their time to field work. It is furthermore held by some that, unless supervised field work becomes a requirement in all universities, students would tend to avoid the one school that insists that it be incorporated into its vocational guidance curriculum.

The latter point is really a conjecture, not a statement of fact. There is little doubt that some potential students would stay away because, for whatever reason, they could not or would not meet the field-work requirement. On the other hand, there may be many students who would be attracted to a university that offers such a programme precisely because they wished to avail themselves of maximum training opportunities. What effect a field-work programme would have on enrollment may have to be determined empirically before any conclusions can be drawn.

The question of students who also hold daytime jobs deserves further consideration. Students who attend college beyond the bachelor's be level can be subdivided into two categories: those who take special course, because of their individual needs or interests, and those who are fully matriculated and are working toward either a master's or a doctor's degree. The first group need not constitute a problem, for the students who take desultory comes that do not lead toward a degree do not have to take fieldwork, any more than any other one subject. The fully matriculated students, however, are frequently those who are able to make various personal sacrifices in order to pursue their objective. Should field-work training become a general requirement for the master's degree with a vocational guidance major, many candidates would probably make provisions for such a curriculum.

Clinical psychology has managed to develop an internship programme and still draw numerous students. Social work, which provides an extensive field-work programme, seems also to have overcome quite effectively the obstacle presented by employed students. The extent of the field-work programme; which incidentally is fairly uniform for all accredited schools of social work, can be appreciated when one considers that the New York School of Social Work (Columbia), for example, requires "six quarters of field work with three full days in the field weekly." The University of Buffalo School of Social Work expects its students to complete 80 days in field work with an agency, during the first year of training, and an additional 100 days in the field during the second year. The University of Pennsylvania School of Social Work requires 3 full days a week during the first year and 4 days a week during the second year of training.

Currently, many social workers are holding positions in their field without the benefit of professional training. As the standards for qualified workers are raised, many of the presently employed workers are returning to school to complete their academic work. It is not uncommon to see middle-aged people with years of practical experience behind them attending classes and studying toward the master of social work degree. Many of them for the first time in their lives discover the value of supervision. At this point one might ask, If clinical psychology and social work can make provisions for additional training and extensive field-work programmes, why cannot vocational guidance do likewise?

It is encouraging, indeed, to witness the growth in importance assigned to field work as an educational medium for counsellors. The APA, for example, states unequivocally, "The practicum is in some respects the most important phase of the whole process of training in counselling. Without this, the student may be unable to apply his academic knowledge or to integrate required skills to understand and help his clients." But a field-work programme is only as effective as the supervision it has of offer. The variety of counselling experience provided, the intensity, or depth, of the counselling situations, and the type of service rendered are some of the media through which field-work practice enhances the student's professional development. Valuable as these experiences may be, they may fall short of their objectives unless they become integrated into the student's inner life. It is held that such integration is facilitated greatly through the intermediary action of the competent supervisor, who endows the entire field-work programme with a new meaning.

The problem of supervised field work in vocational guidance appears to be sufficiently pressing to require a careful examination. It cannot be dismissed arbitrarily as impractical without a thorough consideration of its theoretical merits. It is entirely probable that, once the profession itself becomes convinced of the desirability of field-work as a part of the professional curriculum, proper steps can be taken to incorporate it into the requirements for a master's degree in vocational guidance.

The Function of Supervision

Two kinds of supervision will be discussed presently: the supervision of vocational guidance students placed by the university, in fulfilment of their field-work requirements, and the supervision of vocational guidance workers already employed by the agency. Of necessity the discussion dealing with supervision in the field-work programme has to be hypothetical to some extent, for, as previously stated, field-work training in vocational guidance has not been generally incorporated into university curricula. On the other hand, such a discussion need not consist solely of idle speculations, for a large body of information concerning student supervision is available to those who will consult casework literature dealing with that subject. There can be little doubt that much casework experience could be applied, either directly or with appropriate modifications, to vocational guidance. We have already seen how certain casework principles and techniques in counselling with clients can be employed beneficially in occupational and educational planning. By analogy, fundamentals of casework supervisor-student relationship would probably prove to be of equal value in vocational counsellor-trainee situations.

It may be well, for discussion purposes, to keep the matters of student supervision and worker supervision separate, for, although the two have much in common, there are also important differences. In student supervision the primary objective is to enable the student to make the greatest use of the field-work placement and of himself as a potential counsellor. The supervisor's responsibility is primarily to the student, just as the counsellor's responsibility is always to the client.

In supervising a worker, the supervisor is endowed with a double responsibility; he has the worker's growth at heart, but he is also deeply concerned with the nature and quality of service the worker is prepared to render to the client. Whereas the student's chief job is to learn, the worker's chief function is to assist the client. Under adequate supervision the trainee can gain a great deal from the field-work situation at little or no cost to the client. That is to say, the client need not suffer because of the trainee's inexperience. The worker, on the other hand, assumes full responsibility for helping the client. It is the supervisor's concern to make certain that the worker is able to carry out competently the self-imposed tasks.

It is most regrettable when students assigned by the university to an agency for field-work placement are used by that organisation for selfish purposes. There have been instances of agencies employing beginning students in lieu of regular psychologists and counsellors because of a shortage of trained workers in those institutions. Such an unethical practice can have no justification. It denies clients the right to be assisted by professionally qualified personnel, and it denies the trainee the right to be a student. Most clients would refuse to be attended by unskilled interns, and most students would resent responsibilities thrust upon them which they were not ready to assume. As if to make matters worse, institutions which because of budgetary limitations or other reasons are compelled to use trainees instead of competent counsellors often find themselves in a position where the already harassed supervisor is too busy as a practitioner. He cannot devote the necessary time to individual supervision, consultation with the university about the trainee's progress, student evaluation, and other related matters. As a result the student may have to rely on his own resources, with detrimental consequences to himself and the client.

The unethical employment of trainees also harms the standards of the profession involved, for it creates the illusion that a competent service can be rendered by students, with only a token number of qualified personnel. Such a practice also tends to limit employment opportunities for the younger counsellors who have completed the requirements for the position in question.

In discussing professional training in social work Robinson speaks of three basic variables that constitute the worker's equipment, *(a)* knowledge supplied by the school, *(b)* skills provided by field-work experience, and *(c)* "the controlled use of the capacity to relate oneself and one's service to people in need." These components, which are the basis for the professional make-up of a social worker, are probably equally important to the training of a vocational counsellor, except for the fact that vocational guidance in its present state of development tends to stress the cognitive aspects of preparation as against the developmental growth of the student. In other words, vocational guidance seems to be so preoccupied with the value of factual information as to overlook the importance of helping the client utilize this knowledge.

Both school and field-work programmes have distinct, although complementary, contributions to offer to the making of the professional counsellor. Whereas the school is concerned primarily with providing the student with information about occupations, psychological tests, personality dynamics, and methods in counselling, the field-work programme is responsible chiefly for the application of this knowledge to specific helping situations. As Rester formulates it in discussing the educational aspects of supervision, "The goals for the learner, in the main, are integration of knowledge, development of skill in practice, and personal emotional growth that enable him to use himself helpfully with other . . . The worker not only requires a body of knowledge intellectually, but must integrate this in such a way that he can use it to help people in trouble". She furthermore maintains that the relationship between student and supervisor is the medium through which such learning can take place. Conversely, wherever a supervised field-work programme is lacking, the student is left to shift for himself. Whether or not he will overcome unassisted his own problems that will arise out of his relationship to the clients and the agency employing him remains a moot point.

The Functions of the Supervisor

The supervisor has several functions to perform in relation to the student and the worker. Among these are administration, teaching, consultation, and evaluation.

Administration deals with the relatively simple structural and technical details. The student or the new worker learns about the physical setup of the agency, gets acquainted with the members of the staff, etc. The supervisor helps the novice to acclimate himself as quickly as possible and to get a general idea of the agency's objectives, policies, practices, and functions. From then on, it becomes the supervisor's responsibility to see that the student has grasped the different fundamentals and is applying them in a manner that is in keeping with the established routine.

Teaching, from the supervisory standpoint, may denote two different activities. The first is the implementation of new information; the second integrates that which is already known by the student. Thus the supervisor may show the student how to administer, score, and interpret a test used by the agency if the trainee has had no previous knowledge of it. He may also introduce the student to new sources of occupational information and to community resources or help him brush up on the *Dictionary of Occupational Titles*.

The integrative aspects of supervisory teaching are more complex. The student or the new worker may report for field-work with a considerable background of information as well as misinformation. The worker, although new to the particular agency, may haw had leaf of experience elsewhere. As he starts on his new job, he is very likely to bring with him the old patterns and attitudes which helped him to function previously. Some of the knowledge or attitudes may have to be altered significantly to suit the new situation. The old dog who cannot learn new tricks may become a real problem in supervision.

The trainee, without previous working experience, may also ring with him certain concepts and mental sets acquired in the classroom. Some of these ideas, although sound in themselves, have not as yet become internalised by the student; he may be eager to employ his newly gained knowledge but does not know how. At this juncture the supervisor may step in and help the student clarify and integrate the various principles and methods learned in the classroom. The probability is that the relearning process is not going to proceed smoothly and without pain. Accepting supervision and taking help have much in common. The dynamics of supervision will be considered in greater detail in the appropriate place. Meanwhile, we may proceed with the third function of the supervisor, which is consultation.

Consultation may be thought of as the process of helping the student make use of what he already knows about the field and of his inner resources. It takes place through the medium of a supervisory conference and is therefore predicated on a face-to-face relationship. There may be considerable exchange of information between the student and the supervisor as they discuss the case at hand. The supervisor will encourage the trainee to express himself freely with regard to what he may have said or done with his client and whether or not he himself thinks he did the right thing. Both the supervisor and the student examine critically the vocational assistance rendered, the techniques employed, and the feelings expressed by the student in the roles of counsellor and trainee.

A written summary of what took place during an interview with a client may serve as an excellent subject for discussion at a supervisory conference. A written statement is decidedly preferable to an electrical recording, for, although the latter is likely to be by far more accurate in the factual sense, it deprives the student of the valuable learning experience of putting down on paper what happened during the interview. In evaluating the relative merits of electrical recording as opposed to transcription from memory, a great deal will depend on the object of such recording. If one is concerned with research which depend, on the factual accuracy of what transpired during the interview, electrical recording will probably prove to be decidedly more reliable than a statement made from memory. On the other hand, if one is concerned with helping the student grow professionally, a written summary is more likely to be of greater value. Some counsellors who have used electrical recording as students in their own training programmes and as supervisors subsequently feel that such a technique provides the learner with a unique opportunity of hearing himself as others hear him. This they hold is a valuable didactic experience that need not be in opposition to the type of personal supervision commonly employed in casework circles. There seems no doubt that electrical recording can be employed as a most useful tool in the educational development of the student-counsellor, especially when he is still in the classroom milieu. The longhand written statement probably lends itself better to supervised field-work practice. Some of its merits will be considered presently.

The beginner frequently encounters considerable difficulty in putting down what he thinks took place during the counselling session. At first he may not know which aspects of the interview to mention and which ones to omit. At times the incidents which he omits are more significant than what he includes. The aspects of the interview in their full meaning may become more understandable as he discusses the summary with his supervisor. He may begin to realise why he "forgot" some portion of the counselling session and possibly overstressed other parts.

Essentially, a case recording is a projective experience. As perhaps in the TAT, the counsellor injects his own interpretations, feelings, and attitudes as he puts down what took place during the interview. In case recording he relives some phases of the interview and simultaneously prepares himself for his supervisory conference. Perhaps he "pulled a boner" which he is not ready to share with the supervisor. He may omit it entirely, modify it to make it more acceptable to himself, or record it as it actually happened. Whichever he decides to do is equally important, for the action may signify the level of his development and his attitude toward supervision.

"Process recording" is of particular value as a supervisory medium for it does not merely state impersonally what happened but reveals the dynamic interplay which took place between the counsellor and the client. A very brief illustration of the difference in form between the more conventional type of recording and process recording may be in order.

Standard recording: Client requested that he be given some tests to help him find out in what occupation he is likely to succeed.

Process recording: Client came in and said that he wanted to take some aptitude tests to help him find out what he is best suited for. I asked him if he had any idea what he would like to do, but he said that he didn't. I then wondered if he thought that I could tell him what he should do in life. Client said that he realised that I could not *tell* him, but he thought the tests might help. I wondered whether he had that much confidence in tests or whether he would like to take tests and also talk with me about his plans in the light of the new findings. Client said that he certainly would not be satisfied with the tests alone but would want to discuss his plans, etc., etc.

Generally, the significant features of process recording appear to be as follows: *(a)* the importance of feelings and attitudes is stressed as against factual events and statements; *(b)* the role of the counsellor is made evident as it is related to what happens between him and the client; *(c)* prominence is given to changes in feeling tone as part of movement; *(d)* the dynamics of client-counsellor relationship are brought into focus; *(e)* the entire vocational guidance experience is expressed as a process contingent upon the client's ambivalences and the limitations set by reality.

As the supervisor and the student discuss the cases assigned to the latter, it is most probable that the trainee will have certain feelings about the client, about his own reactions, and about the comments and suggestions made by the supervisor. Almost imperceptibly he will become drawn into the process of counselling and being counseled. A classification of the student's feelings, especially if they interfere with his job performance, is an important aspect of supervision. We have already discussed the numerous psychological needs and personal characteristics of the counsellor that may retard the progress of a counselling relationship. In a supervisory relationship these feelings may be given new meaning and new poignancy, for now they are brought out and examined critically by the supervisor. This reexamination of what transpired between the counsellor and the client may set into motion a new set of feelings directed toward the supervisor. The supervisor becomes an important figure in the life of the student. Unlike the teacher, he is not primarily an impersonal source of information. Nor is the supervisory experience analogous to attending a lecture in a crowded auditorium. The relationship, although professional, is also personal, and the anonymity of the classroom is shattered by the face-ta-face proximity.

Evaluation is the final function of the supervisor to be considered separately. This is not solely the supervisor's evaluation of the progress of the student, for such an appraisal, although useful to the school, may not be particularly beneficial to the trainee. However, an evaluation can be made a part of the growth experience by causing the student to assess his own development. Evaluation can be seen as a jointly undertaken venture intended to contribute to the trainee's growth.

McCaffery suggests four criteria by means of which the student's progress in field work can be evaluated. Quite obviously these standards would have to be modified to meet the particular needs of a vocational guidance service, and perhaps those of a shorter field-work programme. The four criteria are *(a)* capacity for professional development, *(b)* capacity to work within agency structure and function, *(c)* development of knowledge and skills, and *(d)* use of supervision.

As one of the early steps in his development as a vocational counsellor, the student has to "modify some of his lay attitudes toward people and about helping them". He must also accept differences in occupational objectives, in standards of living, and in attitudes. He must learn to see the world through the client's eyes and respect the latter's ways of handling his own problems. Somewhere during the initial stages the student has to demonstrate sufficient self-discipline to enable him to abstain from lecturing, moralising, and advising. It should also become apparent that the trainee has a genuine desire to help the client make use of his abilities, interests, and special aptitudes. It is not enough to be merely receptive or permissive, or even pleasant and encouraging. The counsellor's responsibilities toward the client, as we have already seen, extend considerably beyond benign passivity.

Capacity to work within the agency may be considered next. It matters little, for the moment, whether the counsellor works within the school system, a private vocational service, or a publicly supported institution. The important factor is that the counsellor (or the student) does not operate as a private practitioner but represents the agency to the client. At no time may the counsellor take it upon himself to render a function that is outside the agency's scope or to proceed with his plans without taking the supervisor into his confidence. As he progresses in his identification with the total structure, he becomes progressively less an "I" and more a "we" in relation to his specific professional responsibilities.

With respect to the development of knowledge and skills, many vocational counsellors, especially those with a psychological background, may feel quite at home. With the universities stressing the value of factual information, such as proper test administration, and the relative merits of interviewing skills, the beginning trainee should not have much difficulty applying what he has learned in school. A less mechanical application of measurements and "techniques" and a greater respect for the client's nonconformity to the dicta set forth in the textbooks may mark another step in the student's growth. At this point one might also mention the student's awareness of the confidentiality of his work as well as of the written records.

How the student (or worker) utilises supervision is a valuable index to his personal and professional maturity. What supervision in counselling is will be discussed more fully in the section that follows. For the present supervision may be viewed as a process which enables the student to develop progressively greater self-assurance in himself and his work. In other words, the student is beginning to assume the responsibility for learning and doing. He demonstrates his confidence in his acquired abilities by sharing his thoughts and ideas freely with the supervisor. Such an action may indicate that he has overcome successfully the initial fears associated with taking supervision. It is an open acknowledgment of his realisation that unless he shares he cannot learn. Sharing with the supervisor also suggests the student's ability to accept criticism and to be able to make a greater use of the supervisory experience. It may take, however, a great deal of time to attain such a level in professional development. Its process aspects will be considered presently.

Dynamics of Supervision

Supervision, if conceived as a helping process intended to promote the student's professional growth, is predicated on a relationship between two people. There can be little question that supervision which attempts to penetrate beyond the intellectual acceptance of facts is also a helping phenomenon. The student who is supervised as a part of his field-work placement is in a sense asking for assistance. In the case of the trainee, such assistance is centred around his desire to gain further knowledge about vocational guidance, his ability to use his professional skills, and perhaps, above all, his will to become a person capable of assisting others. Since vocational guidance is a helping discipline, the vocational counsellor has to learn not only to offer assistance but to receive it as well. Competent supervision should provide the trainee with an opportunity to demonstrate his potentialities for both giving and taking help.

Although individual students will differ from each other in their attitudes toward the programme and the supervisor and in the degree of their "supervisorability," they will also have a great deal in common. Supervisors, too, may reveal considerable variation in their professional competence, temperaments, and attitudes toward the different trainees. Some of the more prevalent dynamics of the supervisor-trainee relationship will be considered presently.

Dowling notes that the development of a student is often characterized by several progressive steps in his training programme. His eagerness to practice, for example, may be followed by retreat, projection, and disappointment as a reaction to his first encounters with the participating situation. The beginner may also have to grapple with self-consciousness and awkwardness during his first few interviews. In his impatience to apply his newly acquired skills to the needs of the client, and in his desire to explain the function of the agency, the student may tend to overlook his own significance in the counselling experience. He may become dissatisfied with the passivity of the situation, the slowness of the process, and the intangibility of results. At this point, he may be tempted to inject himself in order to promote some visible activity. It may take considerable time before the student is able to work out for himself a modus operandi which will help him see himself, the client, and the agency in their proper perspective.

This brief statement by no means exhausts the gamut of attitudes and feelings beginning trainees may evince during their field-work assignment. Individual students may have greater problems with supervision in one area than in another. Robinson, for example, speaks of our levels of learning in field-work supervision. These are response to custom, or the structural routine of the agency; change in attitude; inability to relate to a new situation because of a fear or blocking; and finally the "will" to learn. These are cogent points that deserve much thought from the would-be supervisor, for, although it may be painful to be supervised, it is perhaps equally difficult to assume the role of the supervisor.

We have already seen that a relationship springs into being whenever two individuals meet in a face-to-face situation. It may be insignificant and fleeting, as when two strangers begin to talk to each other in a bus, or it may be meaningful and lasting, as in a supervisory experience. The supervisory relationship commences with the tacit understanding that both individuals participating assume certain responsibilities toward themselves and toward each other. The student goes through the supervisory process in order to acquire new knowledge and in order to learn how to apply the skills already in his possession. The supervisor's responsibility is to assist the student to grow professionally. The field-work situation is essentially an experience in change. Both the supervisor and the trainee expect something to happen as a result of the latter's participation. It is different from what takes place in a classroom, for the student can no longer find security in the number of classmates, nor can he resort to orderly note taking, conscientiously done homework, or intellectualisation. A change, as we have seen in the preceding chapters, is always threatening. The supervisor therefore becomes the chief source of danger.

But there is also the desire to learn, the wish to become the supervisor, the will to become a professional counsellor. The mutually antagonistic drives set into motion a learning process that is unique in the experience of the trainee. Subtle psychological forces begin to go into action. Cautiously and without necessarily being aware of it, the student may begin to test the supervisor's strength. Is he really what he appears to be? Does he mean what he says? How much can the trainee "get away with"? But the student's reactions to supervision cannot be all negative. There must be something positive to sustain the relationship. The student identifies himself with the supervisor. He may find common points of interest or belief; he may seek some similarity in attitude. The student may go so far as to imitate the supervisor's gestures and mannerisms or endow the latter with purely imaginary positive qualities.

Simultaneously the trainee may project on the supervisor his own "badness," or those characteristics which he wishes to deny in himself. The supervisor may suddenly become "dogmatic," "lack sensitiveness," or take "unfair" advantage of his greater knowledge or authoritative position. The student may impute to the supervisor a nonexistent virtue, only to react with disappointment when he cannot find that which lived only in his imagination.

Hostility toward supervision may become more pronounced among counsellors who have been in the field for a number of years but have never gone beyond the traditional diagnostic or advisory phase of vocational guidance. Unlike the novices, they are individuals who may pride themselves on their extensive experience, their familiarity with the subject matter, their professional status or advanced academic degrees. They wish to be treated as equals and may resent strongly the very thought that a competent supervisor may be able to contribute to their growth. Learning something new implies to them that they perhaps do not know very much. It is a genuine threat which they will combat actively By learning something new is not meant getting acquainted with an obscure projective test or discovering an unsuspected correlation between two variables. This type of learning is not only entirdy acceptable but fully in keeping with the tradition of scholars. What is referred to is the kind of reeducation that necessitates the use of oneself. It is a process which enables the student (or the worker) to take and' to incorporate help, in the form of supervision, and to render professional assistance to the client as demonstrated through genuine counselling.

Such personalised learning experience has to be. acquired at first hand. It cannot be learned through books, it cannot be attained through role playing, nor can it be gained through a critical examination of electrically recorded interviews. Granted that these techniques are valuable instruments in the classroom and the counselling laboratory, they cannot take the place of field-work supervision. The student simply has to go through the labour pains of supervision in order to be reborn as a professional counsellor.

Parenthetically, this raises the question of whether or not pain is necessary in the learning process. Pain, as such, not only has no constructive purpose in supervision and counselling but is very likely to produce an inhibitory effect on the learning and growing process. But it would be wonderful indeed if the client or student could rearrange his internal psychic forces as easily as one can shuffle a deck of cards. It would probably also help immeasurably if the counsellor could induce a hypnotic trance which would remove the fears, anxieties, and emotional blocks that tend to spring up whenever one attempts to handle affectively charged material and still help the client make his own decisions, take responsibility for his action, and move in the direction of his own choice. Unfortunately this is an impossibility. It matters little whether the counsellor is a devotee of Freud or Rankempirical evidence suggests that a change in one's make-up is invariably accompanied by a correspondingly strong urge not to change. The anxiety and ambivalence engendered by these contradictory forces are the pain experienced by the individual.

In discussing student and worker supervision and especially its implications in the training of the professional counsellor, one cannot overlook the fact that the majority of practitioners in vocational guidance have never had the benefits of a supervised field work programme. Nevertheless, there exist over 10,000 counsellors (frequently designated by different occupational titles) who enter daily into professional contact with human beings in need of some form of assistance. It is extremely difficult to appraise the numerous implications merchant in this situation. One may speculate that perhaps a large portion of practicing counsellors are engaged in activities considerably beyond their professional capabilities and training. One may also conjecture that academic preparation and supervised field-work are not essential in the preparation of a counsellor. The two hypotheses appear to be mutually exclusive. If one assumes that professional training is indispensable for the performance of an adequate job, it follows that those not having such training are not in a position to render an acceptable service. As a corollary it can be postulated that with most variables held approximately constant, the degree of professional competence is a function of the extent and intensity of professional training. The dictum is especially true if one allows the term "training" to include not only academic preparation but also learning which takes .place during the actual practice of vocational counselling. This may be called "on-the-job training," or "experience."

There can be little doubt that vocational counsellors, even with limited academic background and no supervision, will in the course of time develop some empirical rationale that will enable them to function in their professional role. It is a truism that not all holders of advanced degrees in vocational guidance are *ipsoita* proficient counsellors. Conversely, some workers with a relatively mager professional background develop into competent practitioners. An intelligent, essentially well-adjusted person, genuinely interested in helping people with their occupational difficulties, may, if given an opportunity, become eventually a satisfactory worker. The inadequacy of such reasoning lies in the fact that too much is left to chance. Too much confidence is placed in the latent potentialities of the would be counsellor. Whereas some individuals may progress almost spontaneously, deriving their strength from daily experience with their clients, most counsellors require academic preparation and supervision in order to grow professionally. Even a charismatic counsellor would probably attain a much higher level of professional development if given appropriate professional training.

What has been said thus far about the value and role of supervision certainly is not intended as a comprehensive treatment of that subject. Social casework which has devoted more attention to this important feature of professional development than perhaps any other helping discipline, is rich in literature that covers field-work training and supervision. Much of this information, gained in daily supervisory experience, can probably be transplanted into vocational counselling with only minor modifications. But simple as such a statement may appear on the surface, it carries within it certain theoretical and practical difficulties.

Some Difficulties in Vocational Guidance Supervision

It is easy to admonish the vocational counsellor as to what he should or should not do in his profession, but the relative ineffectiveness of such a procedure has been pointed out throughout this work. However, certain principles that hold good for individuals may also be valid when applied to groups.

The dynamics of individual counselling and supervision conceivably may hold good for vocational counsellors when considered generally: *(a)* there must be a feeling of dissatisfaction with the present methodology and objectives of vocational guidance; *(b)* counsellors must want to do something about their dissatisfaction; *(c)* vocational counsellors must be able to work through their ambivalent feelings of wishing and not wishing to change their viewpoints; *(d)* the will to learn must triumph over the powerful tendencies to retain the *status quo*. These are some of the theoretical considerations that may affect the growth of vocational guidance as a profession. A certain receptive attitude or psychological readiness is essential before one can begin to change. It is a truism that no one was ever convinced of anything against his will. Vocational guidance, too, in order to grow has to be ready to give up much of its former self, painful as this may be, in the interests of acquiring that which is relatively unknown and psychologically threatening.

The practical considerations, especially as applied to field-work and supervision, present further obstacles to the development of professional vocational guidance. Let us assume, for the moment, that vocational guidance has come to the conclusion that field-work training under appropriate supervision is desirable. Let us furthermore assume that the heads of counselling services and guidance departments within the universities are eager to launch such a training programme at once. There still remain several problems that must be solved, at least partially, before training can become a reality.

The chief obstacle to a field-work programme probably is the absence of training facilities for vocational guidance students. By and large, universities that offer courses for counsellors have not developed an intimate working relationship with vocational guidance agencies which could serve as field-work training resources. Privately supported vocational community agencies, state vocational services, and the high school systems that offer vocational guidance to the student body rarely have more than a nodding acquaintance with the local schools that assume the responsibility for turning out professional counsellors. Each body which either teaches or practices vocational guidance is quite independent of all other similar institutions. The general objectives, the standards, and the techniques may vary greatly from one group to another. For example, high school counsellors may have their own professional organisation, their own requirements for becoming a vocational counsellor, and a completely independent philosophy as to the aims of vocational guidance. The Veterans Administration, the state employment service, and the community-supported vocational agency may differ fundamentally from the school guidance system and from each other. The nearest university, which in some instances is miles away from the centre of guidance activity, may be but dimly aware of what is actually taking place in the various institutions that practice vocational guidance. Frequently there is relatively little professional exchange between the professor and the practitioner. As previously indicated, the majority of university teachers of guidance and counselling do not even hold membership in professional guidance associations. There is still less integration between the school and the agency at the administrative level. By integration is meant a coordinated purposeful activity that involves organically each participating body.

A field-work programme for vocational guidance students would probably necessitate close cooperation between the university department that offers counsellor preparation and the agencies or institutions that practice vocational guidance. The university would have to explore the field-work placement resources in the nearby communities, the type of service offered by a particular organisation, and the kind of supervision the student might be expected to receive there. Thus a student planing to work within the high school system might want to be placed as a trainee in high school, whereas one interested in working with adults might do his work in an agency that concerns itself primarily with the out-of-school population. Until a closer liaison can be established between the vocational guidance department of the university and the organisation that offers vocational guidance as a service, field-work practice for vocational guidance students may have to be restricted to the minimum.

A second practical limitation imposed on vocational field-work practice is the dearth of competent supervisors. At the present stage of development in the field of vocational guidance in general, few vocational agencies could assume the responsibility of providing the kind of supervision envisioned in the present chapter. Although the profession may pride itself on having developed excellent counsellors, there are few competent supervisors. Student supervision as an aspect of counsellor training has not been generally accepted in vocational guidance. The very counsellors who have demonstrated their abilities as vocational workers have not had an opportunity to sharpen their skills as supervisors. This situation cannot be remedied overnight, but it need not be considered entirely hopeless. A modest beginning can be made, with the hope that in the course of time some of the present counsellors will develop into skilled vocational supervisors. Once the need for this type of training is recognised, the personnel to carry out the tasks can be developed. What is needed is that additional opportunities for supervision be made available to the more experienced counsellors and. vocational workers who may be presently engaged in some supervision.

The last point to be discussed in connection with the field-work programme has already been touched upon. It deals with the question of students accepting field-work training as part of the vocational guidance curriculum. Some students would probably oppose such a programme; others might welcome it. It is entirely probable that if field-work training became a trend among universities offering degrees with a major in vocational guidance, the majority of the students would try to adjust their personal lives in order to these requirements. Raising the academic standards in any profession rarely deters capable students from entering it. Teaching, clinical psychology, and medicine are fields which have raised their educational standards in recent years and still are attracting a large number of qualified students.

In conclusion it may be said that the problem of field-work and supervision in vocational guidance is both real and pressing. It would be naive to assume that it can be solved in haste or that a supervised field-work programme can spring into being at the waving of a magic wand. If field work and supervision in vocational guidance are to become a reality, they must first be accepted in principle by the profession. The practical difficulties may have to be overcome slowly and one at a time. A great deal of compromising may have to be done at first. Much tolerance will be needed to live through the errors and failures that are bound to occur. It may take years before the profession will have attained the levels of development.

❑❑❑

9

SOME ASPECTS OF ADOLESCENT DEVELOPMENT

It has been indicated previously that the present work aims to assist the professional counsellor to gain a better understanding of vocational guidance dynamics as they may arise mainly in counselling adult clients. This part on helping the adolescent has been added because so much vocational activity is carried on with young people, because even less is known about helping the adolescent than the adult, and finally because principles valid for adult clients need not hold good in working with adolescents. Much of what is to follow may have to be reexamined and empirically tested, for it is presented primarily for whatever heuristic value it may possess.

Volumes have been written about adolescence by poets and psychiatrists alike. The medical profession has time and again described the momentous endocrinological changes during this period of growth, stressing the accompanying psychological metamorphosis. Considerable information is available about the psychosexual development of young people and the effect of culture on growth, not only in the Western world, but in distant Samoa as well. Although there exists a great deal of knowledge about adolescence in general, relatively little is known about helping the individual adolescent and still less about assisting him in the occupational area. This insufficiency of knowledge becomes particularly acute when one deals with the normal adolescent who is never seen by a psychiatrist or a family caseworker. Although normal young people are interviewed daily with respect to their educational or vocational problems by school counsellors, occupational literature is almost completely devoid of references to the vocational helping process or the dynamics underlying the counselling situation. For that matter, even so comprehensive an index of literature in the field as the *Psychological Abstracts* contains only a few references to this important subject. It is generally recognised that adolescents are perhaps the hardest group to work with. Young peuple seem to find it particularly difficult to share their problems with professional workers or with their parents or take any kind of help. Ginzbery *et.al.* summarise the situation aptly when they comment. The adolescent is also in the throes of a struggle to free himself emotionally from the dictation of his parents as well as from his own attachments to them. In view of this, it is obviously difficult to seek-their help on any problem, including that of occupational choice, no matter how much he may need, help and irrespective of whether they are in a position to provide it". Counselling with adolescents therefore frequently becomes a problem in counselling adolescents *and* their parents. This involves a fundamental understanding of dynamics of help taking in general and helping the adolescent in particular. For example, the counsellor may have to be particularly sensitive lest he identify with either one of the participants against the other. The counsellor may also have to assume the difficult task of assisting the parent not merely to accept the adolescent's vocational choice but actually to help the latter bring about its fulfilment.

Although the vocational counsellor is usually concerned with aiding the individual adolescent, a general understanding of adolescents as a psychological group is desirable. Josselyn lists a number of characteristics that are common to young people in our culture. It is not claimed that the attributes mentioned provide a complete list. Other writers in discussing the various facets of adolescent development use at times a different nomenclature. It is of interest to note, however, that despite the varying terminology and degrees of emphasis there appears to be a consensus with regard to the major aspects of that period of growth. Josselyn finds that (*a*) most adolescents are engaged are in struggle for independence and oppose vigorously the protective rule of the adult group. While asserting his independence, the young person does not know how to handle or use his new freedom and is making simultaneously demands for dependent security. (*b*) The "peer" group dominates his thinking. The opinions and pressures exerted by the friends and acquaintances of his own age group may dictate his attitudes, interests, vocational aspirations, and even the colour of socks which he wears. (*c*) His sexual behaviour is confusing to the observer, the choice of his love object being unpredictable and changeable. (*d*) His verbalisations and his actual behaviour are often in contradiction to each other. (*e*) His relationship with others is unstable. Love and hate may become interchanged at a moment's notice. (*f*) His attitude toward his parents may vacillate between rejection and idolisation. (g) The adolescent is secretive about himself and his feelings, but he may bare his soul to the chosen few, revealing dreams, guilt, and conflict.

Among the outstanding characteristics of the adolescent are his self-contradiction and his unpredictability from day to day. Some of the early childhood patterns of adjustment may become revived as he becomes aware of a new world and begins to see significance in events that had no particular meaning to him a few years earlier. In panic he may turn to his parents (or other adults) for support, only to become ambivalent about his "childishness." The Oedipal triangle may become temporarily reestablished, contributing further to the emotional instability of the entire organismic structure.

These inner turmoils lead to insecurity as well as a revolt against "infantile conscience." The latter, however, enables the adolescent to renounce his unrealistic fantasies and to plan for the future in terms of his abilities and the opportunities of reality. This transformation from an unstable and self-contradictory stage to young adulthood is of particular significance to the educational and vocational counsellor. It has been suggested that a sudden academic improvement in the freshman year in college may be due to the resolution of some of the adolescent emotional conflicts, freeing the individual for constructive and purposeful attainment.

It is against such a conflicting background that one must attempt to understand the dynamics of counselling adolescents. From the therapeutic standpoint the adolescent has always been relegated to the status of an orphan. Psychotherapy, in the medical sense, became interested in the treatment of the adult first. Through the contributions of Freud and his colleagues attention shifted somewhat from the immediate problems of the adult to the dynamics of infancy. The genetic approach to personality disorder pointed the way, quite logically, to prophylaxis and thence to therapy with children in general. A great deal of knowledge and many techniques extant today come from the various clinics that offer psychiatric services to children. The adolescent, however, is frequently overlooked, for, in a sense, he is neither a child nor an adult. When an adolescent does come to the attention of a psychiatrist psychologist, or caseworker, it is often in connection with a serious problem such as a total personality breakdown, delinquency, or some aspect of socially unacceptable behaviour.

Some workers see vocational adjustment as a process of growth. It is asserted that the normal adolescent goes through different phases of educational and occupational adjustment until he reaches adulthood. Boys, because of the role assigned to them by our society, may need a different vocational orientation from most girls. Milner, for example, holds that early adolescents develop typical group and sex personality characteristics. These become modified as the child grows older. Different levels of maturity may suggest that in working wth adolescents the counsellor may expect different levels and degrees of participation, depending on the age and the sex of the client.

With respect to the latter it may be well to bear in mind that "for most women marriage, rather than a job, forms the centre of life." This is frequently apparent in vocational counselling with women. Marriage appears to be distant and unreal to many adolescent girls still in the early teens. They day dream of lofty professions without much regard for statistical facts and reality. As they become older, however, they begin to see themselves as potential wives and mothers. A successful marriage rather than a good job suggests an answer to their vocational problems. Some of them desire, indeed, to learn more about certain occupations or their personal vocational potentialities, to enable them to prepare for and to select a suitable job. But the work experience itself is considered to be of temporary duration, something to occupy the young woman until she can fully assume the role of a wife and mother. Consequently the entire question of career planning has a different meaning for most girls from what it has for boys. Needless to say, the vocational counsellor will in the course of his work encounter women who for whatever reason do not plan to get married, women who are no longer young who are not likely to marry, and finally middle-aged and elderly women who, although married, are compelled to augment their income or, because of various circumstances, must be completely self-sufficient economically. To these women, vocational planning may be quite real. Choosing a suitable occupation acquires the importance it has for most men.

Working with the adolescent girl around her vocational or educational problem presents the counsellor with situations that are peculiar to her sex. Although she may share with the boy certain attributes and characteristics typical of adolescents in general, her attitude towards carrier planning and work will be affected strongly by the dictates of society, her immediate cultural milieu, and her family.

The variations in levels of maturity that may arise out of differences in sex or age certainly do not justify the unprofessional practice in many high schools which assigns men counsellors to boys and women counsellors to girls. Such a practice implies that the counsellor is assigned to his professional role not because of his training and other qualifications but because as a man (or woman) he is more likely to identify himself, or "understand," a member of his own sex. It also implies that the young client can form a more frank or intimate relationship with one of his own sex. Such an attitude completely denies the professional part the worker may play in the vocational process and substitutes in its stead a lay "big brother" or "big sister" relationship. It is an anachronism that dates back to the days when the football coach was deemed the logical person to assist the boy with his problems and the kindly home economics teacher was assigned to help the girl with hers.

It would be a sad situation indeed if male physicians were permitted to treat men patients only and women physicians were restricted to women patients. And yet at one period it was unlawful for a male physician to deliver and obstetrical cases were handled exclusively by midwives. Psychiatrist, psychologists, and caseworkers, who are sometimes charged with the responsibility of helping clients in matters of psychosexual adjustment marital incompatibility, and similar emotionally charged problems, do not as a rule distinguish between the sexes as they carry out their professional obligations. In clinical practice, however, situations do arise at times where therapy is hindered unless the psychotherapist and the patient are of the same sex. These instances are comparatively infrequent and tend to occur among individuals seriously disturbed in their psychosexual development. Generally, it is assumed that a professionally trained and disciplined practitioner can be of equal assistance irrespective of the sex of the patient or the client. School counsellors, however, apparently feel that they cannot apply their skills with the same degree of effectiveness to members of the opposite sex. In the light of the above discussion one cannot help wondering whether the division into male and female counsellors does not stem from a fundamental professional insecurity and a basic lack of confidence in teacher-counsellor as professional workers.

It is apparent that vocational guidance as a profession will have to learn a great deal more about counselling the adolescent before a comprehensive rationale can be established. Thus far, as Boynton notes, too much concern has been expressed over counselling techniques and not enough over the helping process itself. Perhaps one of the reasons why relatively little is known about the dynamics of vocational help giving and help taking as applied to adolescents is the fact that such services are offered almost exclusively by the schools. The schools, however, as a rule do not provide an opportunity for the study of adolescent reactions in a counselling situation. Furthermore, the average teacher-counsellor is not professionally equipped to make investigations of the psychological client-counsellor dynamics. Hence, one encounters a predominance of articles dealing with measurements, techniques, and specific hints and very little material that deals with the actual vocational guidance helping process.

It would be inaccurate to suggest that all adolescents are indifferent toward their educational and vocational future. Studies dealing with the problems that beset young people reveal that most adolescents show some concern over their occupational choice. In some instances the young man or woman may take career planning very seriously. To some the quest for a sound vocational plan represents more than a choice of a suitable occupation. Anxious and insecure adolescents may see in vocational selection an answer to their feeling of total inadequacy. Knowing definitely what they are going to do vocationally offers them some consolation and support in the future, especially if they find it difficult to define their place in the present.

There can be little question that many of the dynamics that enter into counselling adults also play a leading role in working with adolescents. But there are important differences, too. The adolescent, by virtue of being young and vocationally inexperienced and going through the transitional stages in relation to his family and society as a whole, presents problems that distinguish him from the fully mature adult. Rall holds that among the major characteristics of maturity are self-security and a capacity to enter into and sustain a love relationship. Many adolescents, precisely because of their age, may experience considerable difficulty in becoming engaged personally in such a process. Such young people may require what she calls a "constructive dependency relationship", which may enable them to weather some of the difficult stages of the counselling process. The counselling, too, by necessity has to be viewed in a new light, not only because of the unique characteristics of adolescence, but because the counsellor-client relationship that is now established takes place between an adult worker and an adolescent client.

Adolescent Optimism

At this point it may be in order to examine some aspects of adolescent personality that make it both" similar to, and different from, adult personality. As a basic premise it is held that an adolescent is a person in his own right. He has needs, drives, and conflicts. He can be happy or disappointed; he can will, and he can become frustrated when his drives are thwarted. Mutually antagonistic impulses arise within him, engendering indecision, anxiety, or guilt. It is entirely probable that because of his limited experience as a conscious human being he feels more poignantly about himself and the events that surround him. Because of his age he has not developed an adequate sense of perspective to enable him to distinguish readily between essentials and trivia. As a young person he does not possess sufficient self-confidence to meet the adult world on an equal footing, nor is he very certain as to what is expected of him. His life is a continuous process of adjustment to the amorphous and frequently threatening environment.

The average adolescent who comes for vocational guidance may, like the adult, experience dis-comfort about his future, show some anxiety regarding his vocational goals, and reveal a considerable number of mixed feelings about the outcome of his educational plans. He may also have some fears about the counselling experience and what it may do to him. Unlike the adult, however, he may be too immature emotionally to appraise the situation or to take upon himself the responsibility for planning, or, for that matter, he may be insufficiently independent of his parents to undertake a course of action solely on the strength of his own convictions. A study conducted by Ryden, for example, reveals that most of the students under investigation regarded their parents as chief vocational guidance counsellors. This same study also noted that the majority of parents estimated incorrectly their children's abilities and interests. Most adolescents do not have the freedom of action enjoyed by adults, and their occupational decisions and preferences are likely to be coloured not only by the kind of thinking that is so characteristic of young and vocationally inexperienced persons but also by the attitudes and aspirations prevalent in their family unit. In a study conducted with preschool children Ackerman and Sobel speak of young children "not as separate individuals, but rather as functional parts of the family group, more specifically, as an expression of the socio-psychological configuration of the family unit." As the child grows older, he becomes a progressively more distinct individual in his own right. By the time he has reached adolescence he has probably given up some of the typical familial characteristics and developed a personality peculiarly his own. But his emancipation is never complete. His vocational aspirations, his attitudes toward work and the various ways of earning a livelihood are still likely to be influenced by the thinking of his immediate family. Thus is not to imply that occupationally he is bound to follow in his father's footsteps. Going in an opposite direction from that taken by his brothers and sisters may be equally suggestive of the part the family unit plays in his vocational choice.

From the standpoint of the present discussion, one of the significant aspects of adolescent development is the boundlessly optimistic outlook on life. The average adolescent believes that somehow, somewhere, his dreams will come true. He usually does not stop to examine the probability of his wishes becoming reality. He is too preoccupied with living in the present. The past is something he wishes to leave behind him as quickly as he can in his efforts to become a full-fledged adult. The future is an enigma, both alluring and frightening, but he is quite confident that he will be able to handle it when the time comes.

Perhaps the wish and reality are not too clearly differentiated in the mind of the young person. The Alluding lamp of childhood has not quite gone out yet, and almost anything may happen if one only wishes hard enough. Wittles, for instance, feels that in our understanding of reality lies the chief difference between childhood and maturity. Vocational counsellors have encountered time and again very mediocre boys who aspire to become statesmen and scientists in the future, while at present they can bardy pass elementary algebra. Physically unattractive girls, who seem to be only too painfully aware of their shortcomings, aspire to become airship stewardesses or television starlets.

In passing it may be worth noting that there does not seem to be much agreement among the investigators who conduct research in vocational aspirations among adolescents. Stubbins, for example, holds that 61 per cent of the young people in his study made an appropriate vocational choice. Myers, on the other hand, reports that in Washington at least 50 per cent of the boys and 55 per cent of the girls intended to enter college and study for a profession despite the fact that only 10 per cent of the total city population were employed in a professional capacity In a certain high school in Buffalo about 90 per cent of the students expressed intentions of going to college although the percentage of Buffalonians having attended college is much lower.

With respect to "glamorous" occupations, there does not seem to be much agreement either. Edmiston and Starr, for instance, found that seventh- to twelfth-grade pupils seemed to regard service to mankind, freedom from political limitations, and effect on health as the most important factors in choosing a career. The least important were adventure and glamour. These findings are not wholly supported by evidence secured through counselling interviews. The explanation for the difference might be sought in the possibility that answers given on a questionnaire need not necessarily agree with attitudes expressed in a counselling session. The questionnaire is likely to elicit the socially more acceptable "correct" replies as against the more candid feelings expressed during counselling.

In all probability this unrealistically positive outlook regarding the vocational future serves as an important adjustment mechanism in the life of the adolescent. He may not be strong enough as yet to face reality as it is, and he has to project himself into an autistic future in order to weather the present. From the counselling standpoint such an attitude is not easy to handle. Nor can the vocational counsellor be certain that it is his responsibility to shatter the occupational dreamworld of the young client. Levin notes correctly that striving to achieve a higher occupational status may engender considerable anxiety. An optimistic outlook may serve as a defence against such anxiety. What would happen if the adolescent client were suddenly compelled to face reality cannot be determined with any degree of certainty.

The Meaning of Time

Closely related to youthful optimism is the meaning time may have in the life of adolescents. It is questionable that, psychological, time as measured by the calendar possesses the same meaning to an adolescent as to adult. Ten years to an adolescent probably does not represent the same amount of time as as middle-aged person. If one considers that a young adolescent may have lived altogether some fifteen years, ten years represents almost his entire conscious life span. The future is far off, and it should therefore not be too surprising if he is not particularly concerned with events so distantly removed from his present. Even an adult with some forty years of life behind him is not likely to become actually disturbed over what may happen to him at the age of seventy. It is this unrealness of the future that deprives the occupational focus of much meaning in counselling with adolescents. There is little emotional involvement in the choice of a career per se.

Many young people would of course like to know in which general occupational areas they are likely to succeed, whether or not they are college material, or what special aptitudes they possess. We have already spoken of curiosity-prompted adolescents who come to the agency primarily for psychometric testing. It is entirely possible that many adolescents cannot use a service that offers assistance beyond occupational information, factual counselling, or individual appraisal of occupational potentialities. The fact that the central theme of vocational guidance is the *future* rather than the present perhaps transforms the entire experience from something that might have significance today to an adventure akin to scientific crystal gazing. The teen-age boy or girl is not always going to draw a sharp line between the psychometric tool and a crystal ball, especially if he is under the impression that either might tell him "what he should do" sometime in the remote future.

Perhaps one of the crucial differences. between vocational counselling with adults and adolescents lies in the fact that most adults who come for occupational assistance have a current vocational problem. When they make plans, these are expected to materialise within a fairly definite and foreseeable future. Adolescents, on the other hand, may have no immediate educational or occupational problem. They are oriented toward the future, but, unlike many adults, their future may be measured in decades instead of months. Some young clients talk glibly of ten years precisely because ten years in the future may have so little actual meaning to a fifteen-year-old.

A case in point is Jack, who during the initial interview expressed a desire to become a psychiatrist.

Jack is a fifteen-year-old sophomore in high school. His father is an optometrist who works for a department store in his professional capacity. Jack has two brothers, twelve and nine. Prior to coming to the agency, Jack had mentioned his interest in psychiatry to his family physician and was told that it would take him approximately fourteen years of preparation from the point at which he was at present. This did not seem to disturb Jack too greatly, since he liked school and appeared to be interested in psychiatry as a profession.

For a moment we left the personal attributes in abeyance but discussed the time factor and its implications. I wondered whether Jack had ever considered being fully supported by his father until the age of twenty-nine. Jack had not thought of that. We then talked about his brothers. Could his father help him financially for so many years and still enable the younger children to go to college too? Jack did not know. Had Jack ever considered getting married and raising a family? How would marriage affect his plans? Had Jack ever thought of following a career that took less time, but one which would enable him to earn a living sooner and become financially independent of his family? Jack acknowledged quite frankly that he had never seen his plans in this light. We then talked about the probability of his being drafted into the armed forces and the effect that might have on his career. Jack had not thought of that either. He still had three years to go before induction. Perhaps he could get deferred. All Jack knew was that there were many years to come. Many unforeseen things would probably happen in the course of time. Somehow everything was going to turn out all right.

Where Jack and thousands like him can be expected to draw a line between dreams and reality is not easy to decide. Nor can the counsellor ascertain the effectiveness of his services with a young client who has given so little thought to the matter at hand. Some young people are undoubtedly disturbed over their educational or vocational dilemmas; others, quite genuinely, do not have a serious vocational problem. Whereas no blanket statement can be made regarding the seriousness with which adolescents regard their occupational future, the competent worker must be read to assist the young client with the latter's vocational problem, whether it can be relieved through psychometric testing or interpersonal relationship. At this point the counsellor has to be particularly attuned to what it is that the young client wants help with. The fact that the adolescent may ask naively for tests need not mean that this is all he wants or can use. On the other hand, the counsellor has to be very careful lest he assume that he knows what the client needs irrespective of what the latter may say.

Time plays another role in counselling with adolescents. We have seen that as a dimension of consciousness it is frequently poorly perceived, especially if compared with either the past or the present. However, the fact that the young person is not always aware of its presence per se does not necessarily militate against its effects. Maturation in general and vocational growth in particular take place irrespective of the adolescent's conscious participation in the process. We have spoken time and again of the adult's emotional unreadiness to accept or to follow a certain idea. It has been implied that such unreadiness can be helped through intensive counselling and that in a course of several sessions the adult can be assisted to overcome some of the difficulties that hold him back. Once some of the emotional conflicts are lessened, the adult client can proceed with his vocational plans. This general principle is probably equally applicable to adolescents whose failure to utilise their potentialities is due primarily to emotional factors.

But the adolescent, precisely because he is still incompletely formed, may be confronted with the phenomenon of unreadiness not as an emotional block, but simply as an aspect of his very youth. Lack of readiness which appears to be due to psychophysiological underdevelopment is not likely to yield to skill ful counselling. Time is perhaps the most important single factor which controls the orderly development of a maturing organism. The counsellor is in no position to bring about in a few hours changes which ordinarily require several years. Hamrin and Paulson make this point when they state, "The youth's final educational choice results from his thinking over a period of many fears rather than from his making an immediate decision at a time of crisis." This is a tremendously important observation, for in a sense it provides counselling of adolescents with a definite frame of reference. Whereas we spoke of process as a significant feature of counselling with adults, process evidently does not play the same role in working with young people. It should be recalled that process was perceived as a growth phenomenon which received its stimulation from the client's desire to effect a vocational change and the counsellor's efforts to help the client to free himself from inner inhibiting influences and thus mobilise and channelise his energies toward an objective of his own choosing. It was furthermore pointed out that the feelings and events that preceded the adult client's visit to the agency could not be considered as a part of such a process, since the counsellor could have no part in it. The question now arises, how much of this hypothesis is applicable to counselling with adolescents? The implications behind the statement of Hamrin and Paulson appear to be that adolescents, because of their psychological immaturity, will tend to follow a course of almost spontaneous development. Whatever may take place between the young client and the counsellor in terms of process cannot significantly modify the physiologically determined rate of ontogenic growth or unfolding. Ginzberg *et al.* express a similar view when they state, "Our basic assumption was that an individual never reaches the ultimate decision at a single moment in time, but through a series of decisions over a period of many years; the cumulative impact is the determining factor". This view poses some very fundamental questions as to the role of the vocational counsellor and the extent of his contribution to the occupational development of the adolescent client. Does the counsellor play a truly significant part in assisting the adolescent with his occupational dilemma, or is he merely one of the numerous "cumulative" factors that will ultimately enable the young client to select a trade or a profession?

Time, therefore, plays a dual role in the counselling of adolescents. It is vague and usually autistic when spoken of as the future; it is barely perceptible, but nevertheless extremely vital, when viewed as an aspect of growth. The counsellor's contributions are of necessity limited, for he cannot endow with the poignant meaning of present that which is in the distant future, nor can he accelerate very markedly the naturally slow maturation process.

Limited Experience with Reality

The young person's limited experience of the world about him is another factor that should be taken into consideration in the counselling of young people. Essentially the adolescent tends to live in the present with little regard for the future. The governing forces, to a large extent, are pleasure and pain; the former is to be sought, the latter avoided whenever possible. The adolescent has not learned yet that there is some pain in every pleasure and some pleasure in every pain. Nor has he learned the simple fact that some discomfort in the present may forestall hardships in the future. Although he has learned, overtly at least, to control his relatively unbridled emotionality, a great deal of maturation is still in store for him if he is to attain the level of a real adult. It is entirely probable that much of his primitive thinking stems from his limited experience of himself and the world about him. In some ways, like a young infant, he still has to experiment with reality in order to be able to distinguish between what he desires should be and what is. The infant explores the physical world by reaching out and placing objects in his mouth. The young person explores the intricate universe of human interrelationships by continuously testing his own strength and that of others.

In the occupational world, the adolescent has a tremendous amount to learn. He may be surrounded by industrial plants, warehouses, and stores, but he knows practically nothing about what goes on inside these. establishments. A surprising number of young people cannot even describe what their own fathers are doing to earn a living. A still larger proportion do not know what the earnings of their fathers are. The importance of work and money is taken for granted, but the adolescent rarely has an intimate understanding of the value of either.

Occupational planning to some young people is no more meaningful than the Pythagorean theorem. Intellectually they have accepted the general premise that it is advisable to plan and to prepare oneself for a worthwhile occupation. However, because of their meager fund of factual information and their emotional unreadiness, such an undertaking does not involve them to a great extent.

Discussions of various occupations, trips to industrial plants, and similar activities may be of some value in providing occupational information and provoking some thought along vocational lines. How much value such projects actually have in helping the individual adolescent clarify his own occupational thinking is not known definitely. We have already talked about the tendency to abstract from any situation only that kind of information which is meaningful. An adolescent visiting a steel plant, for example, is likely to come out with the impressions about the industry which he had entertained prior to his visit. This is not to deny the fact that in some instances learning and acquisition of new knowledge and attitudes do take place. However, such a change is going to be contingent upon the individual's personal maturity, his need to learn about new occupations, and his ability to translate the objective evidence into personally meaningful material.

Although most adolescents require a great deal of information about the world of work before they can plan realistically, such information will not be particularly helpful if conveyed on a purely intellectual level. An overall psychological readiness is essential. Although many counsellors may feel that factual information is the clay out of which the young client will mold his vocational future, many young people do not share this view. In a characteristically adolescent manner they may tend to disregard that which is deemed so vital by the counsellor, only to become absorbed by inconsequential trivia.

Adult criteria cannot be applied to basically immature young people. In order to do effective counselling, the value and meaning of adolescent experiences must be gauged from the standpoint of the adolescent, not from that of the counsellor. The counsellor has to accept the adolescent client for what he is and try to be of help to him on the level understandable to a young person. Counsellors who insist on viewing the vocational problem from their own, rather than the client's, point of view cannot be very helpful to either the adult or the adolescent client.

This raises the important concept which sometimes is referred to as the phenomenological approach to behaviour. In essence it postulates that to be helpful to the client, the counsellor must attempt to see the world in terms meanings that exist for the client. Whatever the client does or says has to be understood from the client's standpoint and evaluated in terms of what such actions or statements may mean to him. At times the very concept of self becomes comprehensible only if considered in its phenomenological significance. Segel makes this point clear when he says, "The *phenomenal self* as used here must not be confused with the physical self. It includes not only the physical self but all the meanings which the individual has attached to the word 'I'—the ideas he has of himself, the things he believes he stands for, the kind of a person he thinks he is".

As a tentative hypothesis it may be postulated that "growing up," or the maturation process, is essentially a movement in the direction of reconciling the phenomenological (or phenomenal) self with objective reality. What we actually are and what we think we are (*i.e.*, how we perceive ourselves) may be conceived as a ratio the limits of which are 1 (lim $a/a' = 1$). The very young child's idea of himself is frequently completely at variance with what he actually is, i.e., a little boy or a little girl. As the child grows older, the reality principle begins to play an increasingly important role in his life. The adolescent is no longer the omnipotent magician of his earlier years, though he still seems to himself quite capable, if not in the present, then certainly in the future. It may take many additional years before the individual begins to see himself as he is seen by others. Actually, he will never reach this point but will merely "approach it as a limit," to express it mathematically.

Reality and its influence on the vocational growth of the adolescent may also be determined to a large extent by the economic forces characteristic of his group. A few remarks about the significance of the socioeconomic status of the adolescent in relation to his occupational planning may be in place. The importance of this subject is frequently minimised in counselling with high school students. It is assumed that in a democracy opportunities for advancement and personal development are equal to all. In practice, however, the counsellor may discover that the socioeconomic background of the individual and his immediate family frequently determines his educational and vocational choice. Most children of the lower-income groups tend to reveal different vocational aspirations from those raised in economically and culturally superior environments.

Special problems may arise when the young client wishes to abandon the general vocational pattern set by his family and attempts to select an occupation that lies outside the experience of his socio-economic group. Such a move may be entirely un-realistic in terms of the support his family can give him in pursuing his objectives. If the young person persists, he may precipitate a serious conflict between himself and his parents. Parents who hold one or more academic degrees each and are in the professional field are likely to be sorely disappointed if their son chooses a trade or decides to become a labourer. Similarly, parents with a minimal educational background may frown upon a son's high professional aspirations. Realistic vocational assistance demands that the counsellor recognise the parental attitudes and the extent of approval and support the elders may give in helping their child with his educational plan.

It is a truism that many young people think of their vocational future with a comparative, disregard for reality. Their selection of a career is often guided by wishful thinking unsupported by the opportunities that would make the choice real. The wishful nature of their vocational aspirations may be revealed by the selection of occupations for which there is little demand, occupations that in practice are restricted to the select few, or occupations for which the young people are personally unequipped. Failure to take into consideration the members of his family and their socioeconomic status in general may lead to serious friction in the vocational area or render the plans themselves utterly worthless. The case of Veronica illustrates the adolescent's lack of realism as related to status in society.

Veronica is a fourteen-year-old girl of approximately average general ability (IQ 103). She has two sisters and one brother older than she. Her father, formerly a trackwalker, has been dead for several years. Her mother and her brother (the oldest child in the family) are employed in industry on a semiskilled level. The two older sisters are in high school. The family is continuously in difficult financial straits. Veronica's brother left high school when still in his second year.

At present Veronica is a freshman in a high school that is attended chiefly by children of middle-class families. Many of the parents are businessmen or are employed in a managerial or professional capacity. Going to college is practically taken for granted by most students in this school. Quite naturally, Veronica, too, is planning to go to college. She wants to become a high school teacher or an airship stew-ardess.

As we talked about the feasibility of Veronica's educational plans, she revealed complete ignorance as to what going to college would mean, how much it would cost, etc. (For example, Veronica thought that it took two years to graduate from college and that it cost about $200 a year.) None of Veronica's relatives ever graduated from high school. Veronica's sisters are taking a "business sequence" course and expect to find work immediately after graduation. Veronica has never discussed her plans with her mother concretely. When she did broach the subject on a few occasions, her mother ridiculed it gently and evidently did not take Veronica seriously. Despite her mother's attitude and the practical improbability, at the moment, at least, Veronica is convinced that she will go to college.

It is fairly obvious that in counselling with Veronica the worker could not take it upon himself to decide whether Veronica should continue with her seemingly unrealistic daydreams. On the other hand, Veronica herself was too young to know what reality might have in store for her and how to cope with it. It, was imperative to solicit Veronica's mother's help to enable. Veronica to plan more realistically. It was suggested to Veronica that a three-way conference might help her with the educational dilemma. During the following visit Veronica told the worker that her mother could not afford to lose a day's pay in order to come to the agency. She was too tired to come after work. Since Veronica appeared to be very much under the influence of her "crowd," all of whom planned to go to college, little progress was made in helping Veronica to appraise the situation more realistically. It was indicated to Veronica that she should feel free to return when she reaches her junior or senior year.

This is a rather pathetic case of young girl of average ability and decidedly below average social, economic, and cultural background who found herself accidentally surrounded by children most of whom were of superior ability and enjoyed many benefits unknown to her. Vocational guidance, college education, and a profession apparently meant little to Veronica's mother and the rest of the family. These concepts were alien to Veronica's milieu and were probably looked upon with understandable mistrust, if not outright hostility. Considering Veronica's adolescent immaturity, it is doubtful that the counsellor could have made significant gains without a real understanding on the part of Veronica's mother, and yet such acceptance was not forth-coming.

Veronica's case was presented as an illustration of the kind of problem a counsellor may encounter in connection with the question of social background. In order to help the adolescent client plan realistically, it is usually necessary to consider not only the individual's attributes but also the values and aspirations prevalent in his particular group.

Changeability

Another attribute of adolescence which is of importance in vocational counselling is the fact that the average adolescent is likely to change his educational and vocational plans several times in the course of a few years, until he finally decides on what he would like to do. The greater the opportunity for occupational selection, the more often will he change his mind, other things being equal. This characteristic, too, seems to be culturally rather than biologically determined. When the vocational opportunities are limited, as they have been in the past or among certain strata today, the adolescent is likely to follow the vocational pattern set for him by his father and his immediate associates. Thus, by and large, farmers' children become farmers, just as the offspring of professional workers usually enter a professional field. However, when the occupational choice is almost unlimited, the adolescent is likely to choose different goals as his interests and knowledge of the world about him mature. Interest patterns vary from decade to decade and from group to group. Young people, who seldom examine critically the basis for their individual occupational preference, are likely to follow the trends of their own socioeconomic "crowd." This may account for the popularity of certain occupations at various periods. Individual experiences in the occupational area, looks about a "glamorous" field, or a motion picture that glorifies a special kind of work are sometimes sufficiently powerful in their influence to sway the impressionable adolescent from one vocational objective to another.

In discussing a theory of occupational choice Ginzberg notes that occupational decision-making can be classified according to three periods: "*fantasy* choices (before 11); *tentative* choices (between 11 and 17); 'and *realistic* choices (between 17 and young adulthood) when a person finally determines his choice". These stages can be further distinguished in terms of basic factors which play a dominant role in determining the choice. Thus interest is of primary importance under eleven. Later on the adolescent takes into consideration his capacities and values. The realistic stage begins with exploration and is followed by crystallisation and specification stages. Ginzberg furthermore notes that at times "the pattern is defective when, for example, a 17 -year-old deals with his choice solely in terms of his interest without reference to his capacities. or his values, as would the typical 11 year old".

The tendency to select an occupation chiefly on the basis of interest is sometimes pathetically revealed at the conclusion of "career days," held by some high schools as a part of their vocational programme. Young students who have listened to eloquent speakers on these occasions often emerge with a feeling that they have discovered their occupational ambition in life. The fact that personally they may be completely unequipped to enter the particular area does not always enter their minds. Nor does it occur to them that had they wandered into another room, where a different field was discussed, they would conceivably have come out with an entirely different choice.

We have seen that objective evidence, especially if it happens to be in opposition to one's fundamental needs, is usually disrearded by the client. The fact that a speaker may have stressed the high standards and rigorous training required by a certain profession does not necessarily deter the high school student from pursuing unrealistic educational goals. Frook's study illustrates this point quite well when he notes that, out of 81 high school seniors planning to enter college, only 54 students ranked in the 50th percentile or higher on the Henmon-Nelson test. As many as 12 students fell in the 25th percentile or below. The fact that some of these seniors were probably aware of their intellectual limitations apparently did not affect their educational plans seriously.

Only recently two young men came to see me about their occupational plans. While still active with the agency they attended the career day held by their high school. Both continued with their vocational guidance programme after that event. A few facts about each case may serve to illustrate how some adolescents seem to decide their vocational future.

Phil is a short, chubby adolescent with wavy, dark hair and thick eyeglasses. His speech is somewhat nasal and not always clear. When he saw me originally, he thought he would like to join his father in a retail clothing business after his graduation from college. He was planning to major in business administration. Phil's average in school is 81; IQ 107; reading retarded by about one year. His measured interests lie in the persuasive and clerical areas.

After the career day, Phil said that he was now interested in television and radio announcing. The speaker at school had told the students that the field of television was expanding, the salaries were good, and the right person entering it would probably do well. Apparently without too much hesitation Phil decided that this work was for him. When asked how he happened to select this particular topic among the different subjects discussed that day, he said simply that he "went along with a friend."

Leonard was the other client who seemed to succumb to the impact of oratory.

Leonard came into the agency to discuss the question of his becoming an attorney. At the beginning of our contact he told me that he had entertained that idea for a few years. Leonard's scholastic average is in the high 80's; IQ 116 reading score on a high average level; measured interests quite pronounced in the persuasive, social service, and literary areas.

After having attended a career-day session Leonard expressed an interest in becoming a draftsman. He, too, was impressed by the glorious opportunities in that field, When I wondered how he happened to attend a session on drafting rather than law, he explained that the room in which law was discussed was filled and, since he had arrived a few minutes late, there was no vacant seat left. There were plenty of seats in the other room, however; so he sat through the session on drafting.

Whether or not the two examples cited above are typical of adolescent vocational thinking in general cannot be determined at the moment, although studies that might provide an answer could probably be set up without too much difficulty. How strong and lasting the vocational interests of young people are is another subject that requires further investigation. The consensus seems to be that for large groups of adolescents over-all interest patterns do not change greatly over a relatively short course of time.

Daily observations suggest that some children develop certain occupational patterns of interest at an early age and retain these general preferences through adolescence into adulthood. Others, for whatever reason, never seem to develop any marked interests in anyone field but tend to vacillate their entire lives. Individual maturity, the home environment, and an opportunity to come into contact with different occupations are probably some of the factors that determine vocational preferences. Chance, too, plays an important part in shaping the ultimate outcome of occupational development. In retrospect, many adults realise that, if it were not for certain accidental events that occurred many years ago, their lives from the occupational standpoint might be quite different from what they actually are. In discussing "accidents" as determining factors in occupational selection, Ginzberg *et al.* note conically that, although external factors (opportunities, etc.) do play a role in choosing a career, the choice itself is never purely "accidental." Certain deep-seated personality patterns usually provide the background that make the "accident" possible.

❑❑❑

10

Some Principles in Counselling with Adolescents

The discussion in the preceding chapter was concerned chiefly with four aspects of adolescent development which may be of particular interest to the vocational counsellor. These were the adolescent's optimism regarding his occupational future; his subjective perception of time, which frequently attenuates the intensity of the vocational conflict; his limited experience with occupations and the working universe in general; and finally his impressionability and changeability with respect to vocational goals. Multiple external circumstances and intrapsychic factors undoubtedly contribute further to the complexity of the situation, thus placing the adolescent among the most difficult groups with which counselling has been undertaken. The relative paucity of information concerning the helping process with young people tends to endow the entire discussion with a hypothetical quality which demands further investigation and verification. The foregoing four attributes of growing up were selected, not because they are necessarily the most important single aspects of adolescent development, but because they appear to be prevalent in structuring and influencing the vocational guidance process. In an occupationally focused client counsellor relationship these attributes tend to appear repeatedly with a Vivid intensity. The question under consideration is not the total personality of the young client but his capacity to benefit from a vocational counselling experience and his ability to use himself as well as the worker in constructive and positive manner. Some principles on which counselling with adolescent is predicated.

The Adolescent's Right to be Adolescent

It has several times seem started emphatically that a client can be helped vocationally only to the extent that he is able to help himself. This does not mean that the client is expected to administer and interpret his own psychological tests or search through, the volumes in a public library to discover the current occupational trends or job opportunities in a particular area. The counsellor has responsibilities to the client in assisting him with a vocational diagnosis or providing him with factual information on which to base his vocational decision. But we have seen that the counsellor's functions extend considerably beyond diagnosis and fact finding. It has been stressed that the counsellor's chief function lies in assisting the client with the assimilation of facts about, himself and the occupational world around him. It is to be hoped that the client can take hold of the process during the helping stages of vocational counselling. How much he will benefit from the vocational experience will depend greatly on the extent to which he can participate in the counselling relationship and on his will to bring about a change. Although the counsellor can offer the client an opportunity to work out some of his occupational problems, he can never work them out for him. Thus vocational guidance is always a self directed process. Hankins stresses this point further when she says, "... it is not enough to have help to offer, it is equally necessary that the helping situation be one in which the recipient can become sufficiently engaged to make the help his own. This is true of people of all ages; it is doubly true of adolescents.

Ingle notes that in dealing with an adolescent the worker can offer him a secure relationship with an understanding adult. With the counsellor's help the adolescent has an opportunity to work out his feelings of ambivalence toward himself and others. This is particularly important when the young client's occupational plans are at variance with those of his parents.

It is difficult to conceive how intensive vocational help can be offered adolescent without the active participation and involvement of his parents. Perhaps this comment needs further qualification. Vocational guidance as it exists today is not always perceived a helping process that demand the fullest use of oneself. We have seen that vocational guidance is frequently limited to its testing (diagnostic) aspects, to a matching of the client's measurable attributes with the prevalent occupational trends, or to suggestions and expert advice. It is on relatively rare occasions that the client is provided with an opportunity to examine his own needs and their subjective meaning and is assisted by the counsellor to overcome his emotional blocking in order that he may formulate his own plans. Similarly, it is only infrequently that the client finds himself in a situation wherein he must assume the responsibilities for his own occupational choice or must develop sufficient strength to become independent of the counsellor. Vocational guidance that is predicated on measurement and a general evaluation of the young client's fitness for a particular trade or career probably does not demand that his parents share actively in the vocational process. To many in-school adolescents vocational guidance is but a fleeting experience. They are too young to plan, and the plans themselves look to the distant future. Hence vocational counselling is deprived of much meaning. The adolescent's contact with the vocational counsellor is at times too superficial to demand that his parents participate in the process. The case of Margaret may be used as an illustration.

Margaret is a rather timid girl of fifteen. She is in her second year at Jefferson High School, where she is maintaining a 93 average. Her father is a pharmacist; her mother is rather active as a volunteer in community affairs. The family lives in a good socio-economic neighborhood. They also own a cottage at the beach.

Margaret came in for aptitude testing as a result of a talk on vocational guidance she heard in high school. In a general way Margaret would like to know what she should take up in college and what she is best suited for. At the moment Margaret cannot think of any problems. She likes school and participates to a moderate extent in extracurricular activities. Tentatively Margaret has thought of social work as a possible career, although she knows very little about the field. Margaret is planning quite definitely on getting married soon after her graduation from college.

The counsellor talked with Margaret about her interests, hobbies, and leisuretime activities. Margaret appeared to be a thoroughly likable, quite well-adjusted young lady. From the occupational standpoint she took for granted that she would go to college (all her friends were planning to do likewise) although she was not certain whether she should major in literature or sociology. (Further discussion revealed that by "sociology" she meant social work.) When the counsellor asked Margaret how she thought the agency could assist her, Margaret replied that she hoped the tests might help her decide what subjects to take in college. The school counsellor whom she heard address some group in school seems to have emphasised the advisability of career planning and the value of testing. Margaret did not appear to have any real educational or occupational conflicts regarding her future. Margaret impressed the counsellor as being somewhat dependent on the judgement of others. When the counsellor raised the question whether Margaret's parents had any vocational aspirations or preferences for her, Margaret said that her parents "want me to be happy and would not stand in my way." Margaret did not think that there was much point in discussing her vocational guidance plans with her mother, especially since the latter was quite a busy person. It was fairly apparent that, although Margaret was curious about vocational guidance, and testing in particular, she was not going to let herself (or her family) become intimately involved in the vocational guidance programme. Prior to coming to the agency, Margaret had indicated to her mother that she was about to make an appointment for some "aptitude tests." Her mother thought that it was "a good idea" but did not regard that event as being of any particular significance.

Cases such as Margaret's are common indeed. The majority of high school adolescents (and their parents) do not view the vocational guidance experience as meaningful events in their lives. Quite the contrary, they tend to regard it as an aspect of the broader educational process comparable perhaps with a field trip to a museum or a library.

The case of Lenore is in sharp contrast to that of Margaret.

Lenore K is fifteen and a freshman at Central High School. Her average is about 96. She is taking a commercial course but is unhappy because a business preparatory course will not qualify her for admission to college. She is following the present curriculum strictly at the insistence of her father.

Lenore's father is a small poultry butcher. He has three other daughters older than Lenore, none of whom is married. Mr. K is quite concerned lest his daughters become a "bunch of old maids." Mr. K does not think that girls should go to college. That, he feels, reduces their chances for marriage. He believes that a girl should work as soon as she is of age. Even high school education is superfluous and an undesirable innovation Mr. K was born and spent his youth in an orthodox Jewish community in Poland. He is resentful because he has no male heir to pray for him after his death.

Lenore, however, has very different views regarding the place of a woman in society. She further more has a definite interest in learning and is determined to go to college, even if she has to attend evening session. Lenore has not worked out too clearly for herself what she could do vocationally but thinks that she would like to become either a chemist or a biologist. She has also considered becoming a high school science teacher.

Several tests were administered to Lenore, on which she attained the following scores.

Kuder Preference Record:

Mechanical ---------------------------------- 83rd percentile

Computational ------------------------------ 90th percentile

Scientific ------------------------------------ 95th percentile

Social service ------------------------------- 86th percentile

Clerical --------------------------------------- 15th percentile

(Other areas fell between 25th and 75th percentile)

Henmon-Nelson Test of Mental Ability ----- IQ132

Nelson-Denny Reading test ----------------- gE16

There can be little question that Lenore possesses many attributes that suggest that going to college is an excellent occupational choice, and yet, because of parental interference, it is unlikely that she will be given an opportunity to utilise her potentialities. The final counselling session was accompanied with considerable weeping. Lenore knew what she wanted, but she saw no way of attaining her objectives. When worker wondered whether Lenore's parents would want to come in for a consultation, Lenore expressed grave doubts. Mrs. K. is apparently a weak, docile woman,very much dominated by her husband. She is quite sympathetic to Lenore's plans but does not dare to oppose her husband openly. There was no point in her seeing the counsellor. Mr. K. on the other hand, would probably refuse flatly to have anything to do with the agency. As a matter of fact, he was quite annoyed when he learned of Lenore's contacts with the counsellor.

Lenore's case, unlike that of Margaret, certainly would seem to require fullest parental participation, and yet such participation could not be obtained because of Mr. K's refusal to see the counsellor. A letter was written to Mr. K, apprising him, in general terms, of Lenore's vocational potentialities, and offering him an opportunity to discuss some of the problems personally, Mr. K did not respond, and the family has not been heard from since.

Numerous other illustrations showing the need for parental participation could be cited. Some parents recognise their role in vocational guidance readily enough and work with the counsellor and their child toward the resolution of vocational conflicts. Other parents themselves need help in order to assist the adolescent with his occupational or educational problems. In working with adolescents the counsellor may have to deal with the young person and his parents, or sometimes he is compelled to work with the child alone. In the latter instance the counsellor must represent reality and help the client clarify his rational and irrational impulses, especially as they may relate to his educational or occupational plans. Ingle furthermore feels that "one of the greatest services caseworkers can offer the adolescent is an adult's secure belief that the adolescent can do things for himself that he can make his own decisions, that he is a potential adult".

The vocational counsellor not experience some difficulty in attempting to reconcile the seemingly contradictory views which, on the one hand, advocate a "constructive dependency relationship" and, on the other, appear to demand considerable maturity and self-directiveness from the adolescent. This paradox may be understood if one re-examines the dynamics of self-determination and the problems of maturing and growing up. The difficulties that accompany adolescence in general and the problems that may arise out of the counselling relationship. Hankins recognises the dilemma when she says, Adolescents need support, too, and the problem is how it can be provided and yet have the young person free to be as responsible for the coming as he is possibly capable of being."

Certain factors and principles inherent in vocational counselling apply to most age groups. Among these are the existence of a conflict, the wish to do something about it, and the right to self-determination. Needless to say, these are not fixed all-or-none entities that are equally expressed by each age group and every individual. The younger the client is, the less likely he is to articulate the nature of his difficulty. The fact that the client cannot formulate clearly and concisely the reason for his coming to the agency or the kind of help he wants does not mean that he does not need help or cannot use it. One of the objectives of the intake interview is to assist the client to verbalise his problem, to help him express his desire for help (which is often so difficult to do), and, finally, to aid him in deciding whether or not he wants to go ahead with the programme.

The necessity for the existence of a problem as a prerequisite for counselling is questioned by some workers in the field. Williamson, for example, seems to feel that the vast majority of in-school youth can profit from vocational counselling, irrespective of whether they have a problem. A similar opinion is expressed by, Berdie when he states, "Counselling provided by a well trained, capable counsellor is an educational technique which can benefit all students. The difference in viewpoints probably, stems from the understanding of the concept of counselling. Certainly a better understanding that various occupations and training requirement is desirable for the student body as a whole. Some objective appraisal of the individual interests, aptitudes, and abilities may also be of value in helping the student formulate the broader aspects of his vocational future. These objectives can be attained through group guidance and group psychometric testing, augmented by an individual interview with the school counsellor. But such guidance activity, although desirable, is not counselling. Counselling signifies a deeper process which cannot be set into motion unless a problem exists and unless the client is sufficiently concerned about it to take some action.

These principles are equally applicable to both adult and adolescent clients, except that adolescents, because of their youth will probably react to the vocational guidance contact in a manner characteristic of their age group. Just as one cannot apply adult standards of behaviour to young children, one cannot measure the adolescent's personality by adult norms. It is the child's right to act as a child and to be a child. The counsellor would not expect a three-year-old to act in a grown-up manner. Similarly, the teenage client should not be required to make decisions, assume responsibilities, and act on his own free will to the same extent as an adult. The adolescent, too, has a right to be adolescent.

The counsellor must understand the hostility that so many adolescents harbour against the adult world. He may have to help the adolescent resolve some of the educational or vocational conflicts that stem from his lack of self-confidence, his dependence, his changeability, and his limited experience and knowledge. Hankins notes, "... if childhood is a period of identification with others, we can think of adolescence as a period of projection." In other words, most adolescents perceive their troubles as caused by parents, school, or events outside their control. They may recognise a need to change the situation around them to buy a new car, move out of the neighbourhood, change friends, etc. rather than seeing the desirability of making an inner change. Perhaps the most significant basis for the relationship between the young client and the adult counsellor is the latter's recognition of and respect for the adolescent's being what he is. If the adolescent is noncommunicative, embarrassed, flippant, or inattentive, if he refuses to enter into a meaningful relationship with the counsellor or cannot do beyond the testing phase, the counsellor must accept these characteristics for what the are. Although it is the counsellor responsibility to assist the young client to become dynamically engaged in the vocational process, he should not deny the adolescent the privilege of remaining adolescent. If an adolescent is to be helped vocationally, he has to be helped as the young person that he is, not changed into an adult.

The Right to be Dependent

It was noted previously that adolescence is a recent outgrowth of our culture. In a sense it represents an extension of childhood with its numerous implications. Statutory laws and unwritten customs make the adolescent basically dependent on the adult for major decisions and actions. Young adolescents cannot marry without their parents' consent, nor can they obtain employment unless they can show their working papers. They cannot travel without their parents' permission or buy a glass of beer in a tavern. Aside from the legal aspects of the situation, the adolescent is dependent upon his home for security, affection, and guidance. Individual parents, without quite realising it, will, frequently foster immaturity in their offspring because of their personal psychic needs. The paternalistic and directive attitude of the school system further discourages the adolescent's efforts at independent action. The high school student has to adhere to a rigid code of rules and regulations that govern his attendance, lateness, homework, and conduct in general. Considering the amount of regimentation that surrounds the average young person, it is not surprising that rebelliousness has been described as an adolescent trait. But rebelliousness does not exist without an element of conformism. The adolescent has a need to assert himself as well as to conform. He experiments with new experiences but also clings to that which he considers his own and with which he feels secure. By and large the average young person has learned to regard his father, his uncle, his teacher as someone in authority, someone whose judgement he can trust and on whom he can depend.

When the adolescent meets the counsellor for the first time, he quite naturally expects to be told what vocational career to follow and how to go about it. This is quite understandable if one considers the fact that he has probably always been told what to do. The more important the issue, the more advice he has received. The counsellor, endowed with an aura of expertness according to the adolescent, is the most logical and the best-qualified person to give such advice. The feeling of dependence in the adolescent, unlike that in the adult, need not stem from some form of psychological underdevelopment or maladjustment. It stems rather from the fact that he is young, immature, and inexperienced. In his naivete he comes to the counsellor for concrete advice and psychoneurotic testing because he has been led to believe that these are the services the counsellor is pared to offer. The average adolescent has never paused to examine the psychological implications of directive counselling, nor does he know anything about psychometric measures. It may be argued, and justly so, that neither do most adults have a particularly clear understanding of the vocational process. There is one important difference, however. The normal adult, presumably by virtue of his age, has learned to a greater or lesser extent to think and act for himself. He has had the experience of making his own decisions when confronted with a difficult choice. The adolescent, on the other hand, does not have the necessary years behind him. He has rarely, if ever, been called upon to make use of himself. When confronted with the need for making an important choice, he has always depended on his parents, his teacher, or the family physician to assume the responsibility for the decision. It is therefore entirely understandable that in coming to the agency for educational or vocational guidance he perpetuates this pattern by expecting the counsellor to the him what to do.

The adolescent may present a problem to the counsellor because the latter cannot be certain how much responsibility the young client is ready and able to take upon himself. He cannot know how much of the dependent attitude stems from the fact that the client is too young to assume the entire burden of planning for himself and how much is an expression of personal immaturity. Unfortunately there are no norms. The counsellor has to decide this important question solely on the basis of his impression of the client and his experience as a professional worker. It is entirely possible that many young clients do not complete their vocational contacts because they find the new experience of deciding for themselves too frightening. We saw previously that many nature adults often find it extremely difficult to participate in a process wherein they are expected to assume the initiative and the responsibility for their action. An adolescent who has led a relatively sheltered and dependent existence will probably find such a situation even more untenable. Some adolescents at the time they first visit the agency are not ready to go beyond the stage of taking tests and being told what specific vocational plans to pursue. They seem to be too immature to participate in the helping process, especially since the entire problem of occupational planning is too vague to enable them to mobilise their emotional resources around it.

Some individual adolescents will undoubtedly derive more benefit than others from the entire experience. The counsellor may have to explore with the young client the extent to which he is able to enter into a personal relationship, the kind of plans that may have meaning to him, and the amount of sharing and independent thinking he is capable of. In discussing diagnosis we mentioned the fact that the counsellor will often be called upon to decide whether the problem with which the client wants help falls within the function of the agency and whether the client is receptive to vocational counselling. The latter decision is based not upon a static concept or a diagnostic label such as "schizoid personality" but upon the client's actual ability to participate in the counselling process. Clients who during the interview reveal that they suffer from delusions or live in a world of psychotic fantasy or in general evince signs of personality deterioration are obviously not capable of benefiting from vocational guidance. Dynamic diagnosis plays a definite part in counselling with any age group. In dealing with adolescents the counsellor is called upon to as certain whether or not a particular young client is likely to gain from the vocational process. A client's youthful, and immature appearance need not indicate that he is not genuinely anxious about his vocational future or is incapable of active participation in the process. Conversely, an older adolescent, because of his individual experience and make-up, may not be ready to gain significantly from the vocational contact. The safest procedure for the counsellor is to make no assumptions about the client but to proceed with counselling and thus empirically determine the extent of his ability to make use of himself and the agency. Frequently one interview will be sufficiently revealing to help both the young client and the counsellor decide whether or not additional appointments should be made. In working with particularly dependent and immature adolescents, the counsellor may have to recognise the fact that even deciding on whether the vocational contacts should be continued may be too big an issue for a particular individual. The young client may insist that the counsellor decide for him whether or not further visits are indicated. Such, an attitude would suggest that he is quite unprepared to take an active part in counselling. A recognition of his unreadiness, augmented by some re-assurance by the counsellor, give the contact a termination which does not appear to be a rejection. The counsellor may indicate that he realises how difficult it may be at the moment for the client to decide whether or not he should return, pointing out simultaneously that he may feel free to continue with the discussion at any time he wishes. A frank statement to the effect that in a year or two the adolescent client may want to delve more deeply into his planning may help him return when he is emotionally more mature. However, simple as such a procedure may seem, the counsellor must be quite certain that the adolescent's failure to become engaged in the process is due primarily to the absence of a vocational conflict and the kind of unreadiness. He must also feel fairly certain that he has provided the young person with every opportunity to explore his needs and to become personally involved. As Korner sees it, it may be necessary to "disengage" (step back from the situation) and to evaluate the counsellor's feelings about the termination of the contact, lest the counsellor's, rather than the client's, needs become the determining motive. Whatever characteristic adolescents may share in common as a group, they still are individuals endowed with unique personalities. The counsellor has to be extremely careful that he does not terminate the vocational guidance contact because the client appears to be "just another kid."

The Focus with Adolescents

An adult harassed by the problems of daily existence will oftentend to bring all his difficulties to the attention of the worker. Considering the dynamic interrelationship in tension-arousing situations, it is never easy to separate problems of economic adjustment from those of family counselling or parent-child relationship. Lack of employment for the head of the family is very likely to affect the intrafamilial balance and give rise to new problems that further intensify the conflict. We have already seen that at times the educational or vocational problem is merely peripheral to a more basic complaint. Although the client may be asking for help on the occupational level, the true focus is often on the total personality.

When an adolescent comes for vocational help, he may have even more difficulty than the adult in delimiting his problem and establishing a focus. This, too, would appear to be his prerogative. A young child tends to think in whole concepts and often overlooks the nuances that make up the details. As he gets older, he begins to perceive the subtler gradations of which the whole is composed. Many adolescents who come for vocational guidance are still at a stage where their difficulties are sensed in a totality, and it may be very hard for them to concentrate on one aspect of their problem. In working with adolescents several foci may emerge. A young man who has conflicts over his choice of a career may attribute his difficulties to his father, who is perhaps actively opposing his son's vocational preferences. Here we have two related foci. Ideally, a caseworker and a vocational counsellor could work jointly on the case and help both father and son. In practice, this is rarely possible. The counsellor may be compelled to assume the responsibility for helping both. When the counsellor sees the father, he will limit himself to the educational or vocational aspects of the problem in the sense that he will try to enable the father to free himself from his need to control his son vocationally. In dealing with the son, the worker will attempt to assist him to gain independence from excessive paternal dominance as related to vocational planning. In both instances the focus is the choice of a career within the framework of reality. The focus is not father-son relationship per se.

At this point a word of caution may be in order. In working with the adolescent and his father (or parents in general) the counsellor may discover that there exists considerable hostility between father and son. Impulsively the counsellor may tend to identify himself with either one and, without quite realising it himself, may work with the adolescent against the father or with the' father against the young client. A counsellor attuned to the danger of such identification can frequently be of greater assistance to both father and son by helping the father understand some of the dynamics involved and may thus secure his support in assisting the young man in working out his vocational future.

The concept of vocational focus may be particularly difficult for the adolescent to grasp, for he has not as yet attained the ability to delineate very clearly. The adolescent's tendency to present and to perceive his problems in a rather diffuse manner may be actually a protective device against the frequently painful reality that emerges when the focus is sharpened. The difficulty in focusing on his occupational dilemma may also be due to the fact that, although he is seeing the counsellor presumably because he wants vocational assistance, actually other than vocational problems prey on his mind. Dumpson quotes Dudley in enumerating the chief areas which are of concern to young people. Dudley states, "The major problems of adolescence are to loosen the emotional ties of the family, to become self supporting, to develop a heterosexual attitude, and to form a definite policy toward life". Although self-support is related to career planning, it rarely constitutes as immediate a problem as sexual adjustment or emancipation from the dominance of the family. The latter problem, Baumann and Hurvitz note, is sometimes so intense as to precipitate socially unacceptable behaviour which may compel another member of the family to seek outside help. Vocational indecision rarely takes on such a dramatic aspect, unless the occupational conflict becomes an outlet for a more fundamental parent-child discord.

Ross and Johnson, too, seem to feel that "the central problem of the adolescent is to emancipate himself from the childish dependence on the parents and to work out good, warm relationships with members of his own sex and then with members of the opposite sex." The relatively secondary role assigned to career planning may explain to some extent why it is sometimes so difficult to establish a meaningful relationship with the young client around a strictly vocational focus. Vocational guidance simply may not appear important to an adolescent specially if, at the moment, he is preoccupied with the problems of finding himself in relation to his family and society in general.

Relationship with Adults

Thus far we have touched upon some of the difficulties that confront both the counsellor and the client when intensive work with adolescents is undertaken. It has been shown that the question of occupational planning is frequently too indefinite in the mind of the young client to engender strong conflicts and a correspondingly intense desire to do something about his occupational future. It has also been pointed out that many adolescents are ready to assume only limited responsibility for their decisions or actions. Lastly, we have discussed the difficulties encountered by many young people when faced with the need to focus sharply on the purely occupational aspects of the problem.

The next point to be considered is the question of the relationship between the adolescent client and the adult counsellor. Perhaps the simplest way of describing this is to say that essentially it is an interaction between the small and the big. In the counselling situation the teen-age boy or girl may assign to himself the role of a dependent, essentially passive, and perhaps helpless person. By contrast, he may endow the counsellor with wisdom, prestige, and authority. The preconceived juxtaposition is likely to influence much of what is to take place during the interviews.

It was mentioned previously that many adolescents regard the adult world with some suspicion and hostility. A denial of these attitudes is not likely to be helpful. Many an adolescent has heard it said only too often that a punishment is for his own good. Similarly, a counsellor's assurance that he is interested in the young client's welfare may not be particularly convincing. To be effective, the counsellor may have to go considerably beyond verbal reassurance and demonstrate to the client that he recognises the young person's right to be different, has an understanding of the latter's feelings, and respects his being himself. But the counsellor must also face the reality of the situation which insists on the fact that the counsellor is an adult and the client is fundamentally a child. By virtue of his youth, the client is less mature, less experienced, more impulsive, and more optimistic. Perhaps if he were not an adolescent, with all the implications, he might not even need vocational assistance. The young client may be coming for help because he wants occupational information and an interpretation of facts and events about him and because he needs the emotional support and security which he cannot find elsewhere.

The fact that the young client may want a warm and understanding relationship with the worker does not mean that he can ask for it in a clear and concise manner. What has been said earlier about the difficulties adults may have about taking help may apply with even greater force to the adolescent. The counsellor, when confronted with an adolescent whose chief contribution to the interview is an apologetic "I don't know," is in a difficult position indeed. Many a young person will just sit, smile sheepishly, and answer with "I guess so" and similar remarks. The harder the counsellor tries to shift the initiative to the client, the more paralysed the latter becomes. Stating the fact that the young client may find it at times difficult to express his ideas will probably meet with a monosyllabic expression of agreement. The situation resembles that in which a policeman comes across a lost child wandering the streets. No amount of coaxing or cajoling seems to elicit the child's name and address. In an exaggerated way, this, too, represents the meeting between the big and the small, except that in the latter case the psychological difference in size is so overwhelming as to preclude even an elementary contact. The adolescent can give his name quite easily. He can also answer any factual question regarding his age, grade, etc. What he cannot always do is relate himself personally to the counsellor. This is perhaps one reason why the adolescent at times adheres so tenuously to the psychometric aspects of the programme. Tests, too, are tangible and less threatening than sharing of feelings.

Finding himself alone face to face with the counsellor seems to have an inhibiting effect on some young people. They become tongue-tied and cannot express themselves freely. The counsellor who, by looking at the client and saying nothing, insists almost mechanically that the client start the conversation is not helping the already timid adolescent. Quite the contrary, he contributes to the client's inability to express himself creating an awkward and embarrassing silence. The counsellor may have to accept the fact that some young people, especially in a vis-a-vis situation, find it almost impossible to formulate their thoughts. The counsellor can help the client relax by temporarily assuming the responsibility for a more or less smooth exchange of ideas. The interview may begin with impersonal remarks and then gradually shift toward the client and his problems.

In this instance the counsellor is not "winning confidence" in the sense discussed previously but is merely helping the young client to overcome his self-consciousness by directing the discussion, for the time being, away from the adolescent toward some neutral subject. Nor is this suggested as a "technique" designed to overcome "resistance" in the sense implied by Davis and Robinson. "Techniques" intended to influence subtly the client's attitudes or actions seem to have about them an unsavory aura of subterfuge and have no place in a relationship predicated on the counsellor's sincere belief in the client's capacity to help himself. The application of a particular "technique" to some end also suggests that the goal, whatever it may be, is the counsellor's, not the client's. This once again seems to violate the principle of self-determination. Perhaps it might be best to abandon the term "technique" altogether and to use the term professional skill when one means the application of knowledge to the helping process.

In the small-big relationship which may permeate the initial stage of the interview, it is important to recognise that "getting started" may be particularly difficult for the adolescent. He may require some time to adjust himself to the new situation before he can be expected to start talking about himself.

At this point a word of caution may be in order. The amount of talking done by the client is in no way indicative of the extent of his participation. Many clients will maintain a steady stream of conversation precisely as a means of keeping themselves out of the counselling process. Extreme "mutism" or profuse verbalisation may be equally indicative of the client's fear or inability to take hold of the help offered. This principle has been recognised in casework and demonstrated further by a study conducted by Carnes and Robinson which led them to remark, "It is not possible to use the amount of client talk as a criterion of counselling effectiveness". There is little relationship between the extent of helpfulness and the number of words uttered during the interview, irrespective of whether they were spoken by the counsellor or the client or by both.

Counselling of young people is sometimes complicated by the fact that many an adolescent client is not likely to surrender his privilege of being "small" The counsellor who denies the adolescent his role as a "smaller," less experienced, and dependent person is not likely to establish a truly warm relationship. Growing up is a process, too. Forcing the young person to become mature overnight, as it were, will probably result in the client's not returning to the agency. An adolescent client and an adult worker can establish a worthwhile counselling relationship provided the counsellor respects the young client's prerogative to remain "small" and fundamentally dependent on the counsellor.

Fortunately for the worker, the counselling process need not proceed in an all-or-none fashion. The counsellor does not have to choose between an autocratic, advisory attitude and one of utter passivity and nondirectiveness. There need not be anything mechanical or rigid about the interview. The counsellor recognises that adolescents, like everyone else, possess individual differences. This means that some young people may feel more keenly than others about their problems. Some may be more ready than others to assume the responsibility for effecting a change. Some young clients are socially and emotionally more mature and are capable of entering into a counselling relationship more readily than other adolescents. The counsellor assumes nothing about the client. A good portion of the first interview may be spent in attempts to discover an optimum operational level. This level is set empirically by both the client and the counsellor. What ensues is a unique relationship wherein the counsellor tries to help the young client to take as much initiative as he is capable of, recognising simultaneously that the client is young and is usually unable to carry the entire burden by himself.

This raises the question of parental participation once more. For example, the counsellor may want to know whether the adolescent has shared his vocational difficulties with his parents and, if so, what their position and attitude were. If he has not taken his parents into his confidence, does he feel guilty about it, and would he be willing to include them in joint vocational planning? Parents can be very helpful in helping the young person carry out his plans. They can be equally hindering if they are unsympathetic to the adolescent's viewpoint. Irrespective of their attitudes they do play a major role in molding the vocational future of their child. It is highly questionable that the counsellor and the adolescent can proceed with vocational counselling and testing as if parents did not exist at all.

But once again the counsellor has to pause and examine what the vocational guidance contact actually means to the adolescent. Does the young client really have a vocational problem? Is he truly concerned with it? Does he want and can he use vocational assistance? It has been stated repeatedly that to many in-school boys and girls coming for vocational guidance is a minor experience in their lives. Some come prompted by curiosity, others because their friends are being seen by the counsellor at the moment, still others because they have nothing better to do that particular afternoon and a bus trip downtown may contain an element of adventure (sic!). These youngsters frequently come in groups of three or four and ask that their next appointments be scheduled on the same afternoon to enable them to visit the agency together again. They are disappointed if they have to come in separately and frequently do not keep their appointments. Any minor activity after school hours may prevent them from continuing or completing their vocation guidance sessions. They frequently forget to keep their appointment and later on are too embarrassed to telephone for another. Many of these young people are completely unready for actual vocational counselling. As the counsellor explains his functions in relation to the adolescent client during the first interview, as he begins to work with the client's feelings and the anxieties that may be Centred in the question of vocational choice, the young person may become so overwhelmed as to withdraw, never to return. After all, the coiling client came to take aptitude tests to tell him what he is best suited for he did not come in order to struggle with his painful vocational uncertainties and indecisions. When the vocational contact appears to be so superficial and meaningless to the client, the counsellor may question not only the need for parental participation but the value of the entire experience for the adolescent.

Quite obviously, not all young people take career planning so flippantly. Many adolescents are genuinely concerned over their vocational future; many are sincerely interested in formulating their occupational plans or bringing about some important change. These adolescents come to the agency because they are aware of an educational or vocational problem and because they want help with it. Realistic planning with these young people does require that their parents take part in the process. To become effective, the service has to be offered not only to the adolescents but to their parents as well.

Process and the Adolescent

Process should not be confused with progress. The former is a growth experience that takes place as a result of interaction between the personalities of the counsellor and the client as they focus around the problem under consideration. Progress, on the other hand, is a judgemental concept which expresses the extent of movement with respect to a fixed point or objective. The degree or amount of process is contingent on several factors, among which are the psychological intensity of the problems, the ability of the client to make use of himself and the agency, and the quality of professional relationship established during the vocational contacts.

Earlier, we dwelt to some extent on the fact that planning for the distant future, as well as the selection of a particular occupation or trade, does not as a rule have very much meaning to the average adolescent. The conflicts around the vocational choice, therefore, are not likely to be charged with a great deal of feeling and consequently will not lend themselves readily as a focus in the counselling relationship. Educational problems that deal with the necessity of deciding whether the client will or will not enter college may have more meaning to the young person. Those adolescents who have conflicts over the alternatives of entering college or going to work are more likely to profit from a guidance programme because their indecision as to what step to take may arouse both anxiety and design to be helped. High school students frequently become genuinely concerned and upset by their fear of failing a subject, by a low mark on a test, or by a teacher's sarcastic or hostile attitude toward them. Those, who feel most strongly about their immediate predicament are probably in this latter group, and they are likely to be receptive to counselling and will probably participate wholeheartedly in the efforts to be helped. The focus, however, is probably not clearly defined, for a low mark on a routine test in elementary algebra, although possibly very painful at the moment, is not in itself sufficiently all-embracing to warrant counselling. It is only when failure in a subject begins to affect the rest of the academic programme that comprehensive counselling may be in order. For example, when a student who is on probation fails a subject, the entire question of his remaining in school may be reviewed. Vocational counselling may be desirable in such an instance, not because of the one subject, but because something must have gone awry with the entire educational endeavour. A reexamination of the student's objectives, potentials, and attitudes may be in order.

We have thus arrived at what appears to be the paradoxical situation of an adolescent client being relatively unimpressed by the need for occupational planning and yet painfully concerned with his failure to attain a particular mark on a school test. Would it be of any avail for the counsellor to try to impress upon the young client the fact that choosing the right career is incomparably more important than the results on a class examination? Obviously not.

And yet can a vocational or educational process be initiated when the chief concern is a situational disappointment and there appears to be little readiness or desire for career planning? Does one take his infant to a physician for every minor scratch, bruise, or bump that is inevitable in the life of a normal child? The tears and screams that may accompany a superficial hurt may be frightening at the moment, only to be replaced by smiles a few minutes later. It may be humiliating and upsetting to an adolescent to remain after school hours as a punishment, and there may be a great deal of feeling associated with the whole episode, but does this in itself warrant educational counselling? The existence of a real vocational conflict, a state of readiness for counselling, and a desire to effect a change are still the prerequisites for an effective vocational process, be it with adults or adolescents.

The adolescent's capacity for participation in the programme is the second point to be considered. Quite obviously, it is related to the first. We have, however, pointed out the fact that the quality of participation may differ from that of adults. The adolescent is likely to be more dependent on the counsellor for concrete information. He is more likely to seek advice or some other form of directive counselling, and, by the same token, he will take less responsibility upon himself. The focus will probably be less sharp and the over-all movement slower and less total. It is necessary for the counsellor to recognise that he is dealing with a psychologically relatively unfocused individual who is in the throes of growth and transition. The values of the adolescent are not always the values of the adult world. The goals and aspirations have not as yet been tempered by reality. It has furthermore been pointed out that the over-all growth process determines to a great extent the ease with which the adolescent can handle his vocational and educational difficulties. It may take years for a young person to become aware of the existence of a vocational problem, to go through the different stages of development from fantasy to realism, and finally to make an appropriate occupational choice in terms of his interests, abilities, values, and employment opportunities.

The foregoing remarks have attempted to sketch in a rather general way some of the difficulties the vocational counsellor may encounter with adolescents. It was indicated that, on the whole, vocational guidance as a profession has not devoted sufficient attention to the problem of assisting the young person with his occupational plans despite the fact that the bulk of all vocational guidance activity is carried on with young clients. To avoid misunderstanding, it may be helpful to recapitulate the statements made previously as to what is meant by vocational assistance.

By no means all vocational counsellors perceive themselves as helpers in the occupational area or, for that matter, conceive of vocational guidance as a helping process. Many vocational workers feel that their primary function is to ascertain (mainly by means of tests) the client's abilities, interests, etc., to inform the client of his general capabilities, and to present him with an accurate statement regarding the prevailing occupational trends, the labor market, etc. Such activity is not synonymous with vocational assistance for it tends to leave the individual client (or the counsellor) out of the dynamic process of giving and taking help or bringing about a change in the client's vocational thinking. Psychometric evidence and occupational information are but supportive attributes in a deeper and broader vocational process which should not be mistaken for vocational assistance in the fuller sense of the term.

The extremely limited familiarity with the theoretical aspects of the vocational helping process as well as an almost complete absence of a sound body of vocational counselling practice make counselling of adolescents a precarious task. We have seen in the preceding chapters that, in dealing with adults, vocational guidance as a profession could rely to a great extent on principles established by other helping disciplines. However, the knowledge accumulated by casework agencies and psychiatric clinics is not especially helpful in dealing with the average in-school boy or girl.

From the vocational counselling standpoint, adolescents are difficult to work with because many of them do not enter readily into a meaningful relationship with an adult counsellor and seem to find it particularly hard to share their problems. The counselling situation is further complicated by the fact that many adolescents are autistic in their outlook on life, are seriously limited in their appreciation of the working world, and finally, perhaps because of their youth, perceive reality in a characteristically immature manner. Other attributes such as impressionability, unstable interest patterns, and the apparent remoteness of the need to make a vocational decision, contribute further to the complexity of the counselling process.

From the practitioner's standpoint, counselling with adolescents presents a subtle problem. The worker is called upon to decide how much support he may have to give without thwarting the young person's freedom to decide for himself. This matter must be handled individually and almost intuitively. The young client must arrive at his own conclusions, and let he has to be assisted to take the responsibility for his choice upon himself. This is much easier said than done and requires perhaps the highest level of professional skill.

Considerable space has been devoted to the adolescent's rights to be adolescent and to be dependent. It was postulated that, although a young person has a will of his own, his total personality still in a developmental stage. Consequently, he cannot be judged by adult standards or be expected to share in the vocational counselling process to the same extent as an adult. The young person may require a supportive and a nondirective attitude simultaneously in order to enable him to take help and yet provide him with an opportunity for self-expression. This is particularly exemplified in the "small to big" relationship, where many conflicting feelings may come to the fore.

In summing up the brief discussion on adolescents and their vocational problems it may be well to bear in mind that what has been said was viewed from the standpoint of a practitioner working within a vocational agency's structure. Personnel workers, parole officers, teacher-counsellors, and others who may be called upon to assist the young person with his occupational problem would probably have to modify some of the outlined principles to suit the particular needs of their own specialization.

Helping the adolescent is too complex a subject to be handled in a dogmatic and supposedly universally applicable manner. There exist theoretical problems which have not yet been resolved satisfactorily. There are also practical difficulties which must be overcome before some of the basic principles can be applied successfully. Considerable research in the area of counselling of normal adolescents is needed before this subject can cease being essentially hypothetical and impressionistic. Currently the United States government is spending over $2,000,000 annually on studies of "human resources" conducted by various universities. Some of the studies in process deal with psychological dynamics as they are encountered in generic counselling.

At this juncture one might ask whether the counselling interview is the most effective medium or whether most adolescents could, perhaps, be assisted in the vocational area through classroom discussions, dissemination of occupational information, and other group guidance techniques intended to broaden their occupational horizon.

Vocational guidance, especially as applied to in-school youth, is rapidly becoming a major "industry." There are those who feel that educational guidance should be extended to the fourth-grade level, and still others who set: vocational counselling as an educational technique which can benefit *all* students". This latter view appears to be in harmony with the philosophy which holds that the teacher's primary responsibility is not only to impart factual information but to help the child with his total emotional development. Novick holds that "even more important, is the teacher's responsibility for the personality and character development of the child." Interestingly enough, the third function sometimes assigned to the contemporary teacher is that of "case finding and referral." The teacher, and this does not mean only the teacher-counsellor, is expected to be able to recognise the more common manifestations of maladjustment among his pupils and to make appropriate referrals. One may go along with Williamson that "counselling is the responsibility of every teacher" provided the term counselling is used in a broad and nontechnical sense. Counselling, however, if conceived as a highly intensive face-to-face professional relationship, is the responsibility only of those who have been trained to assist people with their problems.

Fortunately the concepts that "guidance is everybody's business" and that guidance is a specialised profession need not be antithetical in practice. General educational guidance, which may assume expression through group guidance programmes, and individualised counselling are not only compatible but actually complementary to each other. Although different in its objectives from personal help, a sound group guidance programme can serve as a source of referral for those individuals desirous of personal vocational counselling and assistance. A vocational group guidance service, however, valuable as it may be, cannot take the place of individual diagnostic testing and individual counselling. Although all adolescents can profit from a general educational guidance programme, not all young people need or can use vocational counselling that is predicated on awintense interpersonal client-counsellor relationship.

The question sometimes arises, At what age is vocational or educational guidance most effective? Unfortunately, there seem to be few studies that could provide a conclusive answer. A great deal would depend on what it meant by "effectiveness" in vocational guidance, what criteria are to be employed, and how movement it is to be measured. It is held by some that at the age of fifteen or sixteen the adolescent is most likely to benefit from contact with vocational guidance. Here, once again, one to differentiate between vocational guidance which is fact-centred and that which is help-centred. By fact-centred vocational guidance is meant the kind of activity which provides the client with general occupational information and factual evidence about himself as revealed through various diagnostic tests and methods. Help-centred vocational guidance is that which emphasises the phenomen-ological aspects of the problem and focuses on the helping process itself. The probability is that at one stage of his emotional development the adolescent client can utilise chiefly factual data. At a later period of growth he may be in a better position to enter into a more meaningful relationship with the counsel or. We have, seen that maturity plays an important role in the extent of the client's participation and his capacity to become responsible for his decisions and actions.

Personal experience suggests that older adolescents. *(i.e.,* eighteen or nineteen years old). generally speaking, are more pressed by a need for occupational planning, tend to become more deeply engaged in the vocational guidance process, and finally arrive at a more definite conclusion as to what they want: to do next. Older adolescents also appear to be more fearful of the counselling contact and will frequently attempt to solve their occupational problems unassisted. Younger adolescents (fifteen or sixteen years old), on the other hand, rarely feel a deeper than intellectual need for vocational planning. Consequently they are less likely to become seriously involved emotionally in choosing a career and will tend to emphasise factual information and test evidence. Since the entire experience of vocational counselling is often not too meaningful to the younger clients, they appear to be less threatened by what is to take place in the office. Ginzberg *et al.* hold that older adolescents are in a better position to utilize the vocational guidance experience. In their own words, "It is only when the period of conflict and tension comes to an end at about the age of seventeen or eighteen, when the individual has succeeded in channeling anew the manifold emotional pressures upon him, that he finally acquires a solid foundation with which to cope with the problems of adulthood. At this point he is ready to relinquish his earlier tentativeness and finally face the fact that he make a definite choice."

From the above discussion it would appear that the age at which vocational guidance is likely to be most helpful will be determined by what one understands by the term vocational guidance, what one holds to be its chief objectives, and what guidance media are to be employed. The next chapter will attempt to deal with some of the basic concepts in working with individual adolescent clients.

❑❑❑

11

HELPING THE ADOLESCENT

Some Problems of the Teacher Counsellor

It has been stated repeatedly throughout this work that the largest portion of all counselling with adolescents is carried on within the framework of the high school system. According to figures published by the U.S. Office of Education for 1946, only 16.4 per cent of all high schools had counsellors and guidance officers. Although the number is woefully small percentage wise, it nevertheless represents 8,299 counsellors. The counsellor student ratio is reported as 384.8, It is easy to see that, should all high schools institute a student guidance programme, the potential number of counsellors would increase to 50,604. Should the present student-counsellor load be decreased somewhat to enable the worker to do a more comprehensive job, the demand for school counsellors would increase proportionally. Thus, if the present average of 385 students per counsellor were to be reduced to 250, for example, the number of counsellors would have to be raised to 77,930. This is a large number indeed. Actually, if the professional standards set by the NVGA were adhered to somewhat more closely, the body of school counsellors would have to be enlarged even further, for, as Baer remarks with respect to the above survey, No distinction was made between full-time and came people Nor do we know anything about the training, experience, or actual duties of those who are called counsellors and guidance officers." The anticipated need for school counsellors can also be gleaned from the fact that it is estimated that by 1960 there will 30,000,000 children in elementary schools and 8,500,000 adolescents in high schools. To meet this situation an additional 250,000 teachers will be needed, many of whom will assume counselling duties. Those not connected directly with public education perhaps do not appreciate fully its vastness and the numerous professional problems that beset the teacher-counsellor.

There exists a definite need for a comprehensive treatment of the general question of the function of the teacher-counsellor, his professional focus, level of competence, training, and relationship to the student-client and the latter's parents. There is a need to reexamine critically the enteire objective of in-school counselling, as well as the practical implications of such an endeavour. If such a project were to be undertaken, it is fairly obvious that it would have to be initiated by people intimately connected with the school system and assisted by workers from other disciplines.

What the school counsellor is, at least in one locality, what he does, and how qualified he is to carry out his functions is presented in an excellent pamphlet issued by the state of California. It would be most helpful if other states were to issue similar publications. It is of interest to note that the authors of the above work do not perceive the school counsellor as a "specialist," in the narrower vocational guidance sense, but rather as "a generalist who works with a *wide variety of adjustment problems* that fall within his own range of competence" (italics not in original). Some of the problems that the school counsellor is expected to be able to assist with are "the acceptance of bodily changes that mark adolescence and a masculine of feminine role, the development of satisfying relationships with age-mates of both sexes, the gradual development of freedom from undue emotional dependence upon parents and other adults, and the defining of educational and occupational goals" In short, "The chief responsibility of the school-counsellor is to assist individuals in solving their various personal adjustment problems."

It is not entirely clear whether such thinking stems from a theoretical rationale which would endow the *counsellor with* what appears to be professional omniscience or from practical consideration based on the fact that there are not enough psychiatrists, psychologists, and caseworkers within the school system. It was pointed out previously that the generic counsellor, by being a Jack of all trades, cannot offer the client the professional services that only specialists can offer. If one considers the fact that adolescents constitute the most difficult and the least explored group in terms of helping relationships, the responsibilities assumed by the teacher-counsellor become stupendous indeed.

A classification of problems handled most frequently by full-time counsellors in California schools is quite revealing. A table from the cited survey is presented below:

STUDENT PROBLEMS DEALT WITH MOST OFTEN BY COUNSELLORS	RANK ORDER
Adjustment to schoolwork	1
The future: educational	2
The future: vocational	3
Home and family	4
Personal psychological	5
Social Psychological	6
Finances, living condition, and employment	7
Curriculum and teaching procedures	8
Health and physical development	9
Social and recreational	10
Courtship, sex and marriage	11
Morals and religion	12

Working with young people demands a degree of knowledge and skills which perhaps surpasses that required in dealing with young children or adults.

Vocational counsellors working within a community supported agency are often at a considerable advantage in that they frequently find themselves in close juxtaposition to professional workers in related helping occupations. This proximity not only permits a freer exchange of ideas but may require that the vocational worker operate closely with a psychiatrist or a caseworker in handling a specific case. The vocational counsellor within an agency setting usually possesses a good working knowledge of community resources and the policies and philosophies of other agencies and frequently knows personally practitioners, supervisions, and administrators in the different related field. Through practical cooperation on a case, through informal discussions and joint conferences, he may begin to realise that problems that beset other helping areas may also apply to his professional problems, that techniques and skills useful in casework or psychotherapy may also be utilised in vocational counselling. In short, the vocational counsellor who finds himself in a help-centred milieu is likely to perceive himself as a helper and the client as a person who comes to him for some form of help.

This orientation is in sharp contrast with the climate that is likely to be encountered in many university-sponsored psychological clinics or in vocational services offered by the public school systems. The average teacher-counsellor usually operates almost exclusively within the framework of the school department. By training and temperament he is presumably a teacher, first and foremost; his qualifications as professional counsellor are frequently nil. In the words of Kitch and McCreary, "Teachers who may handle successfully the typical group situations that are characteristic of the classroom do not necessarily possess the qualities that insure success in handling the person to person relationships which are the basis of the counsellor's work". Much of the school counsellor's thinking is influenced by the educational structure of which he is a part. Whatever the objectives of education may be, they are different from those of a helping profession such as, perhaps, casework or vocational guidance. Furthermore, teacher-counsellors as a group seem to find security in their homogeneity and tend to regard other professions with some understandable (from their standpoint) mistrust.

It is probably significant that most schools require their potential psychologists and counsellors to be teachers first. "Outsiders," even if recognised for competence in their own professional circles, are usually ineligible for the position of school counsellor unless they have had previous teaching experience within the school system. By pursuing such a sectarian policy, the schools not only deprive themselves of the services of some excellent workers but actually erect a wall between themselves and other helping professions. The effects of such an ideological isolationism are felt already and will probably become more serious as teacher counsellors become more fully cognizant of their professional role and responsibilities. If the teacher-counsellor is to become a truly professional worker, he will have to establish a much closer ideological as well as working relationship with members of the older helping professions. It is questionable that the school system alone can provide him with the necessary orientation and on the job training that are essential to one who assumes the responsibility of helping others.

The rationalised distrust for nonteaching professions is clearly demonstrated by the fact that "eighty-five per cent of the counsellors reported they believed that teaching is not only desirable but essential in preparation for counsellors." At no time was training in psychology, casework, or vocational guidance deemed nearly as important as preparation for teaching, and yet there can be little question that workers in these areas have much more to contribute to face-to-face counselling than teachers have.

It is but recently that some teachers have assumed the part of helpers. In their new role as counsellors many of them strive to reorient their thinking, acquire new information and skills, and professionalise their work. According to the previously quoted Californian survey, 94.7 per cent of full-time counsellors in that state took one or more courses in the various areas of psychology, sociology, statistics, counselling techniques, mental hygiene, and other related subjects. This is very encouraging indeed. The sole limitation of such a training programme is the tendency to equate academic credits and degrees with competence in counselling. It has already been pointed out that subject matter, although essential to one's professional development, is incomplete without a correspondingly intensive programme of supervised field-work training. Personal professional maturity, self-discipline, and the respect for the client's right to make his own decisions are some of the characteristics of a trained counsellor. Bios, for instance, notes that many teachers are apt to respond to the student in terms of their own struggles during adolescence. "This often accounts for the teacher's sensitivity to and selective awareness of adolescent problems in his group, for his unusual understanding of one student and his complete lack of understanding of another." Whether or not taking courses at the graduate level will help the counsellor to differentiate between his own problems and those of his client is a moot point. Genuine insight into one's own motivations and needs is essential in the development of a counsellor. As Ruth Strange aptly remarks, "The counsellor's understanding of his students seldom goes deeper small his understanding of himself."

The school counsellor's problems frequently become complicated because helping facilities within the school system are either limited or completely nonexistent. The teacher-counsellor may therefore be compelled to broaden his functions considerably. Thus, in addition to handling problems in educational guidance, he may be expected to help students in matters of personal adjustment and emotional disturbance, intra-familial difficulties, and similar problems which are enough to challenge the skills of an entire clinical team. Very frequently, the teacher-counsellor, who is already taxed to the limit by the responsibilities vested in him by face-to-face relationships, may be expected to be in charge of an occupational library, show films on career planning, conduct vocational guidance group sessions, assist with attendance records, and make home visits.

There can be little question that there exists an acute need for an expanded professional guidance service available to in-school youth. Although the urgency of conditions may vary from locality to locality and the quality of service may differ from one school to another, there exists a nationwide shortage of vocational counselling facilities prepared to handle the occupational needs of young people. The Midcentury White House Conference on Children and Youth summarised the existing situation by stating, "Adequate guidance services are not yet available to most of the youth of our country. Many existing programmes tend to be not only inadequate, but uncoordinated. It was agreed that guidance, in the sense of personal help in meeting life situations, should be given by trained personnel and start early in the school programme. . . In some schools, the only attempt to provide guidance is made through teachers who have little or no special training, and who continue to carry heavy teaching loads."

As a professional worker, the teacher-counsellor may find himself seriously handicapped in several ways. Frequently, he is the only teacher-counsellor in the entire school. This automatically precludes professional supervision as practiced in agencies where there several workers. Being alone also means absence of staff conferences where specific cases may be studied, new knowledge acquired, or older attitudes modified.

The fact that there does not appear to be a unified rationale as to the functions and responsibilities of the school counsellor makes his task difficult and at times ambiguous. The structure within which the teacher-counsellor is expected to operate is often left to the discretion of the school superintendent or the principal, neither of whom is likely to be qualified to administer a vocational guidance programme. Quite often little distinction is made between matters of policy, administrative duties, and professional responsibilities. What the school counsellor is going to do is likely to be determined largely by the local school and the principal's understanding of what constitutes vocational assistance.

For illustrative purposes one might mention a few problems that can be classified under policy, administration, and professional responsibilities. The reader can undoubtedly amplify each list without much difficulty.

Policy. Should every student be seen by the counsellor at least once during the term? Should every student be tested at least once? Should cumulative records be kept for every student? Should parents be invited to participate in vocational planning? Should out-of-school referrals be made by the counsellor when deemed necessary? Should disciplinary matters be handled by the counsellor? What functional and structural relationship should exist between the counsellor and the school nurse, the attendance officer, the classroom teacher?

Administration. Who should interpret the type and objectives of the vocational programme to students, their parents, and the community? Who should solicit parental participation in "routine" cases when a referral to an outside resource is contemplated? Who should be responsible for the correction of minor infractions or major breaches of discipline? Who should be responsible for settling differences that may arise between the counsellor and another member of the faculty over a specific case?

Professional Responsibilities. What tests, if any, should the student be given? Should the counsellor undertake helping the particular student? In what area should assistance be offered? What counselling techniques are to be employed? What conclusions can the counsellor reach on the basis of evidence before him, and what recommendation can he make at this point *(e.g.* suggestions for a realistic educational plan; recommendations on leaving a child behind in his class, advancing him, or giving him instruction; recommendations for psychiatric treatment or further clinical testing, etc.)? What ethical principles should be adopted by the counsellor *(i.e.,* confidentiality of records, not divulging IQ and similar technical data to the client, etc.)?

Whatever may be said about the professional difficulties that are likely to beset the teacher-counsellor, one fact stands out as undeniable reality: the school counsellor is often the first and sometimes the only person who will ever offer professional counselling help to the student. From the practical standpoint it matters little whether the student himself requested to see the counsellor about his educational plans or whether he was referred by a classroom teacher because of academic failure or odd behaviour. What-ever the problem may be or however difficult it may appear, the counsellor is likely to be the first professional worker to meet the student. The school counsellor cannot retreat to an ivory tower and refuse to offer help to a student because the problem does not fall within the range of his professional function. Nor can he attempt to make a referral to a casework agency or to a psychiatric clinic simply because a student may want assistance with some difficulty that arises at home or seems to involve the total aspects of personality. A blanket policy of referral for all students who confront the teacher-counsellor with other than educational or vocational problems would be not only completely impractical but probably harmful to the individual client.

The teacher-counsel often finds himself confronted with a genuine professional problem. Essentially he is a teacher trained to teach subject matter in a classroom. By virtue of additional courses in psychology, vocational guidance, and testing, he may have taken on the job of school counsellor. Now in his new role he is expected to assist young clients not only with educational and vocational problems but also with conflicts that may arise from interpersonal relationships from difficulties in emotional adjustment, and from intrafamilial difficulties and with what may be precursors of a total psychic breakdown. The school counsellor may be aware of his limitations as either a diagnostician or a therapist but may still be forced into a situation which demands his active participation. The troubled student as a rule does not have a choice between a highly trained "expert" and a comparatively less well equipped generic counsellor. The reality of the situation presents the student with a choice between a school counsellor, with all his limitations as a professional helper, and no helper at all. Unfortunately, this situation is not restricted to any particular portion of the country but appears to be typical of the nation as a whole. The White House conference mentioned previously makes the following significant comment: "Almost universally, teenage youth seek a mature, understanding and trained professional person with whom they can discuss fully their vocational, educational, social and personal problems. Few communities have provided adequate resources to help our young people effectively along the crucial path from school to work, or through the perplexities of their early work experiences. Hence, it was agreed that all community resources should be expanded and used to the fullest to give youth the guidance needed."

Having to deal with the variegated problems of the adolescent is a tremendous responsibility thrust upon school counsellors. Most professional workers in related fields would shun a position that in a sense demands that they be vocational counsellors, caseworkers, psychologists, and psychiatrists all in one. And yet this is precisely what is expected of teachers who, for whatever reason, chose student personnel work as a part of their high school activities.

There can be little question that many teachers are but dimly aware of the magnitude of the responsibilities they undertake when they decide to become school counsellors. Nor are they always cognizant of the complexity and the intensity of training that is required to enable them to do a professional job. In an article dealing with in school counselling Dresden gives a portrayal of the situation that is candid and very much to the point. She reports, "We started with one psychological counsellor. She was an experienced teacher, having taught all the grades in state grade schools, and having taught social studies in a Milwaukee high school for many years [sic!]. In February another counsellor was added to the staff, she specialised in primary children these seem to be the chief professional qualifications possessed by the good women. What they may have lacked in a academic or clinical training was more than compensated by their zeal. The same article furnishes a table of problems handled by the two counsellors. It is presented without further comment.

MALADJUSTMENT	TOTAL
Social	120
Emotional	152
Physical	31
Others	7

The foregoing brief discussion on counselling with in-school youth has attempted to suggest several premises around which a more comprehensive student counselling service could be established. The basic tenets are *(a)* There exists a real need for vocational guidance among high school students. *(b)* There also exists an acute need for counselling in personal areas not necessarily related to occupational planning. *(c)* A job analysis of the school counsellor's functions is imperative to permit him to prepare himself for and to assume the responsibilities of a helper. *(d)* An advanced educational curriculum must be evolved to equip the student counsellor as well as the practitioner with the knowledge and skills required by his profession. *(e)* There must be a fuller exchange of professional thinking between the school counsellor and workers in other helping areas outside of the school system proper. *(f)* The counselling services offered to individual pupils must make provision for the inclusion of their parents whenever this is deemed necessary, *(g)* Research and investigation into the dynamics of counselling .with adolescents are imperative for the formulation of a total helping rationale.

Objectives in Working with the Adolescent

The central theme of the present work has been helping the individual client attain a satisfactory occupational adjustment. Such help has been conceived as a process in which the client, with the aid of the counsellor, works toward a reduction of his indecisions and conflicting feelings and by employing his own, strengths finally embarks upon a course of action or a plan. It has been stressed repeatedly that a client can become engaged in a self-helping process only if the problem at hand is sufficiently disturbing to force him to seek professional assistance and if his will to effect a change is stronger than his desire to remain unchanged. It is held that this principle is equally valid for adults and adolescents and is applicable to occupational planning as carried on in either an agency or a school.

In practice, however, counsellors frequently discover that there is a basic difference between working with adults and working with clients who are still in their early teens. The distinction stems not from theoretical considerations alone but from the fact that for many adolescents planning their future does not constitute a particularly meaningful emotional experience. Why this is so has been discussed previously and need not be repeated here. The subject under consideration at present is not the young client's rather limited capacity to profit from a vocational guidance contact but rather the fuller utilisation of whatever capacities he does possess. Although the young client may not be able to enter into the same kind of relationship with the counsellor as an adult, and although the occupational conflict may not be so disturbing and pressing, he still may want assistance with his vocational dilemma. The question then becomes, How can the counsellor offer the a adolescent client the kind of vocational service which he can use at a level acceptable to his adolescent personality?

Perhaps the first principle is not to assume anything about the young person but to help him formulate his own thinking as to what it is that he wants help with. In other words, what does he think is the problem, how does he believe he can solve it, and what does he propose to do about it? It may be very difficult for the counsellor not to project into the situation what *he* thinks the problem is and how the client should go about solving it. In his inexperience and psychological naivete the adolescent may see his difficulties as something relatively simple, a temporary condition that may be remedied by sound advice or diagnosed through an aptitude test. Frequently, he is not even much disturbed by his problem but is in a state of mild disquietude which he hopes the counsellor can relieve for him. If the counsellor cannot wave a magic wand and take it away, he still need not be greatly upset, for, in the first place, the, problem is not necessarily vital, and second it will probably take care of itself in the course of time.

The counsellor cannot tell the adolescent client that the latter's problem is more serious than he imagines and that he ought to do something about it. It is the client's prerogative to feel about himself and his difficulties as he does. If the young client feels strongly about some matter, reassuring him that "it's nothing" is no more helpful than telling him that he should be concerned over something that has little meaning to him even if the counsellor considers it important. What the counsellor can do is offer the adolescent an opportunity to discuss and to think through his occupational dilemma. If at the end of such a process the client still feels that all he wants is' factual information or psychometric verification of his potentialities, the counsellor will have to accept such a programme, even if he himself holds that the client needs a different or more intensive service. The case of George illustrates this point.

George was referred for vocational guidance three years ago when he was fifteen by a child care agency. At that time George was having a great deal of difficulty with his foster home parents and in school. Vocational counselling did not appear to mean too much to him. On the various tests he attained uniformly low scores, although he did not impress the examiner as a dull boy. At the conclusion of the counselling sessions the counsellor's opinion was that George was an emotionally disturbed adolescent of at least average intelligence who because dinner difficulties was unable to use the vocational service to any great extent.

George telephoned for an appointment recently. He had developed physically and appeared to be able to relate himself somewhat better to the counsellor than on previous occasions. He had just entered his senior year in high school, where he was maintaining an 85 average. He came in primarily to get help in finding a job for the summer. As the counsellor wondered whether George would be interested in assistance with his occupational future, George became very defensive, saying that he was "doing fine," that he "did not want to take any test,," and that he knew that he was going to enter college. When the counsellor asked what George intended to major in, he replied quickly that he would study either engineering or law. The counsellor assumed an accepting and noncritical attitude but also asked George if he thought his abilities lay in those areas, especially since the two professions he mentioned called upon rather different talents. Again George assured the counsellor that he was aware of the implications and that all he wanted at present was a summer job.

From the foregoing brief summary one may infer that the counsellor felt that George could profit from further vocational counselling. George apparently did not share this view. His nonreceptiveness verged on negativism, and it was obvious that, had the counsellor insisted on his opinion that George was sadly confused vocation ally and probably needed further counselling and testing, George would become completely unaccepting of the counsellor. Perhaps absubtler approach might have been more effective in dealing with George. This, however, is not the question, The crux of the issue lies in whether a counsellor can decide for a client what should be important for the latter. It has been said repeat that sometimes the client must be helped to take help, This is true, but in offering help the counsellor must also respect the client's right to refuse it. In the above illustration, George came in exclusively because he wanted a job for the summer. Apparently he was fearful of becoming involved in a counselling process. He probably considered the entire matter beforehand and decided that it was a job not vocational guidance—that he could use at present. The fact that the counsellor recognised that he was dealing with a disturbed adolescent who had no clear picture of his vocational future does not in itself suggest that George was either aware of the seriousness of the problem or desired to do anything about it. Although some workers feel that acceptance of factual data is essential in counselling, such acceptance, despite its importance does not embrace the total dynamics of vocational assistance. This is perhaps why little confidence, despite its importance, does not embrace the total dynamics of vocational assistance. This is perhaps why little confidence can be placed in interviewing techniques designed in advance or similar practices intended to create a special "atmosphere" conducive to counselling. The uniquences of every individual tends to preclude a postulaion of static principles.

During the first contact the counsellor will want to convey to the young client the feeling that he has confidence in the latter's ability to handle his dilemma, that the counsellor's role is not to solve the problem for the client but to help him come to some decision. At the same time the counsellor will show the adolescent client an understanding and sympathetic attitude based on recognition of the fact that the client may find it difficult to put his problem into words and that he needs factual information about himself and the world around him in making his occupational plans. Lastly, in working with a young person, the counsellor will not only offer assistance but will try to help the client get hold of the process, even if on ever so simple a level.

It is entirely possible that, if the client is still too immature at the time of counselling or is not too much in conflict over his vocational choice, the client-counsellor relationship will never develop into a momentous experience in the client's life. What the vocational guidance contacts will mean to the client will be determined not only by the kind of service offered by the counsellor but by the intensity of the vocational problem and the extent to which the client can use the service and himself.

Most vocational guidance sessions with high school freshmen and sophomores, although generally helpful, do not as a rule develop into particularly meaningful relationship processes. As a result of such contacts, the young client may gain a somewhat better understanding of occupations, possibly a clearer conception of his own interests, abilities, and aptitudes, and, it is hoped, a stronger drive to do something about his vocational future. It is not uncommon to have a young client complain at the end of the counselling sessions that now he is more confused than he was when he started. This need not indicate failure. Such a statement may suggest that the client have moved from a point where he expected the counsellor to advise him what to do to one where he is beginning to think about the problem himself. It is entirely understandable that the client is somewhat frightened by this new development and is anxious to bring about a change without knowing exactly how. The counsellor may want to remind the client that the counselling relationship need not come to a final end and that the young person is welcome to return at a later date. At any rate the client is given a choice, either to continue for another session or two, or to try to resolve the newly aroused anxieties unassisted.

Thus far we have dealt chiefly with difficulties encountered in counselling of adolescents. What, however, are the goals of such counselling? Perhaps the primary objective is to provide the young client with an opportunity to work out for himself his vocational plans. This means defining the problem, bringing out its conflicting components, and resolving it, at least partially, in a realistic manner. To do so, the young person may need factual information about the issue at hand, some understanding of his own potentialities, and, above all, sufficient maturity to enable him to integrate the objective facts with his phenomenal self. At this point it should be recalled that the average adolescent can rarely function as an isolated individual. Most young people are strongly dependent on their families, and especially their parents, in deciding on a vocational plan. An occupational programme that has been evolved solely as the result of interaction between the young client and the vocational counsellor is likely to have a dreamlike quality about it unless it meets with the acceptance and support of the client's parents.

In vocational counselling with adolescents factual information plays a greater role than in occupational planning with adults. By factual information is meant psychometric and similar test evidence about the individual, knowledge about various occupations, familiarity with college curricula, entrance requirements, etc., and some idea about opportunities in the different fields. It can be assumed that, because the average young person has lived a shorter time than the average adult, the former's knowledge of the working world with all its implications will be less inclusive and less detailed. Since many young people have never worked in their lives, their understanding of jobs and professions is likely to be influenced by wishful fantasy rather than firsthand experience. Both adults and adolescents need facts from the counsellor around which they can build I their vocational plans, but adolescents need them more, because, at the time they see the counsellor they are likely to have fewer lets at their own disposal.

Another reason why objective information plays a more important role in vocational planning with young people is that, by virtue of their youth, greater educational and occupational opportunities are open to them. Frequently several equally sound vocational possibilities are at the disposal of the young client. A better factual understanding of each area, coupled with the scientifically established probability of his succeeding in it, may help the young client to decide in favour of a particular career. Similarly, when confronted with a choice of several career plans, an adolescent sometimes can, with the aid of test evidence, rule out those fields in which he appears to lack the necessary attributes for success and simultaneously select that area for which he may have special aptitudes. Adults, conversely, rarely have so broad an occupational choice. If psychometric testing is indicated, it can often be confined to the narrower problem at hand. It is rather uncommon for a mature adult to come to the counsellor with the statement "I would like to find out what I am best suited for. Most adults who have a vocational problem have usually given it considerable thought and, in discussing it with the counsellor, tend to limit themselves to a specific occupational area. Testing then may become centred in the fields under consideration.

Testing is likely to be less fruitful with adults than with adolescents because the adult client can convey to the counsellor much information about his vocational present and past that, from the practical standpoint, may be more valuable in vocational counselling than abstract psychometric data. An adult client with a family who has .worked for twenty years as a labourer is not likely to decide that he is going to become a psychologist because on a test he attained an IQ of 120."

The last point to be considered in connection with factual information is the fact that the majority of young people are vocationally more flexible than most adults. Given certain information about themselves or an occupation, they are more likely to use it than one who is "set" in his ways. From the standpoint of vocational planning, the young person possesses great motility. He is not encumbered by the excessive baggage of the past. There is less to unlearn, less to give up, and more to gain. Not only are the opportunities greater for the young pioneer, but he is less bound by tradition, by personal ingrained patterns, and by responsibilities. Like Walt Whitman he can say "Afoot and light-hearted I take to the open road. . . ."

The Parents Role in Vocational Counselling

The practical difficulties in counselling with adolescents are increased by the fact that to a large extent many young people are dependent on their parents for vocational support. Counselling with adults is predicated on their ability and desire to make use of the vocational service offered. The counsellor's responsibility is to help them move in the direction of their choice. It is presupposed that the adults who come for vocational assistance are relatively free to come to a decision and are in a position to carry out their plans. This is not to say that it may not at times be extremely difficult to make a particular choice and even more painful to carry it out. Most people cannot change jobs or their occupations lightly. There is always some ambivalence about every major step. If it were not so, there would be little need for counselling services. However, by and large, the assumption is that, in a free society, the average adult can carry out his vocational plans when he is determined to do so. The majority of adolescents, on the contrary, are still dependent on their parents, not only financially and emotionally, but occupationally as well. Few high school students can leave their studies at will or, for that matter, decide on occupations that are at variance with their parents wishes. Aside from the purely practical considerations, there is also the question of the counsellor's right to enter into a meaningful relationship with the young client without the parents' consent, participation, or encouragement. Perhaps situations that limit themselves to brief educational testing and superficial guidance do not burden the counsellor with too much responsibility. The likelihood is that a perfunctory and occasional contact with a school counsellor is neither particularly beneficial nor harmful. Vocational counselling that is predicated on the intensity of a relationship, on the other hand, poses certain basic questions that demand careful consideration.

It is fairly obvious that few, if any, adolescents would take it upon themselves to visit a social work agency or a mental hygiene clinic without discussing the matter thoroughly with their parents. Coming for vocational guidance, however, rarely evokes more than a passing mention. Choosing a career or taking an aptitude test has a positive connotation for many. It is free from the stigma that is at times connected with social agencies or mental hygiene clinics. Implicit in the attitude is the feeling that occupational or educational planning is not as taxing on the individual's inner resources as may be casework or psychiatric treatment. There is good reason for this belief, for, by and large, vocational counselling as it is practiced today rarely constitutes a significant emotional experience. The strong emphasis on psychometric testing, case histories, and the professional authority of the counsellor tends to leave the client out of the process. Diagnosis, rather than help, is still the major focus in the field.

When vocational assistance becomes the chief objective of the guidance process, an entirely new situation is created. The problems of counselling are particularly accentuated when the client happens to be an adolescent. How much joint planning can the worker and young client do without consulting with the parent? Can the counsellor assume that the adolescent is free to follow his inner vocational promptings without parental consent and help? If the counsellor should encourage independent thinking, will such action create a conflict in the child parent relationship? We say child deliberately, for, in the eyes of most parents, adolescents are still considered children, though the situation sometimes is revered and the parents tend to view the physically mature adolescent as an adult. Some parents overlook the fact that emotional maturity does not always parallel physiological growth. Although large for his age, the adolescent may not be ready to take a job, regard his studies seriously, or become genuinely concerned with his vocational future. Neither an apathetic nor a hedonistic approach to life need suggest that the adolescent is a "bum" in the making. He may be simply following his ontogenetic rate of growth. But both he and his parents may also be in need of professional assistance lest the problem in emotional maturation become one of family relationship.

In psychotherapy for younger children it is not uncommon for the psychotherapy to treat the child while caseworker works with parents (usually the mother). It is assumed that therapy for the child alone is not sufficient unless the parents, who are so close to the child, are also helped to understand the nature of his difficulty. In a vocational guidance situation such an understanding cannot be restricted to intellectual conceptualisation alone. The parent may have to help the adolescent grow up vocationally by supporting him in the feelings and attitudes that may accompany a change. But since the parent himself may not be in a position to offer such support, he may have to receive some assistance from the vocational counsellor. Counselling of an adolescent may therefore easily develop into a three-cornered relationship between the counsellor, the child, and his parents. It certainly is not implied that every vocational guidance case be handled by both the vocational counsellor and a case-worker. As a practical compromise, however, it may be very desirable for the counsellor to confer with the parents while working with their child. Experience has shown that some adolescents actually use the counsellor as a force against their parents. Deliberately or otherwise, upon returning home they may misrepresent what actually took place in the office, attributing to the counsellor statements they themselves made. Greater tensions may be created at home, and what was intended to be a helping experience may develop into an intrafamilial conflict. Thus the counsellor in working with an adolescent has a responsibility not only to his client but to the latter's parents as well.

The matter of parental participation and the role the parent may play in vocational counselling have been raised by the various Jewish Vocational Services on several occasions. In 1949 at a National Conference of Jewish Social Workers at Atlantic City, I presented a paper on the subject to stimulate further discussion on this important topic. Despite the genuine interest and concern revealed by a number of counsellors, the matter was not taken up at the subsequent meeting. It seems that the establishment of a well-founded rationale that would harmonise fully with the principles of self-determination and vocational immatunty of adolescents still need, to be formulated.

We have seen that vocational guidance for adolescents is by no means an all-or-none process. There are levels in the intensity of the occupational conflict, levels in the extent to which the young client can become engaged in the professional relationship, and finally levels in which he can make use of himself. Individual vocational services may range from the imparting of simple factual information to a vocational process that may involve all the resources of the ego. From this it follows that the extent of parental participation may vary from the case where there is none at all to the situation which necessitates working with both the child and his parents simultaneously.

Working with a parent around a vocational focus is by no means easy. On the one hand the counsellor is bound by the professional confidentiality of his work with the client, and on the other he is prompted to violate that confidentiality because of his responsibilities to the young client's parents. Extreme skill and tact may be required best the client lose confidence in the counsellor or begin to identify him with his parent. Under no circumstances should the counsellor do anything "behind the client's back" or divulge information without the client's consent and approval.

School counsellors who take it upon themselves to offerr assistance beyond the occupational area will probably find the question of parental participation even more pressing and vital. Problems in the areas of personal adjustment, social functioning, or familial relationships almost invariably call for the fullest participation on the part of the young client's parent. Social agencies, as a rule, will not attempt to work with a child parent or marital counselling case unless both persons involved are willing to discuss their differences with the worker. Casework experience has demonstrated fairly conclusively that in an interpersonal relationship conflict it is almost impossible to render assistance to one person only.

In counselling with adolescents, even a strictly vocationally focused counsellor will occasionally encounter individuals whose occupational difficulties apparently stem from a total personality disorder. The counsellor may have reason to believe that the client's interior performance in school or on tests is due not to intellectual deficiency but to emotional factors, Sometimes the degree of disturbance is so pronounced as to become obvious to any psychologically trained worker. Such a situation may confront the counsellor with new difficulties as related to the question of his responsibilities to the adolescent client and the latter's parents. In theory, at least, the counsellor may have three possible choices he may do nothing, which might indicate a callous disregard for the client's welfare he may help the young client accept a referral to an appropriate agency, such as a casework agency or a mental hygiene clinic or he may attempt to secure the parents' cooperation in working out a suitable diagnostic and therapeutic plan. Should be attempt the second possibility, he may incur considerable and just criticism for failing to apprise the child's parents of the problem and his action, whereas tact with the client's parents would probably enable the worker to be of maximum service to the client by making an appropriate referral. Such a step, by bringing the parents into the picture, would probably lessen somewhat the tensions that a referral is likely to arouse.

A psychiatric or family casework referral is at times very difficult to make and often taxes to the maximum the counsellor's professional skills. It is not easy for most parents to accept the fact that their child is so severely disturbed as to require a psychiatric consultation and possibly treatment; nor can the parents face without difficulty the realisation that their own relationship to the child may have resulted in his failure in school or other activities. The tendency to blame oneself and simultaneously to reject the guilt feelings is likely to produce severe conflict in the parents. They will probably "fight" the worker's suggestion that other than vocational service may be indicated. While the counsellor and the parents are struggling with the acceptance of the referral, the adolescent cannot be overlooked either. If a referral to a psychiatrist is indicated, this cannot be presented to the adolescent with the promise, "A man will play some games wish you," as is sometimes done with very young children. The young client's cooperation has to be enlisted and his fears handled in order that the referral may become a positive rather than a damaging experience.

In passing it may be interesting to note that some parents will accept a psychiatric consultation more readily than a family counselling referral. This may be due to a wider acceptance of psychiatry than of casework. Social work is only too frequently associated with the "needy" or the economically underprivileged. Coming to a social agency for any kind of assistance is associated in the minds of some people with "relief" and "public welfare" in general. Psychiatry, on the other hand, does not carry the stigma of poverty quite the contrary, in some circles it has an aura of sophistication. Possibly, psychiatry, with its traditional emphasis on genesis, is less threatening to some than casework therapy, which is likely to focus on the painful aspects of the immediate reality. Lastly, some parents can accept more readily the idea that it is their child, rather than they themselves, who needs help. One hears much more about problem children than problem parents.

There are also, of course, those parents who will sooner face a caseworker than a psychiatrist because they associate the functions of the latter with psychosis. In such instances the case-worker becomes the lesser evil. Whatever the feelings about psychiatry or casework may be, a referral to either is invariably fraught with a great deal of apprehension and ambivalence. The counsellor may have to spend several sessions with the parents and the adolescent before making any referral.

The question of parental participation in vocational counselling of adolescents has to be viewed from the standpoint of what such participation may mean to the young client. Some adolescents may actually ask that their mother or father be included in the process; others may resist this emphatically. Parents themselves differ in their attitude toward participation in vocational contacts. Some parents make the initial appointment for their child and accompany him on his first interview; others fail to respond even when the counsellor writes suggesting that they come in to see him. Whether parents should or should not be seen is not so much a question of agency policy as a matter of professional discretion. Generally, in counselling with adolescents, the agency should maintain an attitude which will encourage parents to want to talk to the worker, although it is not necessary to see the parents of every adolescent. .

The seriousness and the nature of the occupational problem, the presence of other nonvocational conflicts, and the client's feelings about parental participation are some of the factors influencing the counsellor's judgement on the necessity for including the parent. The parent's desire to take part in the planning stage, or at least to be apprised directly of the diagnostic findings and tentative decisions, may be considered as within his prerogative. At times the young client may want to keep his mother or father out of the vocational process. When this happens, it may be suggestive of a difficulty in the parentchild relationship, which may be considered outside the functional scope of the vocational counsellor.

The preceding discussion on adolescence has sketched the outlines of a complex and imperfectly understood process, designated in the present work as counselling with adolescents. No attempt has been made to provide the vocational counsellor with a genera blueprint to assist him in his daily professional activities, nor have all the facets and aspects of the subject been considered. If the reader should feel that the foregoing discussion has stimulated his thinking on vocational guidance and has possibly challenged some of his cherished tenets, the objectives of the present work have been fulfilled.

❑❑❑

BIBLIOGRAPHY

E.L. Tolbert, *Introduction too Counseling* (New York: McGraw-Hill, 1959).

Edward C. Roeber. Garry R. Walz and Glenn E. Smith. *A Strategy for Guidance* (Toronto: Collier-Macmillam, 1969).

Buford Stefflre (Ed.). *Theories of Counseling* (New York: McGraw-Hill, 1965).

Donald H. Blocher, *Development Counseling* (New York: Ronald Press, 1966).

Carl R. Rogers, *On Becoming A Person* (Boston: Houghton Mifflin, 1961).

Robert R. Carkhuff and Bernard G. Bereson, *Reyond Counseling and Therapy* (New York: Holt, Rinehart and Winston, 167).

Rogers, *op. cit,*

Carkhuff and Berenson

Rogers, *op cit*

Ibid.,

Louis E. Raths. Merrill Harmin. and Sidney B. Simon. *Values and Teaching* (Columbus, Ohio: Charles E. Merrill, 1966)

Horace B. English and Ava C. English. *A Comprehensive Dictonary of Psychological and Psychonalytical Forms* (New York David MaKay 1958). Used by permission of David MacKay Company. Inc.

Julius Gould and William Kolb (E.ds), *A Dictionary of the Social Sciences* (Toronto: Collier-Macmillan. 1964).

Solomon E. Asch. *Social Psychology* (Englewood Chiffs. N. J. Prentice-Hall, Inc., © 1952)

A. H. Maslow, *Motivation and Personality* (New York Harper. 1954).

William C. Schutz. *The Interpersonal Underworld* (Palo Alto. Clalifornia Science and Behavior Books, 1966)

Francis P. Robinson. *Principles and Procedures in Student Counseling* (New York: Harper & Broo. 1950)

Gerald A Gladstein, *Classification of Non-Verbal Leads,* College of Education University of Rochester (Rochester, N.Y.). mimeograph.

LeDa E. Tyler, *The Work of the Counselor* (New York, Appleton-Century Crofts, 1969).

Arnold Buchheimer and Sara C. Balogh. *The Counseling Relationship* (Chicago: Science Research Associates, 1961).

William C. Cottle and N.M. Downie, *Procedures and Preparation for Counseling* Englewood Cliffs. N.J.: Prentice-Hall, 1960.

E.G. Williamson, *How to Counsel Student* (New York: McGraw-Hill, 1939)

Edward S. Bordin, "Diagnosis in Counseling and Psychotherapy." *Educational and Psychological Measurement.*

Robert A. Apostal and John G. Miller, *A Manual For the Use of a Set of Diagnostic Categories* (Columbia. Mo.: University of Missouri Testing and Counselling Service, 1959), mimeograph.

Ethics Committee (APGA). "Ethical Standards." *Personnel and Guidance Journal* 40:204-209, October, 1961.

Leon E. Tyler, *The Work of the Counselor* (New York: Appleton-Century Crofts, 1969). third edition.

Henry Weitz, "Counselling As a Function of the Counsellor's Personality. *Personnel and Guidance Journal* 35:276-280, Jaunary 1957.